WALK IN MY
COMBAT BOOTS

A list of titles by James Patterson appears at the
back of this book

WALK IN MY
COMBAT BOOTS

JAMES PATTERSON
AND MATT EVERSMANN
WITH CHRIS MOONEY

C

CENTURY

1 3 5 7 9 10 8 6 4 2

Century
20 Vauxhall Bridge Road
London SW1V 2SA

Century is part of the Penguin Random House group of companies whose
addresses can be found at global.penguinrandomhouse.com

Copyright © James Patterson 2021

James Patterson has asserted his right to be identified as the author of this
Work in accordance with the Copyright, Designs and Patents Act 1988

Names and identifying details of some of the people portrayed in this book
have been changed

First published in Great Britain by Century in 2021

www.penguin.co.uk

A CIP catalogue record for this book is available from the British Library

ISBN 9781529135305 (hardback edition)
ISBN 9781529135312 (trade paperback edition)

Printed and bound in Great Britain by Clays Ltd, Elcograf S.p.A.

The authorised representative in the EEA is Penguin Random House Ireland,
Morrison Chambers, 32 Nassau Street, Dublin D02 YH68.

Penguin Random House is committed to a sustainable future for
our business, our readers and our planet. This books is made from
Forest Stewardship Council® paper.

CONTENTS

To Rory Patrick Hamill

PART ONE:

A CALL TO DUTY

MIKE LEVASSEUR

Mike Levasseur grew up outside Hartford, Connecticut. When he graduated from high school in 1997, he joined the US Army National Guard. He served as a civilian firefighter and paramedic for twenty years alongside his military service. He was deployed eight times, three of which were combat missions. After sustaining multiple injuries, Mike retired at age thirty-eight and went on to earn a master's degree in emergency management from Georgetown University.

We're not going to make it."

This from Jackson, the squad leader of my platoon. He's referring to the forty-plus Humvees on the base in Kuwait, which in 2004 is nothing but a big mess of tents in the middle of the desert. The vehicles are all soft-shell. Not a single one has armor on it.

It's 2:00 a.m. I just stepped off a plane.

Jackson opens his duffel and removes two Gatorade

bottles—the big thirty-two-ounce ones. He hands them to me, then looks back down at the bag, thinking.

"Better make it three," he says, and grabs another one. "Follow me."

Twenty-four hours ago, I was at Fort Drum, in upstate New York, training with the US Army National Guard and freezing my ass off in forty-five-below-zero weather.

I haven't slept since I was pulled from the field. No soldier does when told you're going to war.

Jackson finds an engineer. "We're heading to Baghdad," Jackson tells him, "and I'd like to make it there in one piece."

"What do you need?"

"Plate armor. Enough to weld the doors and cover the underside in case we drive over an IED on Military Supply Route Tampa. I also want to line the inside floor of the Humvee with sandbags."

Jackson holds up a Gatorade bottle. "Brought you one of each. Vodka, gin, and bourbon—the good stuff, not the cheap stuff. We have a deal?"

Five hours later, we're driving a jerry-rigged Humvee in a convoy heading north on this main highway that goes from Kuwait all the way up to Mosul. The road is flat and blackened from explosives. Smoke from a burning hulk of what looks like a car billows into the hard blue desert sky, taking me back to my time in Bosnia. I was there, working an ER shift at the base hospital, when 9/11 happened. We watched it live on a TV in the hospital's waiting room. When we saw the second plane crash into the building, right then we all knew we were going to war.

Jackson comes to a stop. We've driven less than a quarter of a mile.

"Possible IED ahead," he says. "Got to wait until the engineers clear it."

We dismount. Everything is flat and dry and unbearably hot. In the distance I can make out the sound of small arms fire. My adrenaline is pumping, my mouth dry. I keep looking around me.

I worked in Bosnia as a medic. I was also loaned out—pimped out, as we call it—to units that needed a medic for their combat patrols. The biggest worry I had was stepping on a land mine. No one ever shot at me.

It takes well over an hour to clear the IED. I get back into the Humvee. The drive to Camp Anaconda, northwest of Baghdad, is over six hours.

It takes us two days.

The first battle in Fallujah happens three months later, in April. Some Blackwater guys riding in an up-armored Chevy Suburban stop on a road by the bridge at the entrance to the gates of Fallujah when they're approached by a group of kids selling gum, candy, soda, and fake Rolexes. A guy rolls down the window to buy some candy, and a kid drops a frag grenade into the Suburban.

The burned, charred bodies of four Americans are dragged from the wreckage and strung up by the bridge. The insurgents declare an all-out war against the Americans in Iraq.

They start slicing people's heads off on TV.

Camp Anaconda, where I'm stationed, is a sprawling military supply base that houses close to thirty thousand civilians, soldiers, Marines, and airmen. Every branch of the service. Even the Navy is there.

Camp Mortarville, as it will become known for the around-the-clock attacks, turns into the most dangerous place in Iraq. Pilots dropping off supplies keep their engines running. Each night when I go to bed in my small A-frame tent, with electricity that works maybe 40 percent of the time and no running water, I wonder, like everyone else, if I'll be alive come morning.

The hospital, one of the largest in Iraq, overflows with casualties, mostly young Marines. The latest casualty is a kid who jumped on a grenade to save his buddies and was KIA. His name was Raphael Peralta, an immigrant from Mexico who came to the US and joined the Marine Corps.

I'm working in the ER on another young kid, his hand hanging on by the skin, when I'm told I've been pimped out for medevac. The kid keeps screaming to hurry up and cut his hand off and patch him up so he can go back to his guys.

Flying in the back of the Black Hawk helicopter, my adrenaline pumping, I'm told we're heading to Samarra. A homemade bomb exploded near an Army guard post. As the Black Hawk lands, I remind myself to be ready for anything.

The bird's door opens to screaming and smoke and blow-ing sand and I'm off and running. Someone is depending on *me* to save his life.

Dealing with trauma on the battlefield, seeing limbs blown off by an IED, the amount of carnage and blood...it's more surreal than anything from a movie. Two Army soldiers have been torn apart by the blast. One is dead. Later, I'll learn his name: Specialist Anthony J. Dixon, of Lindenwold, New Jersey. He was twenty years old.

The other is still alive. He's on his back, blinking up at the harsh Iraqi sun. I drop to my knees and begin to apply a tourniquet around the stump of his missing leg.

His name, he tells me, is Armando Hernandez. "I need you to level with me, Doc." He licks his lips, his eyes sliding to mine. "Is my junk still there?"

Gallows humor. It's the only thing that keeps us sane.

"Still there," I tell him.

Hernandez tells me he's from a farming town in the desert of California. Volunteered to serve his country. He's twenty-two and has kids of his own. I've got him stabilized. As we fly back, I keep looking at his uniform—he's Army, like me. I've been on that road at his guard post at least one hundred times. This could have easily been me lying here.

Hernandez is alive when we land, and he's alive when we bring him into the ER.

I'm on my way to clean up when a grave-faced combat surgeon finds me.

"No," I tell him, shaking my head. "Don't tell me—"

"There was no way he was going to survive, not with those wounds. I was amazed he was still alive when you brought him into the ER." He sees I'm not buying it and adds, "Trust me when I tell you that you did everything you could."

I believe him, and yet some part of me *refuses* to believe him.

The surgeon sees that the indecision is eating me and says, "Mike, if this had happened on the front steps of Walter Reed, he wouldn't have survived."

I try to take some solace in that as I head to the showers.

It's Marine Corps–style, cold water only. You get wet, wash, turn the water back on, then get out. Nothing refreshing or relaxing about it. As I scrub down, washing away the blood of a brother, I have no idea what this war will end up costing me.

In my upcoming year here in Iraq, I will spend half of my time outside the wire. Years from now, I'll end up with a pretty nasty case of PTSD. I'll suffer permanent brain injury from having gotten blown up several times. I won't be able to run, and there will be days when I can barely stand. I'll have memory and sleeping issues, and my future wife will catch me every now and then clearing the house in my sleep, even kicking in my own closet door. It's one of the reasons why I won't keep guns in my house.

But I will never have a single regret. I will think of Armando Hernandez and Anthony Dixon and Raphael Peralta and the young Marine screaming to cut his hand off so he can go back out and fight with his brothers and sisters. I will think of them and all the brave soldiers who served with me in Iraq, and my heart will swell with pride and sadness, and it will haunt me that I'll never be able to accurately describe their sacrifices to others.

JASON DRODDY

Jason Droddy and his twin brother, Kevin, entered the Army on March 18, 2009. They served six years with 3rd Ranger Battalion, 75th Ranger Regiment; deployed six times; and executed more than 150 missions each. Jason got out as a sergeant. His real estate company, the Droddy Group, helps veterans buy and sell their homes.

I'm okay with dying. You have to be okay with it, consciously or subconsciously, to be good at this job. If I'm not okay with it, I'll hesitate, and I *will* get killed. There are no second chances.

My Ranger missions involve looking for and capturing certain high-value Iraqi targets. We go out mainly at night. It's a lot of kicking in doors and rushing into rooms, not knowing who—or what—we'll encounter. Each time it's a mystery. I get into a lot of firefights, some of which are pretty intense.

My twin brother, Kevin, who is also a Ranger, is in a different part of the country, doing the exact same thing I'm doing. This is the first time we've ever spent any extended time apart.

When I'm having a weak moment, tired, anything like that, I think of Kevin. Back at basic training and during Ranger school, we never showed weakness because we wanted to be strong for each other, always. I have to be strong and focused so I can return home to my family.

And there's no question in my mind that Kevin and I are coming home together.

One night I'm given a mission brief about a high-value target hiding inside a compound. Our guys have been watching this compound all day long, and certain individuals who appear to be guarding the compound walk back and forth from the perimeter to a wood line that is basically facing the compound. From comm chatter, we find out there's a heavy World War II–era Russian machine gun sitting somewhere in the wood line.

"Protect the machine gun," we hear these guys say. "Don't let it get wet. Make sure someone is watching it at all times."

That night we do a landing within three hundred meters of the compound. I run off the back of the helicopter. The rotor wash is intense, and the brownout is bad; I can't see anything, and it's loud, chaotic.

The bad guys don't know we're here. They're staying low in the poppy field as we creep toward them. I see one guy hustling away from the compound to the wood line, and because of all the radio chatter I know he's going for the big machine gun. I can't let him get to it. I need to protect the force at all cost. Now.

I fire with my squad automatic weapon (SAW), a machine gun that fires long six-to-nine-round bursts, and end up trading shots with the bad guys. It's the first time I initiate combat.

The guys I'm with—we're tough, trying to be manly men and acting like we're not scared or worried, but they know how close I am with my brother. Anytime the leadership finds out Kevin is in contact with the enemy, they always invite me up to the Joint Operations Center (JOC) to watch the intelligence surveillance reconnaissance (ISR) feed from the drones so I can keep an eye on what's going on, watch what's happening. It's tough to watch Kevin in a fight but there's also a relief in being able to see him and know he's okay.

We start doing some remain over day (ROD) missions, where we infiltrate one night and then move to the target compound and set up shop right before sunrise. We remain over day in a compound and then fight, pick fights, or just wait for a fight. The next night we move on to another target, or move through some trench lines and into some really bad areas.

I'm with a private, the two of us walking point on a trench line running from one fighting position to another fighting position. We're walking along the interior edge when he says to me, "Hey, keep your eyes open. We saw some movement here during the day."

I work my way down the trench system. Then it makes a

little shape, like an S. I look down the trench, but I can't see all that much. I move, trying to stay as quiet as possible.

I hear talking. I'm thinking it's one of my guys just being loud, like telling everyone to back off, try to spread out more. Then I listen a little closer and hear the voices speaking Pashto, the Iranian language of Pashtuns—and they're close, really close. I have an adrenaline dump and stop dead in my tracks.

I jump on the radio. "I've got voices around this corner."

A first sergeant responds. "Get over the wall. Keep it between you guys and see if you can spot where these guys are at."

I back off a little bit. My squad jumps the wall and then I continue toward the S turn. As soon as I get around it, I hear machine-gun fire open and pepper the wall the squad is ducking behind.

We basically get up on this wall, throw the machine gun up over the top, and press fire. We shoot two of the guys who are trying to flee. I know there's a third one somewhere. Every time I peek over the wall, I see a muzzle flash from below, where this third guy is shooting up at us.

My SAW jams. I take every grenade I have and throw them over the wall so I can buy myself enough time to fix the jam.

The bad guy stops firing. I wait.

It's quiet.

"Push over the wall," the first sergeant says. "Make sure you have support."

We set up support. The guys in 3rd Squad push over the wall and begin to clear the trenches.

We jump over the wall. Right in front of us is a dirt walkway that drops down into a six-foot trench. We stand topside, looking down into it. As I walk, I find a little mud bridge that crosses the trench. Down to my right, my squad leader sits down on the edge of the trench, looks underneath the bridge to make sure the third guy that was shooting at us isn't there.

I cross the bridge. On the other side I find a stockpile of guns the enemy tried to cover up. We're in a bad area for IEDs, so I leave the stockpile alone, come back across the bridge, and start working my way down toward my squad leader. He drops into the trench, and I see gunfire coming from underneath the bridge.

I immediately turn and go to jump the wall to get cover. Then I hear my squad leader scream, and, knowing he got hit, I turn and run back to the trench line, where I see my private pulling my squad leader out of the trench. I jump down and give them suppressive fire, focusing on the area underneath the bridge. I can't really see where the shooter is, so I just shoot everything to give them time to pull out my squad leader.

As soon as I know he's out and clear, I jump out and jump back over the wall. Immediately we back off enough so the birds can drop fire.

I catch my breath and think to myself, *I don't think I can walk anymore.*

I fall over.

I've been running on straight adrenaline, it was the only thing keeping me going, and now I'm starting to come off of it and my body realizes how tired it is, and I collapse.

I lie on my back in between rows inside a grape orchard, waiting for the fire to come, and I start thinking about Kevin. I pray he's okay, wherever he is. Safe.

We're going to go home, together, I keep telling myself.

The birds arrive and destroy the trench line from one end to the other.

JODI MICHELLE PRITCHARD

Jodi Michelle Pritchard's father was in the Air Force. She was born in Ohio, and when she was six months old she moved to Berkeley Springs, West Virginia—a one-horse town that had one stoplight. An only child and a self-described tomboy, Jodi loved playing in the dirt with G.I. Joe figures, and at an early age she fell in love with the military. Her great-grandfather served in World War I, her grandfather in World War II, and her father volunteered to go to Vietnam. Jodi wanted to continue her family's military legacy and, like her father, joined the Air Force. In August of 1998, with a certification as a national registered paramedic, she attended basic training at Lackland Air Force Base in San Antonio, Texas. She's a flight nurse in the West Virginia Air National Guard. Her current rank is major.

My turn comes in 2003. I'm going to Iraq, as part of Operation Enduring Freedom.

We board the C-141 military transport plane with our

medical equipment bags, flight gear, and chemical gear. IV pumps, cardiac monitors, and all the critical medical equipment we need are already all laid out, but we have to configure the space by hanging straps and putting up poles for our litter stations.

I also have my personal bag with me. It contains my death letter, my final message to my loved ones. I hope to God I don't need it.

I'm a senior airman but, at twenty-three, the youngest of the group.

Tonight, we're flying to Baghdad, which is not only the safest, most secure spot for us to land, it's also the most central location to collect our patients: wounded soldiers, children, even prisoners. We'll load them up and make the six-hour flight back to the Ramstein Air Base in Germany.

Our pilot briefs us before we take off. "Listen, when we get into Iraqi air space, we have to go dark."

"What does that mean?" I ask.

"We kill the lights and go in under night vision. You guys will have to use your goggles. Then we're gonna do an assault landing."

Oh, my gosh. I've done a practice assault landing on a C-130. A 141 is a completely different plane. A 141, I've heard, has to basically do a spiral in order to get to the ground.

When we hit Iraqi air space, everything goes black—no lights, just night. I'm buckled in. The loads block all the windows, and we can't get up and see what's happening outside.

I put on my helmet and flak vest.

The loadmaster looks at me and says, "You have to sit on it."

"Sit on what?" I ask.

"Your flak vest," he says. "When we spiral down to land, they'll shoot at us, and the bullets can potentially come through the plane. Because of their direction, if you're sitting on your vest, you'll have a much better chance at not getting shot."

"Well, why do I gotta wear a helmet then?"

Everyone starts laughing, including the loadmaster. It's a comical moment, but I'm thinking: *What the hell did I join?*

We're all sitting on our flak vests when we go radio silent, though we can hear our strapped-down loads clattering against the plane floor.

There's no chatter among us, but on our headsets, we can hear the pilot, copilot, and engineer synchronizing, going through their checklist. "Okay," I hear the pilot say to the copilot, "we're starting our descent."

The plane starts a hard-left rudder turn.

Starts to bank.

Then we start to do a spiral. It's like a huge corkscrew—a roller coaster from hell.

And it keeps going and going and going.

The pilot says, "Gunfire, eleven o'clock."

I can hear it, the gunfire happening outside.

They're shooting at us.

The copilot says, "Gunfire, two o'clock."

Even if the windows weren't blocked, I couldn't see the gunfire because I'm not on night vision. But the pilots can see it, and the plane is spiraling and spiraling—

Bam, we're on the ground, pulling back the engines.

I have no idea what's about to happen next.

They lower the ramps. A representative from the hospital and one from MASF—the Mobile Air Staging Facility—come on board, hand us paperwork, and start talking, only we can't hear them because the plane's engine is still running. *Why haven't they shut down the plane?*

I quickly find out why: the airport is hot. The base is getting hit by multiple mortars.

"I can't hear you—we can't hear you," I shout. *"Just bring them on board, we'll deal with it."*

We load the patients and take off. We have to corkscrew up for the same reason we had to corkscrew down—to avoid the antiaircraft threat.

Ten of our twenty patients are stretched out on litters. Good God, these poor things—some of them are all shot up, and some have lost limbs. One soldier is in a torturous-looking metal traction device locking together the ball of the hip to the femur bone. The contraption looks straight out of the horror movie *Saw.*

We run around with rolls of white medical tape, tear off an inch or two, and stick it to each pillow. On the tape, we write the patient's pain scale, the wound location, the medication and dosage he receives.

We have to treat the patients while also dealing with the stresses of flying—like the g-forces which can be a detriment to a patient's IV bag. We're constantly adjusting IV bags—and we're constantly looking in on the man in the traction device. His leg bones, held together by pins, rattled during takeoff, and they rattle every time we hit turbulence, causing him massive pain even though we're trying our best to keep his leg as padded as possible.

Someone screams to use the rest room. He wants to get off the litter but can't because he's missing a leg.

Someone screams for narcotics. Beside him, another patient sits quietly, staring. With all that's going on inside his head, he can barely answer our questions.

I check on a soldier who is missing half of his face. He looks up at me and says, "Ma'am, I need to know when this plane's going to land. I need to know when I can get back to Iraq."

"You've been shot, honey. Why don't we give this some time, okay? You've been through a lot."

"No, I want to go back."

"I understand that. I get it. And I want you to go back. I do. But first we've got to get you to Ramstein so the doctors can take care of you. Let your body heal, and then we'll get you back."

"I'm good, I want to go back, I'm ready."

He's not the only soldier who says this to me during the flight. All the guys on board want to go back. Every single one.

That same year, our commander brings us into a room to explain our next mission.

"Your crew has three critical care nurses, and you're one of the most highly qualified teams we have here at Ramstein," he tells us. "We have three patients who are pretty sick."

"How sick?" I ask.

"They're going to die. They're going home to die. We need to fly them to Bethesda, Maryland. You need to keep them alive until you get to Walter Reed."

You can do this, I tell myself. "Okay," I tell the commander. "We've got this."

We're given the plane's tail number. The crew—all five of us—get out of our car and find the plane without a problem. I step on board.

Freeze.

What the hell is going on?

The front half of the plane is filled with caskets. Six of them.

Soldiers are draping an American flag on each one.

We stand there, in shock. I take a deep breath and turn to my captain, Gino Crotchwell. "Okay," I say to him. "Obviously, we're on the wrong plane. I'll call and reconfirm."

I radio in the tail number. The answer is quick: we're on the right plane.

Joining us for this mission is a critical care transport team. We get the plane configured for our three patients, who come on board unconscious and unresponsive. After we get them settled, we find out they're being accompanied by what we call PAX—meaning passengers.

I pull Gino aside. "Putting people on a plane with a flying ICU on one half and a flying morgue on the other—they won't be able to handle that."

"I hear you," Gino says. "But we've got to get these guys home."

"They won't be able to sit with us, because of all the medical equipment—and we need room to move around so we can care for our patients properly. That means—"

"I know."

"—they'll have to sit close to the caskets."

Gino nods in understanding, takes in a deep breath. Holds it.

"We've got to get these guys home," he says again.

Before the passengers board, I gather the small group—mostly male soldiers and one woman dressed in civilian clothing. I gently explain what to expect inside the plane and then ask them if they're okay with this.

The men say they are. I look to the woman and say, "Ma'am, are you okay?"

"Yes," she replies. "I'm okay."

We take off. A couple of hours into the flight, some of the passengers get up and move around a bit. I walk over to the caskets to say a prayer. A soldier is standing next to one, his head down, his face etched in grief.

"That's a medic right there," he says, nodding with his chin to the casket in front of him. "It was his last mission."

He takes a deep breath, his voice shaky when he says, "I was with him when he got shot and killed."

He shows me a picture of a man wearing sunglasses and his full uniform. Blond hair, just as young as can be.

"I'm sorry," I say. "I'm so sorry. Is there anything I can do for you?"

"No, ma'am. I'm taking him home." He swallows. "I'm just going to take him home now."

I quickly gather myself and then return to check on my patients. They're doing fine. The woman in the civilian clothes, I see, is crying. I tell my crew I'm going to go up there to make sure she's okay.

"Ma'am?" I gently ask. "Would you like to go up to the cockpit, get out of this environment?"

She shakes her head. "I don't need to go anywhere."

"Are you sure?"

"That casket right there," she says, pointing. "That's my husband."

Oh, my God.

"He died in the UN bombing," she says. "I had to come over and identify the body. Now I'm bringing him home."

I can't even begin to imagine the nightmare this poor woman finds herself in. "Ma'am, I'm so very sorry for your loss. If there's anything I can do—*anything*—please understand I'm here for you."

"Thank you," she says.

When we land, we accompany our patients to Walter Reed in an AmbuBus, a supersized white ambulance painted with a big red cross.

We arrive at the hospital, get our patients sorted out inside, and return to the bus to retrieve our equipment. We're all exhausted. We've been up and working for nearly sixteen hours.

I grab a heart monitor. I'm rolling it out of the AmbuBus when I feel a tug on my flight suit. I turn around and see a little girl with curly hair. She's five, maybe six. It's night and chilly out, and she's wearing only little white stretch pants and a little white shirt.

I also notice a frantic woman standing directly behind the girl.

"Is this your mom?" I ask the girl.

She nods. "Did you bring my daddy home?"

I get down on one knee. "What's your daddy's name, sweetheart?"

She tells me.

Her father is one of the patients I brought home to die.

"I did," I say, feeling sick all over. "I did bring him home."

"Is he okay?"

I glance at the woman. It's obvious she hasn't seen her husband yet but is fully aware of his grave condition.

"Can I see him?" the girl asks me. "Can I tell him I love him?"

"Sweetheart," I say, "you'll be able to go in to see him soon."

And then I lose it. The woman does, too. I know I'll carry this moment with me for the rest of my life.

The rage and everything else that memory drums up, the way it makes me feel inside—I don't want to talk about it with anyone. I *can't* talk about it even now, all these years later.

It's become a problem.

A friend of mine suggests I seek counseling.

The psychologist is awesome.

I learn that it's okay to feel angry. Or hurt or sad or whatever. Feeling these things doesn't mean I'm beneath anyone or that I'm a social outcast. I'm not a detriment.

What I am is human.

And humans are not invincible. And while that may seem like common sense to some people, there are those of us who bury our feelings about difficult topics. Then, when we're reminded of these feelings, we think we're not right. We think we'll get labeled by other people as someone who has mental problems.

"But you're not," the psychologist tells me several times. "You're human, and it's okay to have a problem."

It takes me a long time to be okay with that.

Takes me even longer to tell this story.

And the remarkable thing? Even though I still feel the hurt as I say the words, it feels good to be able to talk about it.

I have a full sleeve tattoo dedicated to the patients I've lost over the years. It's a reminder of what I've seen overseas, what I went through over there. It's also a reminder for me to remember that it's okay to feel the way I do.

I wouldn't trade my life for anything in the world. I love wearing the uniform.

DON STEVENS

Don Stevens grew up in the Cincinnati, Ohio, area. His father served in the Air Force for twenty years, first as Security Forces and then, during the second half of his career, in physical fitness, where he trained Air Force boxing teams. When Don graduated from high school in 1990, he decided to follow in his father's and brother's footsteps and join the Air Force. That November, he began basic training. He deployed multiple times to Iraq, Afghanistan, Lebanon, Jordan, Turkey, and central Africa. He is a chief master sergeant in the US Air Force's Special Operations Command. Don is also the chief, or senior enlisted leader, for the Special Tactics Training Squadron, which takes care of training combat controllers, pararescue men, special operations, tactical air control parties, and special reconnaissance operators.

You've got to be ready every day. *Every single day.* There are no excuses.

When I land at the Bagram Air Base in Afghanistan in 2008, I drag my boxes to my mud and rock accommodations.

It looks like the Alamo. It's got a metal door with a latch and that's it.

I've been on the ground for maybe an hour and a half when the base starts receiving 105-millimeter rockets—big, gigantic rounds that shake the earth.

This is my second trip to Afghanistan. I'm a war-fighting singleton—a JTAC, or joint terminal attack controller. I control aircraft and, using sensors and aircraft imagery, pinpoint where the enemy is and put ordnance on targets.

I meet my new teammates. As we go out on our mission to find these rocket cells, my lungs remind me that I'm now nearly thousands of feet above sea level. These guys have been here for four months, so they're acclimated.

On top of that, I'm wearing the required plates and armor, carrying a radio and batteries on my back, so I'm not as light as the others. I'm really glad I've put in the effort to get in physical shape.

I'm also thirty-seven, older than most of these guys. Back in late 2003, when I was thirty-two and working in the Air Force's Security Forces, I decided to make a drastic career change and made the move to combat controller—a rigorous two-year retraining process.

I'm physically and mentally prepared—which is good because these guys are watching. They don't want a liability on their team. I've got to earn their trust and develop relationships.

My vehicle rolls over an IED. The vehicle behind me gets the brunt of the explosion, but the blast still jars my skull.

I look out the doors and hatches. Fortunately, everyone appears to be okay.

Right now, I'm basically in a black hole, without any aircraft support. I scan for threats.

I don't see any.

What I do see is a nearby hill. If I'm going to establish comms, I'll have to make my way up the higher ground, get a signal. I exit the vehicle.

We get ambushed.

Start taking effective fire.

To get out of this alive, I'll have to run up that hill.

I have no choice.

I make my way up the hill. Rounds flying all over, I use my satellite radio to call our command and control (C2) node while returning fire. It's not easy, but it's what I need to do in this moment of conflict. Prioritizing my part in a given mission has become second nature for me—as it does for every soldier. I have to protect myself and the team.

"You've got two F-18s en route," the C2 node says. "They'll be on station between five and ten minutes."

Relief washes over me.

Then I see the enemy. They're very close to me, their faces vivid. One of them looks like a kid. He could be nineteen, maybe even twenty-five, but to me he might as well be fifteen or twelve.

I take him out. I don't even think about it.

The F-18s push the enemy back. When I get to the top of the hill, I get an aircraft on station, and together we get a clearer picture of the area. Dropping a bomb is out—the area is too densely populated to handle that—so the team uses an MK-19 grenade launcher to take out the rest of the rocket cell.

We're only six klicks away from the Forward Operating

Base, or FOB, so we bring in an armored vehicle that can tow our damaged vehicle. I have an AC-130 overhead for support. Nobody is going to mess with us now.

An 18 Delta medic on my team took a 7.62-round right below the base of his skull. It cleanly passed through his neck, just underneath his jawline. He barely even bled.

The fact that he survived is pretty remarkable.

When I arrive back at the base after the firefight, it takes me a while to figure out that I need to stop, take a knee, and talk to a psych doc, chaplain, whomever. I need to get over what I did to that kid. I wish it hadn't happened, but those men were trying to kill me—kill us.

In 1994, when I was a young airman stationed in Turkey, two Black Hawk helicopters carrying twenty-six people were shot down in a friendly fire incident in northern Iraq. I was part of a team that had to deal with handling the remains.

About 50 percent were in body bags. The rest were charred parts and pieces. We had to recover them, these body parts of people I knew—people I had been playing cards with the night before. It was my traumatic PTSD-type experience.

These days, formations are staffed with clinical psychologists and clinical social workers. Proximity to danger and violence affects different people in different ways. The sight of a 105-round exploding a hundred meters away might scar one person for life. Other people can simply move on. And there are others who can't—or won't—talk about it.

The Air Force hasn't lost as many as the Army or other forces. I can't imagine coming back from a deployment and finding out half your guys are gone. On the other hand, the Air Force is a lot smaller, so any loss is huge to us.

Two guys I know from the Air Force are killed in action. One guy, Tim Davis, gets blown up by an IED while I'm in Afghanistan. I help load Timmy's body onto the plane for dignified transfer back to the States.

During my next rotation, I train guys at home, at the Special Tactics Training Squadron, to get them ready for combat. I work with a kid named Danny Sanchez. We do everything we can to get him ready.

I end up deploying with him and the rest of the guys to Afghanistan. When I redeploy back home, I find out that on his first mission, Danny was shot in the back of the head as he got off the helicopter.

The next of kin haven't been notified. I get on a tiny plane, along with a chaplain, the commander, and another officer, and fly to El Paso, Texas, so we can tell Danny's mom and little brother that he isn't coming home.

When we land, we get to the Suburban and change into our blues. My heart is pounding. *Man, I don't want to do this.*

It's evening when we pull into Danny's neighborhood. As we get out of the vehicle, we can see his neighbors looking out their doors, wondering what the hell is going on. They're a tight-knit community. They know Danny is a combat controller and that he's deployed overseas.

I rap on the door. A little boy answers it. He turns his head back inside the house and says, "Mommy, there are soldiers outside."

You can hear the oxygen just leave the house. And a gasp. Just a gasp, as the mom comes to the door to learn the fate of her son.

MARIO COSTAGLIOLA

Mario Costagliola was born in Brooklyn, New York, and grew up on Staten Island. Mario was attending a Memorial Day parade as a high school senior in 1981, at the peak of the Iran hostage crisis, when the sight of a tank from the local Staten Island National Guard Battalion made him want to enlist. He joined the National Guard and did ROTC while attending college. He later served in the Army. After nearly thirty years of service, Mario retired in May of 2006 with the rank of colonel.

My two-year-old daughter wakes up crying. She's sick. I turn on the TV so she can watch cartoons. I'm debating whether I should go to work or take her to the doctor when the house phone rings. My brother Tommy is on the other end of the line.

"They're bombing us," he says, his voice filled with terror. "They're bombing us."

"What are you talking about?"

"I heard a jet go right over the building. I think it hit us with a rocket."

My brother works at the World Trade Center. He was there during the terrorist attack in 1993, when a truck bomb detonated below the North Tower.

"Where are you now?" I ask.

"Inside. I heard the jet and the explosion, but I can't see anything and—"

"Get the hell out of there right now."

I hang up my phone, about to go to the TV when I get another phone call, this one from one of the non-commissioned officers (NCOs) leading my Staten Island training unit.

"Hey, boss," he says. "You better put on the news."

I hang up and see that the news is on every channel.

One of the towers is burning, just like in a story I heard when I was a kid of the B-25 bomber plane that crashed into the Empire State Building during the early forties.

Has to be an accident. That's the only explanation.

A second plane slams into the building.

Then I find out the Pentagon is burning.

Oh, my God, this is it.

We're at war.

I put on my uniform. I grab my two 1911 45s and just start loading every magazine I have. Then I use the phone to call up my guys in the unit.

I can't get through to anyone. All the phone lines are down.

The buildings fall.

I know deep in my soul that my brother is dead.

*　　*　　*

The news is advising everyone to stay inside. Cell phones and landlines are basically down. All roads and bridges are closed. Screw that. My daughter can stay home with my wife. I'm going to try to get into the city. It's almost 10:00 a.m. when I hop into my little red BMW.

When I hit the road, all the traffic is pulled aside to make room for first responders. I follow, doing 120 mph.

Cops have set up a barricade. As soon as they see me in my uniform, they wave me through. When I get to the bridge, the toll guy says, "It's about time they called you guys up."

I'm on my way to my unit when I remember that my brother's wife also works at the World Trade Center, at Cantor Fitzgerald on the one-hundred-something floor. I don't have a cell phone, so I can't call her—and even if I did, I wouldn't be able to get through.

She's dead, too, I think. *She's a workaholic, never takes a day off. There's no way she made it out of there alive.*

I veer off the road and drive to my brother's house.

I'm frantically ringing the doorbell when the door opens.

I feel like I've just seen a ghost.

Tommy's wife is standing there. She knows what I'm thinking and says, "It's the kids' first day of school, so I took it off. Tommy's all right. He got away. As soon as the first plane hit, he took off. He wasn't up high, so he was able to get out. He's on his way to the ferry."

Back in my car and driving to my unit, I'm wondering how I'm going to call everyone in.

When I get there, I realize it doesn't matter that the phones aren't working. I didn't have to make a single call. My unit has already arrived—and they're not alone. Military guys from all services home on leave, veterans—everyone has shown up, ready to help.

September is a big time for people to go on leave because, until the end of the month, it's use your time or lose it. A lot of key players are at a global training conference in Little Rock, Arkansas. My division, the 42nd, is at a conference at Fort Leavenworth for Warfighter, our major training event. The headquarters is in Albany, New York. A lot of those people are out of town—and now they can't call in.

We wind up getting limited communication with some of the higher-ups. Each one says the exact same thing:

"Don't do anything."

The two battalion commanders and I say the opposite: "Hell, no, we're going." It's been a long time since there was a major National Guard event, and the senior leadership is afraid of making a decision.

We end up losing communication with higher head-quarters.

It's the best thing that can happen. It allows us to focus on search and rescue. These buildings fell, there's a bunch of people alive in all that rubble, and we've got to dig them out. We muster supplies and then head out to the local Home Depot.

The manager comes over to us and says, "What do you guys need?"

"Listen," I say, "I don't have the authority to authorize purchases—"

"We're donating. Just tell us what you need."

The Home Depot guys empty the store of gloves, rope, eye protection, chain saws, pry bars—everything we could possibly want. They load up two box trucks full of supplies.

"God bless you all," the manager says. "Go do great things."

Two firemen walk in the front of the store.

During fire season, these guys have to deal with their fire trucks getting stuck or sinking when they go off-road to fight brush fires on Staten Island. We've helped them out using our HEMTT wreckers and an M88, which in civilian-speak is a tank recovery vehicle. We've developed a good relationship with these guys.

The two firefighters are distraught. All their buddies are missing, and as I listen to them talk, it's the first time I realize the magnitude of the loss we're dealing with.

"Here's the plan," one of the firemen tells us. "The ice-skating rink on Staten Island is located right next to the ferry terminal. We're going to set up a morgue there and we'll do triage at the baseball field next door. Can you give us all your medics, anyone with any medical training?"

Our unit has a medical platoon, and we have guys with civilian jobs as nurses and EMTs. We round them all up and send them down to the baseball field.

We were expecting to head into the city, to dig people out of rubble. What we end up doing is organizing first responders—firemen and cops—to help deal with the people coming off the ferry. We set up a field-expedient morgue to collect the remains.

By early afternoon, the fire department puts out a call

for generators because lower Manhattan has no power, and darkness is coming. When the ferries and volunteer boats drop people off at Staten Island, we put the generators on the boats to be brought back into the city.

I'm still trying to figure out what higher command wants me and the other units to do when I get a call from Brigadier General Ed Klein.

"Get your guys and get in there," he says. "I don't know what's going on down there. But if you do nothing, I'll fire you."

That's all I need to hear.

Our vehicles are already loaded up and the whole battalion is ready to roll.

A few hours earlier, one of my guys sent forward a captain to the city. He comes back and gives me a full report on the crash site. "There are body parts everywhere, people dead," he tells us, "and the fires are still raging."

Less than twenty-four hours later, at first light on the morning of September 12, we roll in a convoy into the city.

The rumor mill is saying that what happened yesterday is just the opening salvo. The cops are telling us that twenty EMT uniforms were stolen from Brooklyn and that they found an ambulance on the Verrazzano Bridge that was loaded with explosives. I've got everyone armed with weapons. The Humvees we're driving have mounted machine guns.

Growing up in New York, I remember watching the World Trade Center—we called it the skeleton building—getting built. When I drive over the Verrazzano Bridge in the lead Humvee, all I see is a burning crater and black smoke.

That's when it really hits me: the World Trade Center is gone.

I break down crying.

When we come through the Battery Tunnel, it looks like it's snowing. A gray ash is raining down, covering everything.

It's nuclear winter.

I link up with a police command post. They give us the perimeter of Ground Zero. We relieve the artillery guys who were there the night before, the medics, everyone. I've got a 113 tank parked in front of New York City Hall and a guy on a .50 caliber watching the Brooklyn Bridge.

The area around Ground Zero . . . it's like time stopped. All the people are gone, and everything is covered with that gray ash. There are shoes on the road and cars and taxis with their doors hanging open. Everybody got out and just ran.

The next shock comes when I see several blocks of twisted, destroyed fire trucks, police cars, and ambulances. The technique to fight a high-rise fire is to set up a command post at the base of a tower. All the cops—specialized high-building rescue, command post guys, all that talent in the fire department—they prepared their whole lives for the day when they'd respond to such a fire, and they were there at the base of the towers when the buildings collapsed.

Everyone loves the military presence. Mayor Giuliani does not. He goes berserk about the tank parked in front of city hall and sends down one of his guys.

"What is this, *The Siege*? *Get that tank out of here!*"

I move the tank to Battery Park, where no one can see it.

As far as search and rescue, it starts to become a bucket

brigade of tiny little body parts: a foot, a rib cage, or a hand, a piece of meat you can't identify. That's all that's left.

Every night, we sleep in Battery Park. Every night, my last conscious thoughts are of my daughter, wondering what news she might have accidentally seen or overheard. We're in this little isolated bubble—no newspapers or TV, limited phones. It feels like the whole world is coming apart around us, and mentally, that preys on a lot of guys.

In the beginning I'd thought, *Hey, we're going to find these people buried in the rubble. We're going to get them out.* It takes about a week for me to realize that nobody is coming out of this thing.

My fellow battalion commander says to me, "You know, we're lucky that we're in the right place at the right time. Everybody in America wants to be here helping, and we're here actually doing it."

I realize he's right.

It also gets me thinking about two guys in my unit: a first sergeant and a mortarman named Tommy Jergens. They work together at the state courts office. When the planes hit, they ran down to the World Trade Center.

Tommy went down into a subterranean level of the World Trade Center to help some people get out. The building collapsed and he was killed, never seen again. The first sergeant got buried in some rubble. He dug himself out, drove home, took a shower, put on his army uniform, and reported to the unit.

JILLIAN O'HARA

*Born and raised in San Jose, California, Jillian O'Hara knew
at an early age that she wanted to fly helicopters. She attended
Norwich, a private military college in New England, and after
graduating in 2013, she went on to flight school. Jillian is an
aeromedical evacuation officer as well as a pilot. She's stationed
at Hunter Army Airfield in Savannah, Georgia.*

I bolt awake to the crackle of the radio inside our shack. It's
dark, unbearably hot, and I'm already jumping off my cot
before a voice belonging to one of our night-ops guys is yelling over the radio, *"Medevac! Medevac! Medevac!"*

My bunkmates are up and scrambling. I went to sleep in
my uniform, so I don't have to waste precious time getting
dressed, and my vest and equipment are close by. When
the call comes in for medevac, you know someone is in
extreme pain, possibly dying, and you can't waste a single
second.

Then I'm told we're about to launch on a Category Alpha mission. That takes the adrenaline to a whole other level.

Alpha is the highest category. A Cat Alpha means a dire emergency. Life, limb, or eyesight.

It's just before dawn here in Jalalabad, a city in eastern Afghanistan. I sprint across the uneven ground full of fist-size boulders, heading for the airfield. My gear is weighing me down, and I'm carrying my weapons. In the crushing August heat, the temperature is already well above ninety degrees, climbing to upwards of 120 degrees by noon.

I'm the pilot of what's essentially a flying ambulance. But I'm not in this alone. I have my Dustoff crew with me: my copilot, crew chief, and medic. We've been training together for the past year. We have each other's backs. This is our first real mission.

And we're going into actual combat.

I take the left seat in the HH-60 Mike—a Sikorsky Black Hawk medevac-outfitted helicopter with a litter system, hoist, and forward-looking infrared (FLIR) cameras. It's a marvelous piece of machinery: swift, efficient, and fast.

I turn knobs and flick switches as I run through a mental checklist. The Black Hawk sat all day yesterday baking in the desert sun, and the cockpit is sweltering.

The twin turbine engines fire.

The rotor blades begin to chop the air. Moments later, the sound is nearly deafening. The only voices I can hear are the radio calls over my headset.

"Dustoff 609," Tower radios, "you are clear to launch."

Wheels up. I grab the stick.

As my bird climbs along with our two escorts, a pair of

Apache attack helicopters, I look to the nearby mountain range housing Tora Bora, the cave complex where Osama bin Laden hatched his terrorist plans. The month after 9/11, bin Laden returned here and then managed to escape US forces. Tora Bora is always in my line of sight, even on the ground.

Bin Laden is the reason I'm here—why we're all here.

Our destination is on the other side of the mountains. When I reach our maximum speed, I radio the ground commander: "This is Dustoff 609. We are en route. ETA six minutes."

"Roger, Dustoff 609. Please be advised patient's life signs have dropped. Anything you can do to increase time will be greatly appreciated."

I increase speed as I climb, keeping my eye on the torque gauge. I can only sustain a high temperature for thirty minutes. Anything longer and the engines will seize.

I've never felt more exhilarated in my entire life.

I knew I wanted to fly since I was five. People would say, "Oh, how cute. Maybe next year she'll want to be a princess or a ballerina." My mind never changed. Then 9/11 happened. Hearing my dad on the phone, distraught as he talked to his family on Staten Island—that sealed the deal for me.

We get a break from the heat, courtesy of the higher altitude. Cool air rushes inside as we fly over the snowcapped mountains at sunrise. Looking down, you might mistake these beautiful peaks for the Colorado Rockies.

And yet I can't reconcile how something so beautiful and peaceful can be so harsh. On the ground, people are living in mud huts and makeshift compounds without electricity, running water, anything. It's a third world country, and I'm humbled to think that back at base we've got plenty of food, shelter, and clean water—we even have Wi-Fi.

I know the bad guys could be lurking somewhere in these mountains right now. Not only are they trying to kill us, they hurt and kill their own, even women and children. They hide there, waiting to take us down with their RPGs (rocket-propelled grenades)—which is why we're flying with a pair of attack helicopters.

Per the Geneva convention, medevac helos aren't allowed to have any weapons installed inside the aircraft. The enemy knows this, which is why they specifically target us. With the red and white medical crosses painted on the bird's sides and nose, we're easy to spot.

But we're not going into this unarmed. Our M4 rifles are stored inside the aircraft, and we each carry an M9 handgun. We can defend ourselves on the ground, if necessary.

I check the speed, and then the temperature. We're good. Only a few minutes away from the landing zone.

Then I get a call from one of the guys on the ground. "LZ is hot. We're trying to clear the area for your landing. Stand by."

As I reach the LZ, over the radio I can hear gunfire, fighting, and I can see bullets hitting the buildings off to our right side.

The guy on the ground says, "Ma'am, you're not cleared. You can't land."

Except I've got to land—and do it *right now*—or the patient won't make it. I also have to consider my team. They're hearing the same radio communication I'm hearing yet they're trusting me to keep them safe.

I've got to make a decision: wait or go into a hot landing zone.

I go in.

My medic throws open the door the second we land and runs off to grab the patient. The whole helicopter is encompassed in dust. I can't see him—I can't see anything.

And we're getting shot at.

Normally, I'm on the ground for no more than a minute—usually less. This time, the waiting feels like a lifetime—and the gunshots are close.

It's the most scared I've ever been.

The medic comes back and loads the patient. Flooded with adrenaline, relief, and the knowledge that I'm helping bring someone home on their worst day, I'm already lifting off the ground.

This is 100 percent the best thing I've ever done and will ever do.

And I cannot wait to deploy again.

PART TWO:

IN TRAINING

LISA MARIE BODENBURG

Lisa Marie Bodenburg grew up in upstate New York, right near Buffalo. In high school, she was an honor roll student and played varsity sports; was a member of the Model United Nations and the National Honor Society; and won multiple academic awards. She is currently a staff sergeant and a 6174, also known as a Huey crew chief or a door gunner.

"You're throwing your life away," my high school history teacher tells me privately, after class. "You're throwing away your talent."

He's not the first teacher who has said this to me. My coaches are shocked by my decision. Nearly everyone in my life is. My mother, especially. I've tried to explain to her—to everyone—my decision to join the Marine Corps.

It's a privilege to be in this country, not a right. I learned this lesson in an AP American history class, and it soon became my passion, driven by my overwhelming need to earn that privilege every day. It starts with my honor to live in this country and extends to my pledge to fight for those who can't earn the privilege themselves.

I felt this way before 9/11, but that strengthened my decision. That morning I was in the hall at school, between periods, when a teacher stepped into the doorway of his classroom and said, "Do you know what's happening?" I didn't. When I stepped into his classroom, he had the news on. I instantly started crying.

All my mother can think about is college. Neither she nor my father (who died when I was young) went, but my two brothers did, and both got full rides. Which is why I've worked so hard in school. My mother doesn't make a lot of money, so I've got to get a scholarship, too, or I have to pay for it myself.

But I've made my decision. I'm joining the Marine Corps. I need something to push me, to drive me, and to bring out something in me that gives me joy. Something that isn't easy. Problem is, I'm seventeen, and my mother won't sign the paperwork. I'll have to wait until I'm eighteen.

Until then, I'll go to college.

In 2005, I walk into the recruiter's office and say, "Sign me up. I want to be a Marine."

"Okay, great," the male recruiter says. *All* the Marines here, I notice, are men. "What do you want to do?"

"I want to be Force Recon."

The recruiter and the other guys kind of laugh at me.

"Okay," the recruiter says. "What do you really want to do?"

I don't understand what's going on. "I told you. I want to be Force Recon."

"You can't do that."

I get defensive. "Why not?"

They stare at me like I'm oblivious.

"Women aren't allowed in infantry billets," the recruiter says.

Women aren't allowed. I'm so angry I get up and leave.

I go back to college and, after I calm down, I do some research. Then I go back to the recruiter's office.

"What's the most combative position I can have?" I ask.

They tell me about this illustrious military occupational specialty (MOS) called a crew chief, or a door gunner. The more they talk, the more I realize it's as close to combat as I can get. It will literally take an act of Congress to change the fact that women can't serve in infantry positions. (They can now. That act of Congress finally happened.)

"Can females hold the crew chief position?" I ask.

"Well," the recruiter says, "we don't know of any women who do have it, but there's nothing saying you can't. If you go in with what we call an open contract, and if you make honor graduate, you'll get to pick your job."

"What's 'honor graduate' mean?"

"It means you have to be the best. You have to graduate number one."

Now I have a goal in front of me.

"Done," I say. "Sign me up."

Boot camp is fun. I love it. I have a great time. I'm good at it because I know I'm a leader. The Marines sharpen my skills. Their no-bullshit attitude creates a sense of self-confidence in me. They solidify what I'll stand for and what I won't.

I am the honor graduate. Number one. I did it. I accomplished my goal.

I tell the battalion commander I want to be a crew chief.

"There aren't any slots for you," she says, "so we're going to sign you up to be crash fire rescue, which is in the aviation field."

After boot camp, Marines either go to the School of Infantry or, if they're not going to be in the infantry, they go to Marine Combat Training (MCT), which teaches the basics of being an infantryman. I'm shipped off to Camp Geiger, in North Carolina.

In boot camp, men and women are segregated. You're not even allowed to look at each other from three hundred yards away. Now I'm going through MCT with the male Marines. We're integrated, and women are going up against men every single day.

And this course has an honor graduate as well. A slot.

The master gunnery sergeant asks to speak to me. I go to his office.

"I hear you're still looking to change your MOS to be a crew chief," he says.

"Yes, Master Gunnery Sergeant."

He stares at me. I know what he's thinking: there's never been a female crew chief who has deployed.

"I don't care that you were an honor graduate at Parris Island," he says. "You're at my school now. If you want that job, you have to graduate honor graduate out of *my* school."

In the platoon, we do land navigation. We do long humps carrying weapons and hundred-pound packs, learning how to survive off the land. I learn to shoot a .50 caliber and a 240. We eat MREs. We don't shower for weeks.

I love it. I absolutely love it—no matter what they throw

at me, no matter how many times they say I'm a brand-new nugget who doesn't know her head from her ass. *You're here to learn,* they keep telling us. *You're here to fight for this country. You signed up in a time of war. You did this willingly, so you better get your head on straight and learn to do it right because the Marine next to you is counting on you to save his life.*

As graduation approaches, I'm neck and neck with another guy for the honor graduate spot. It comes down to the final test—a gun test on the 240 heavy machine gun.

I score number one.

Graduate as honor graduate. They finally change my MOS to crew chief.

But I still have four more schools to go through before I can actually hit the fleet.

Next stop: the Naval Aircrew Candidate School in Pensacola, Florida, where I'll learn to become a crew chief. Half of the course is extremely strenuous PT qualifications.

I'm the only female.

I learn about the fixed wing and rotary aircrafts. There are a lot of attack helicopters, but the Huey is the one I want. Its primary mission is combat.

I finish the course and graduate as the honor graduate—again. Now I get to choose.

The gunnery sergeant walks down the line and asks each graduate his choice.

"Hueys," I tell him. That will put me in the fight.

He shakes his head. "No, I'm going to put you on 46s."

I'm a nobody lance corporal, and he's a gunnery sergeant who's also a Huey crew chief. The reason he doesn't want me on the Hueys is probably because it's a good ole boys club.

I speak up. "Respectfully, Gunnery Sergeant, I was told that if I graduate honor graduate, I get to pick. And I pick Hueys."

"Why do you want Hueys?"

I tell him. He stares at me for what seems like hours. My heart is racing, blood pounding in my ears.

"You can dig your own grave," he says.

Next stop: SERE school. Survival, evasion, resistance, and escape. They blindfold us and put us on a bus where the windows are blacked out. They drop us off at some undisclosed location in California, where we learn resistance methods if we're ever captured.

I get beat up a little bit as I learn how to survive. But still, I'm loving it. Same with the next school, CNATT—the Center for Naval Aviation Technical Training. I love the challenges. I love proving people wrong. And I love proving myself wrong, too—there are plenty of days when I hang my head and think, *Man, I can't do this.* But then I wake up the next day and push myself more and more.

I'm honor graduate at both schools.

My last school is all about flying. It's studying how to be crew chief and then passing not only written examinations but practical examinations, like going down into the flight line shop, checking out the right tools, setting up your aircraft properly, and being able to say the correct things on the flight.

This is where you'll find out whether or not they'll let you fly.

At every school, the men have made it clear that they don't want a female graduate in the door gunner position. At each school, they make it harder and harder for me to succeed. The pressure is constant. I turn it into fuel for my fire. *Oh, you don't want me here? You don't think I can do it? Well, guess what? I'm going to do it and I'm going to do it better than everyone else.* CMT school is even more intense. All day, every day, I'm being told by my male instructors and by other men who are there to supposedly help me and lead me that I don't belong here. They tell me I can't be a door gunner. That I'm not going to make it.

It's the first time I don't like being in the Marine Corps.

I spend a lot of nights scared. There are a lot of tears and plenty of days when I have zero motivation. On those days, the only thing I know how to do is take the next step. When the alarm goes off, I get out of bed. Next step, I put my boots on. Next step, I walk to class. It's all about that next step—these small, everyday victories. It's all a mental game.

And I am *not* going to quit.

One instructor makes me believe I've flunked out. Then the scores are posted.

I'm *the* honor graduate.

I've made it.

Now it's time to go to the fleet. There, no one cares if you were the honor graduate or the bottom of the barrel. None of that matters. You start again from zero. It's time to put all your training into action.

And you better deliver.

I show up to my first squadron, HMLA-367 Scarface, in California. I'm the only female. As I check in, the guys on the squadron glare at me like, "Wait a minute, you can't be here. This is a good ole boys club. Absolutely not. She ain't ever gonna fly on my aircraft. She ain't ever gonna work on my aircraft. She's just a walking mattress. She's not good for anything."

We deploy together in nine months.

In 2008, we fly into the Al-Taqaddum Air Base in Iraq.

The training to get here was the most intensive thing I've ever experienced. Over those nine months, I learned how to be a mechanic. Learned how to test the aircraft and how to make adjustments to the controls, the fuel, how much gets dumped into the engine to make sure we're within limits. Putting weight on the blades, changing the pitch of the blades, making sure it's smooth. Making sure the engines run properly. How to pull a transmission, replace an engine, fix an engine and fuel cells.

On top of that, as a crew chief I studied all our weapons and the proper calls I have to make when flying. I had to know weapon tactics. The fundamentals of aerial gunnery. What happens to the round while it's inside the weapon and what happens when you shoot it from a moving platform. Terminal ballistics and aerial ballistics—I had to learn it all.

The studying never ends. It's incredible, the vast amount of knowledge required in order to simply do our jobs.

And, of course, there was target practice. We flew over the ocean, and I shot at multiple targets with the Huey's minigun. The weapon fires three thousand rounds a minute. It's fairly easy and smooth—a thing of beauty. But if it jams, then oh, God, it's the devil. But still, I love it. It's my favorite weapon.

Now I'm in Iraq. No more practice. I'm about to do it for real.

Our job is to fly around supporting convoys and the ground guys, giving them an escort into or out of a situation. The country is very flat and brown; it never changes color, ever. You can fly for hundreds of miles and it all looks the same.

Most of our missions involve saving the lives of Iraqi civilians—and even our enemies. If an enemy is injured in battle and lays down his weapon, it's our duty to help him, and we do.

During my second tour of Iraq, I switch to another squadron: the Vipers. A small group of us go out and meet another squadron—the Gunfighters—in Al Asad, where we dismantle their aircraft, load them on a transport plane, fly everything to Kandahar, and then rebuild the birds.

The terrain in Afghanistan is different from Iraq. Here there are mountains and a river and patches of green. There are small towns and ones that have what seems like millions of homes and millions of people crammed into a space the size of a football field.

When I return to Afghanistan again, in 2009, for my third deployment, my sergeant major wants me to be a part of the Lioness Program.

"We need female Marines with the ground units," he explains.

"I thought women aren't allowed on the ground side."

"They aren't, technically. But we need them there, to do all the grunt stuff, because of the culture. Our male soldiers aren't allowed to search, let alone touch, Afghani women."

My CO won't allow it. "Absolutely not," he tells the sergeant major. "She's a crew chief. If she leaves, it will take an entire crew out of operation. We don't have enough people, and we're flying every single day."

Not only that, but there are now limits on the number of hours we can fly per day.

Our flight surgeon is downing us all the time. She's constantly checking on us because we're going over the allowable hours every single day. We have daily, weekly, and monthly regulations, and we're superseding all of them. We're trying our hardest to do everything by the book, but it's impossible.

Besides, what am I supposed to tell the guy downrange who's in danger of getting his head blown off? *Sorry, man, I can't come save you because the book says I have to sleep.* I get the rules, they make sense. If we don't rest and do the right things, then we're going to crash out of the sky and die. But the war doesn't care about our sleep schedule or the fact that we only have so many crew members and pilots. If we're at the end of our shift and the alarm goes off and the new crew isn't there yet—or even if they are and haven't set up their bird—we have to go even if we've worked a sixteen-hour day.

The flight surgeons have a solution: they give us uppers and downers.

And we take them, because we need the help. We have to stay awake in the aircraft or behind the weapon. When we get back from a mission, our adrenaline is through the roof. We clean up our bird and talk to the ground guys and maintainers, then realize we've got to be back to work in six hours—so we take a downer so we can hopefully get some sleep.

Somewhere in this haze, I turn twenty-two.

On the morning of October 26, 2009, the last day our squadron is flying together, I'm running the desk when I get word that two Marine helicopters—a Huey and a Cobra—have collided, and four Marines I've come to know very, very well—four great men—are dead.

It's an extremely tough deployment. But the relationships, the brotherhood, the closeness, the fun and joy we manage to find in the shittiest situations—these are the things I'll never forget. I'll hang on to them, and the memories of these four heroes who died that day, for the rest of my life.

My five-year contract is coming to an end. I return home and fly across the country, attending funerals. I'm ready to reenlist, but first I have to get surgery on my knee. My work is very, very, very hard on the body, and my knee is really damaged. I've been putting off the surgery for a long time.

I'm also having some sort of heart issue. I'm told my heart has suffered some damage from inhaling too much toxic smoke from the burn pits in Iraq. The doctors put me on what's called a temporary up-chit so that I can deploy again—and I definitely want to deploy.

I'm at the top of my game. I'm now a staff sergeant. I picked up all my qualifications, I'm good at what I do, and I've proven myself to all the guys. I'm ready to go to WTI—weapons and tactics instructor, the highest level you can acquire as a crew chief. I have my package in for MECEP—the Marine Corps Enlisted Commissioning

Education Program. It will pay for me to go to a four-year college and become an officer—and a pilot.

Health issues aside, I couldn't be happier.

Then, as I'm going through physical therapy post knee surgery, everything is ripped out from under me.

I'm told I'm never going to run again. Because of that and the damage to my heart, I'm also told I'm never going to fly again.

For eleven months, I fight their decision. My CO joins my fight. During that time, I'm stuck running the desk, so I'm not flying anymore. I work as a mechanic, fixing helicopters when they break, and I launch them when they have to perform a mission. I'm watching my nuggets go and fly, knowing that there's a strong chance I will never fly again myself.

Six weeks before the end of my contract, my CO walks me over to medical and pulls aside the battalion commander, a woman. My CO and I discuss all the reasons why I should fly again. Why I *can* fly.

"She will never fly again," the battalion commander tells us.

It's October of 2010. I leave the Marine Corps in January of 2011.

My life turns upside down.

I head off to Southern California and end up bartending. I meet someone, a fellow Marine, and we start dating seriously. I stay in Southern California while he deploys. When he gets back, we move to central California, stay there for a year and a half, and then we move to Annapolis, where he's going to be an instructor at the Naval Academy.

I become a volunteer boxing coach at the academy—as

a civilian. I got into boxing in California so I could stay in shape without running.

For some reason, I get it into my head that maybe I can still run. Ten minutes into it, I collapse. The pain is so bad I have to call someone to come pick me up because I can't walk.

In 2013, I split with my boyfriend. I stay in Annapolis and get my college degree. When I graduate, I use my Marine Corps security clearance and land a six-figure job with the National Security Agency, working as a facility security officer and contract specialty officer.

I hate it. There's no way I can do this for twenty years.

I leave the NSA and become a personal trainer. I've always trained Marines, and I have a passion for fitness. I work for a Gold's Gym for about a year. Then, as I'm preparing to go off and run my own business, I get a phone call from a Marine Corps recruiter. His job is to call all prior service Marines and try to get us back on duty, either active or reserves.

"You're getting a fresh start with your medical record," he tells me.

I'm stunned. Speechless.

"There's no record of anything, good or bad," he says. "I'm telling you this because if you can pass all the physical requirements, you can come back to the Marine Corps."

As he tells me about life in the reserves, I'm thinking about my civilian life. I have a home. I bought a boat. I have a new career and money in the bank. But I'm still miserable. Something's missing.

"Just try it," he says. "If you don't like it, you can quit."

I check out the reserve unit and sign a nonobligating contract.

I pass all my tests.

I rehabilitate myself physically, and even though it's very, very painful, I'm able to complete the three-mile run that's part of my PFT—the Marine Corps physical fitness test.

I get my flight status back.

The feeling is incredible.

I burst into tears.

I've made it. After all this time, I've made it back.

During the drive to my first reserve drill weekend, the gunnery sergeant of the shop calls to make sure I know where I'm going. At the end of the conversation, he says, "Welcome back to the gun club. Your reputation precedes you."

His tone is clear: my reputation is a good one.

Around this time, I start getting Facebook messages from women who don't know me. They reach out and tell me that they've heard so much about me, and they want to know if I can give them any advice on how to be a crew chief. They thank me for paving the way for them.

Hearing their heartfelt words makes all the bullshit I went through fucking worth it.

And I would do it all over again in a heartbeat, because I love the Marine Corps. I love leading Marines. There is nothing greater, no greater feeling, no greater responsibility or achievement.

RYAN LEAHY

Ryan Leahy comes from a long line of military officers, starting with William Leahy, a five-star naval officer who was the head of the Joint Chiefs of Staff under FDR. His grandfathers both served in Army Air Corps during World War II—one as a gunner on a B-17, the other an engineer who was involved in liberating the Buchenwald concentration camp. His uncle was a Marine who served in Vietnam. Ryan grew up in a small town an hour south of Chicago. When he was on active duty, he served as a chief petty officer. He's currently an ensign in the Navy Reserve.

In 2001, my best friend gives me a ticket to attend his graduation from Navy boot camp. This kid is like a brother to me, and sitting in the stands and seeing him looking impressive in his Navy dress uniform makes me reflect on the current state of my life.

I'm eighteen and driving a forklift at a frozen food warehouse. Not the most glamorous job in the world, but I'm making thirteen bucks an hour and I've got my own place and a car. The guys I work with are all grown men who eat ketchup sandwiches because they can't afford a whole lot. They all cram together into one pickup to get back and forth to work because they can't afford gas. Things are okay for me right now, but watching these guys makes me think this job isn't really going to take me where I want to go.

After his graduation ceremony, my buddy gets something like twelve hours of liberty. On the way home, he tells me, "I got paid the whole time I was in boot camp, and now I've got all this money saved up—and they're going to send me to nuke school. I'm going to learn a trade, and they're going to pay me to do it. This is such a great gig."

"How long are you in for?"

"Six years," he says. "Six years and when you get out, you're pretty much guaranteed to get a good job."

Six months earlier, when 9/11 happened, I had reached out to a Marine recruiter because my uncle was a Marine, and he was pretty proud of his service. I set up a time to meet with the recruiter to talk in person. I waited for nearly three hours, but the guy never showed up, and I never heard from him, either. I figured maybe joining wasn't the right idea and went back to my life.

Listening to my friend now, I'm thinking that maybe joining the Navy would work for me. First thing Monday morning, I walk into the local recruiting office and say, "What do I need to sign?" I tell them I want to go to nuke school, same as my friend.

I go to a Military Entrance Processing Station and take the Armed Services Vocational Aptitude Battery test—the SAT for the military. My score is high enough that they guarantee me a slot to go to nuke school, but they can't guarantee whether I'll be an electronic technician, an electrician, or a machinist mate. I'll find out which one during the last week of boot camp.

In my high school, there was no diversity at all. Boot camp is a complete melting pot. There are people who have never seen snow before or swam in a pool. There are some people who literally can't read or write. One guy, who's twenty-five, never learned to shave. We have to sit him down and actually shave him.

America's best and brightest, I realize, don't enlist in the military. There are a small percentage of people here who want to serve the country, but the majority are poor to lower-middle-class kids the country kind of forgot about. Kids who drank too much in college and failed out. Kids who didn't get a great education. Kids from flyover states in the middle of nowhere who couldn't get a job with the carpenters' union or whatever.

Mostly, I find, they're all really, really good people who really, really care about their country and want to do the right thing—but at the same time, they don't have a whole lot of options. What the military does well, I think, is develop the best version of a meritocracy.

As boot camp draws to a close, I'm told my job. It's the same one as my best friend. I'm going to be a nuclear electronics technician.

When I show up to my first ship, an aircraft carrier three football fields long, I stand on the flight deck with all the other new guys and watch as we pull out of San Diego.

All the people who have been around for a while are smart enough to know that it's time to go grab a nap.

We set sail. Once we get past the breakers, the front end of the ship drops. *Oh, my God, we're going to fall off this thing.* A handful of us literally turn around and start running to the other end of the ship. We don't get very far before the ship stabilizes.

The people watching us start bawling from laughter.

We stop in Hawaii first. Standing on the deck and pulling into Pearl Harbor is very powerful. I can see the *Arizona* and the wreckage of other ships under the water. The hairs stand up on the back of my neck. I'm getting to see this very hallowed and solemn place from a perspective that most people never will.

We're not allowed to go out on the fantails on the back of the ship because the fighter planes land like fifteen feet above your head, but I like to sneak out there and sit underneath the flight deck to watch the planes take off and land. Feeling the temperature change fifty degrees from something that's seven hundred feet away from you, causing so much power, is unfathomable.

We go to China next. When I step off the boat and look around, I'm thunderstruck by everything. Never in my wildest dreams did I ever think I would visit this country.

On the ship, I'm part of a reactor department—the third largest department, consisting of nearly six hundred people. When you're a brand-new sailor, like me, you're only really allowed to hold a broom and a bucket. My life for the next eighteen to twenty-four months is to qualify, qualify, qualify—first basic qualifications, then qualifying for different watch stations. On top of that, there's school, where I have to get certain grades each month, and I also have to complete a certain amount of combat exercises to get what they call deployment ready.

The schedule—the pace—is grueling.

Sometimes in the middle of the night, even when I'm not on flight ops, I walk out on the back of the boat. There are six thousand people on board, and the only thing you can hear is the rumbling of the propellers underneath the water. The back propellers kick up plankton and a bunch of bioluminescent marine life, and the lights underneath the boat turn the water a beautiful shade of blue, the wake seeming to stretch out for miles.

I come out here a lot to relax, take it all in, alone. Just a kid from a small western town standing on the back of a multibillion-dollar warship chugging along in the middle of nowhere.

In June of 2005, we leave Guam and go to Bahrain. The place is dusty, drab, and run-down. Miserable. There's some guy yelling in a language I can't understand, pointing us around with his AK-47. We stop on the base, where you're allowed to buy one single six-pack of beer. We spend pretty much the whole time at the hotel because there's nothing to see or do.

One day six of us decide to venture out to a movie theater showing *Wedding Crashers*.

We get a cab, and our driver immediately pegs us as military. It's no secret when a carrier pulls into town. You've got thousands of people descending into the city; everyone knows who you are and what you're doing there. He asks us why we joined the military.

"Do you just want to kill Muslims?" he asks.

The question doesn't come from a hateful place. It's honest, and it's clear he wants to understand why we've chosen a profession that he believes leads to death across the world.

"I don't want to kill anybody," I explain. "I don't hate anybody. But I do want to protect my country and my way of life. I do want to protect people who don't have the ability to protect themselves."

English isn't his first language, so I have no idea how much he understands. When he drops us off, he shakes my hand and says, "God bless you and thank you for explaining things to me."

I have no idea if he actually means it. For all I know, he's going to go home and say he had stupid Americans in his taxi. Still, I try to show a different side of the US military not only to the taxi driver but also to anyone I encounter.

When the six of us walk into the movie theater, everyone stares. The collective look on their faces is pure hatred. Like if we dropped dead right here, they wouldn't have a problem.

An older gentleman holding a little kid's hand says, loud enough for everyone to hear, "Don't look at the Americans! They'll take you to Guantánamo like your father!"

The six of us look at each other. This isn't a good situation. There are forty to fifty people in this movie theater, so we're severely outnumbered. We're also unarmed.

"Listen, guys," I say, "we've got to get out of here."

The rest of the team says it's fine, don't worry about it. He's just an angry old man.

But I am worried about it. "I'm leaving," I say. "And at least one of you guys has to leave with me."

We have to travel in pairs. When you sign off the ship, you have to go with what's called a liberty buddy so that no one ever travels anywhere alone. "You don't have a choice, so who's it gonna be?"

The team decides to leave. When we go out in the parking lot to get a taxi, I see that two cars have blocked the entrance and exit. We venture onto the street as someone yells, *"Fuck you, Americans! Fuck you, killers!"*

We manage to hail a taxi. The driver wants to charge us a hundred and sixty dollars for a two-mile ride. There are people walking toward us, screaming, and the driver wants to haggle over our cab fare.

We pull out a bunch of money and literally throw it in the front seat. He drives over the median and hauls ass out of there to get us back to the hotel.

Every year on Memorial Day I visit the Arlington National Cemetery and leave feeling pissed off.

I've never seen combat. I'll never be the guy pulling the trigger on anything other than a paper target. I want to do more for our country. Why didn't I go back to that Marine Corps recruiting office?

In 2007, during the Christmas season, I'm sitting at the end of a bar, dressed in my uniform and having a drink, when a Vietnam vet wearing a Marine Corps hat comes over to me.

Ah, shit, here we go. He's going to give me crap about being a Navy guy.

He grabs my hand and shakes it.

"Thank you," he says.

"You're the one who actually did something and saw some stuff," I tell him.

He glares at me. "Don't you dare say that. I'd have kissed a Navy guy right on the mouth if I got the chance in Vietnam. You guys saved my life more times than I can count. I can't tell you the amount of times we would have been dead, but we were able to pick up the phone and you guys came in and got everyone out."

I use this moment as I rise through the ranks, start doing more mentoring and coaching with some of the guys. I tell them, "Listen, you're not pulling the trigger, you're not doing what you see in the movies, but most people aren't. What you're doing by keeping a reactor up, getting that F-18 off the flight deck—you're literally saving people's lives. You're only one or two degrees away from physically saving some-one's life, so have a little bit more onus and understanding and pride in what you do. It might not be the sexiest, the most Hollywood and whatever else, but you're still doing an important thing for people."

I was a skinny, dorky kid who grew up without many friends and pretty low self-esteem. And now here I am get-ting up every morning and, with my chest out and chin high, putting on a crisp uniform. I'm proud of myself. I'm ready to walk into the world and conquer anything.

NICK BLACK

Nick Black's parents were in the intelligence community. Growing up, he spent nine years in various parts of Africa, followed by four years in London, England, before coming back to the States to attend high school. When 9/11 happened, Nick made up his mind that he was going to serve. He attended Johns Hopkins University, played football, and joined the Army ROTC. He went on active duty in 2007, as a field artillery officer. He got out in 2011 and did two years of North Carolina's Army National Guard.

Every morning, starting at 4:30 a.m., two sadistic captains work hard to try to kill us all the way up until 8 p.m.

That's the goal of Ranger school. There's sixty-five of us vying for seven slots.

It's the hardest physical thing I've ever done in my life, and I'm not good at it. I always come in last in everything. I'm so far behind everyone else.

Four months later, after weeks and weeks of pure hell,

I'm one of eight left. And now it's time to face my personal physical fitness nightmare: dead-hang pull-ups.

I'm horrible at them. I played college football, and we never did a single pull-up. Now I have to do twelve of them.

I manage nine.

I fail.

I'm not going to Ranger school.

It's 2007. I request that they send me to war. They say I'm needed in Afghanistan.

I arrive in the middle of the night at a base somewhere on the border of Pakistan, to serve with the 173rd, one of the Army's most prestigious brigades. Because I tried out for Ranger school, I'm two weeks late—and I'm the only leader who doesn't have a Ranger tab, which is really hard for me.

The next morning, I wake up to beautiful snow-covered mountains.

"You're going to Attack Company," I'm told. "There in those mountains. They just got in a four-hour firefight last night."

Holy shit. What am I going to do here? I'm a twenty-three-year-old newbie field artillery officer who is going to have to call for fire on the enemy, and the only training I have is what I've read in my field manual.

I decide to seek out one of the NCOs. My dad, who worked in intelligence, gave me a great piece of advice: *As soon as you show up, go find the NCO you're paired with, talk to him and earn his respect, and then everything will work out for you.*

I'm six foot three and a big dude. The staff sergeant stands six foot five, and with his shaved head and tattoos, he looks like a Russian mobster. The guy's neck is flexed, and I know he's going to tear me a new one the moment I'm done speaking.

I quickly gather my courage and say, "My name is Lieutenant Nick Black. I'm not quite sure what I'm doing, and I'd truly appreciate it if you'd help me."

That big dude just looks at me.

Melts.

"All right," he says. "First of all, sir, your kit is all fucked up. Let's start with that."

He gets me trained and up to speed. Takes care of me. We become partners.

I soon discover I'm surrounded by an incredible group of guys. There's 120 of us, and all I can think about is that I don't want to let any one of them down. I don't want to screw this up.

I run into an acquaintance after my tour, a guy about my age—twenty-three—and when I tell him I've just gotten back from Afghanistan, he asks, "Did you join the Army because you couldn't get into college, or did you just want to do this?"

I'm taken aback.

"Where did you go to school?" I ask him.

He tells me. It's some horseshit liberal arts school in the South.

"That's cool," I say. "I went to Johns Hopkins."

"Then why would you want to go in the Army?"

My parents have dealt with this sort of thing—people coming up to them and saying they're so thankful I went to war so their kids wouldn't have to go overseas and fight. There's this weird segment of the population who can't understand why college-educated people like myself would want to willingly go overseas and risk their lives to fight the fight. They can't comprehend what it means to live a life in the service of others.

We drive somewhere, dismount, and then walk up the mountain to an overwatch position to observe a bunch of Taliban guys, we're told, who are clearly up to something.

I spend a good chunk of my first day walking up a big, deep shale-covered mountain while carrying nearly a hundred pounds of gear. It's brutal, hotter than hell. Same with the second day, when we take a watch position and observe a village.

Nothing happens.

On day three, nothing is happening—and we're running out of water. Then, as the day starts to wind down, we start taking on rockets from a kilometer or two away. They fly over our heads while we take small arms fire from another mountain range, maybe three or four hundred meters away. The gunfire isn't all that effective, and we can't see the guys shooting at us.

We assault our way back up the mountain, which is exhausting, and when we finally reach the top we see where the incoming rockets are coming from. The company commander looks at me and says, "Time to do your thing."

I crawl up to my position, thinking, *Oh, God, I don't know what I'm doing.*

Which is why I brought along my field manuals.

The company commander sits next to me, watching as I

take out my manuals. I'm fresh out of school, and I need the manuals to make sure I get the math right.

After I make the necessary calculations, I call in the artillery.

The artillery comes in and, thank God, shoots all the targets.

It gets dark.

Then pitch-black.

We're at the top of the mountain and we have zero illumination—and zero water. We haven't had any all day. And now we've got to make our way back down the mountain, dehydrated and in the dark.

It's brutal. I'm so parched, I don't even have saliva in my mouth.

I misstep and fall off a ten-foot cliff.

I hit my head and pass out.

When I regain consciousness, I find one of the NCOs sitting next to me.

"How long have I been out?" I ask.

"Three hours." He helps me back down the mountain.

The base is completely isolated. We can't drive anywhere (there aren't any roads—and even if there were, there isn't anyplace *to* drive), and because the area is so remote, there's no resupply route, so no one is coming to help us.

Sometimes a Black Hawk will come screaming by to kick out body bags full of water. But because they're being dropped from fifty feet up, they hit the ground and explode, and we're left trying to cup in our hands whatever's left to drink.

We're alone—120 guys from random parts of America, all under twenty-five. It's like we've been left on an island to fend for ourselves. In a lot of ways, life has never been simpler. I've never felt more invincible, or had tighter bonds and connections with the people around me, guys I completely trust—and yet, at the same time, life is bad. Humans hunting other humans.

During my long fifteen-month deployment, I'm a part of long, grueling missions hunting bad guys on the mountains. Every time I go out, my rucksack is packed with ammo, high-calorie protein bars, and high-calorie electrolyte powder to mix in my water.

We've taken over a little ranch compound, with walls made of brick and mud, located three hundred meters away from the Pakistan border and about twenty kilometers north of our main base. This place is supposed to be this really big infiltration route for the bad guys to come into Afghanistan.

We have an observation post on the nearby mountain, about thirty meters away from the Pakistan border. For two months, we rotate guys in and out, about fifteen at a time, and aside from a couple of scrapes, nothing big happens.

Then one night, when I'm at the observation post, I wake up at around 2:00 a.m. to what sounds like a popcorn machine going off.

The entire mountainside is lit up with gunfire from RPGs and machine guns.

We start going at it. One hour turns into three and then six, and the enemy is moving closer and closer and a lot of us are running out of ammo. B-1s and A-10s come on station, fly in and unload everything they have, and fly away.

The enemy comes through the wire. They're literally getting into our perimeter, and a group of them is trying to overrun the observation post. Our guys hold fast. The leadership of the staff sergeant, the way we all come together—it's incredible. Despite the circumstances, I've never felt such an intense level of satisfaction.

By some miracle of God, all fifteen people on the observation post make it out alive. We're all going home.

The week after I get back, I find out that one of the three intel guys attached to us in Afghanistan killed himself. Two exits before Fort Bragg, he pulled off and shot himself in the head.

I can't reconcile that. How do you make it through fifteen months of combat only to come home and kill yourself two weeks later?

I have another eye-opening experience when a good friend of mine from Johns Hopkins ROTC sends me an email with a startling statistic: the numbers of service members we've lost to suicide is far greater than the number of service members killed by the enemy.

How the hell can that even be possible?

I don't know, but it pisses me off so much that I start a non-profit called Stop Soldier Suicide. Through years of grinding, suffering, and just trying to do the right thing, my staff and I are fortunate enough to have built it into an organization where I no longer have to take phone calls in the middle of the night from veterans in need.

But we have to get all the best minds in the room, come up with a solid plan of action to reduce the national average of veteran suicides, attack this problem, and then go out and do it.

I want to see a day when veterans have no greater risk of taking their lives than any other American.

GREG STUBE

Greg Stube grew up as a Navy brat. His father served for thirty years, and all of Greg's brothers joined the military. Greg started ROTC at the University of Tennessee. He enlisted in 1988. He was a Special Forces medic, 18 Delta. After serving twenty-three years, he retired from the Army as a sergeant first class.

You're not going to make it," everyone in my armor battalion keeps telling me. "Hardly anyone makes Special Forces."

I'd rather go to Ranger school, but my leaders won't let me. It's not a priority for them; they don't want to spend the money in their budget. If there's ever a Ranger-qualified guy in an armor battalion, he always comes from somewhere else. Which leaves Special Forces as my only option to get out of my battalion, because I'm woefully disappointed by most of the people around me.

Being in the military is nothing short of a calling for me.

I work very hard to max my PT test. Then, when I begin to train for my Expert Infantryman Badge, my attitude is, the harder I train for it, the sooner in my career I can get it.

A lot of the sergeants and senior guys in my platoon—guys who are more established, have been at it longer—work hard training me. I am the only one who passed, and that creates some bitterness. What I discover along the way is that just because I want to excel at everything doesn't mean everyone else feels the same way. Some guys just want to get through each day, then crack open a Budweiser.

I'm not criticizing people who are happy with the status quo, but that's not me. I want to be a warrior. But the harder I try to advance my personal goals, the more resentment I get from people who believe I'm making them look bad. They act like I think I'm better than everyone else.

I'm not. There are plenty of people who have the ability to do just as well as I do. They just don't want to put in the effort.

It's true that the odds of me getting selected for Special Forces are low. If I fail, then I'll have to go back to my armor battalion and face everyone who said I'd never be a Green Beret.

I put in my packet.

Get selected to try out in 1992.

I'm the baby in the program. In many ways, I know I don't belong here. I end up being behind on a lot of things. I'm physically fast because I'm light and small, but the weight-bearing training exercises are hard on me. Near the end, both of my feet are nearly broken. And I don't have a lot of the emotional maturity that's going to be required of me.

But I make it through. I get selected.

The next part is out of my control: my specialty. They go through everyone's packet and decide what it is you're going to do in Special Forces.

"Eighteen D," they tell me. "Special Forces medic."

They send me to learn surgery, anesthesia, trauma management, minor dentistry, and veterinary medicine. The last two, I'm told, are designed to help win the hearts and minds of local populations in other countries. Pulling a painful tooth for someone who has never been to a dentist before can be a life-changing thing. Same with their livestock, which can be hard for them to get help for. Performing these services can help build rapport really quickly.

Learning all these things helps expand my mind—and it's also very humbling. Up until this point, everything I've accomplished in the Army has been top-notch. Nobody has beaten me at anything. Now, though, I'm doing my best, and I'm in the bottom 20 percent of the class.

After completing the medical portion of my training, I'm sent to Special Forces language training—the last step in becoming a qualified Green Beret. For the next six months, I learn Russian. That right there pretty much destines me to go to the 10th Special Forces Group.

At twenty-five, I'm the youngest in the group. Everyone else is significantly older—the average age is thirty-five. What I start to notice right away—what I love and respect about these guys—is that everyone pitches in and helps each other out.

Still, it's intimidating, and there's a lot I have to learn. The real technical and tactical proficiency starts now. We're preparing to go to Bosnia.

The country is at the tail end of its five-year civil war, and there's a lot going on when we arrive: genocide, mass killings, and an unbelievable number of amputations from land mines. There are well over six million land mines planted in the ground around our operational area.

I see the trauma up close when a six-year-old girl picks up an antipersonnel mine. It had a plastic body on it, and she thought it was a toy. When it blew, the bomb traumatically amputated her arm. I complete the amputation by removing devitalized tissue, up to and including the lower half of the cubital (elbow) joint. This allows for a more functional amputated limb, or stump.

Treating her, pulling teeth for some of the locals, providing prenatal care, reducing the infant mortality rate—all these things wind up helping our relations in the community and help further our objectives in the area. I try to maturely wrestle with everything I'm seeing, wrestle with these mortality issues, but all I do is become arrogant and narcissistic. I believe I'm ten feet tall and bulletproof. I believe the rest of the world will never fully comprehend what I see and do every day—and probably couldn't handle it anyway. I have no idea my maturity is going in the wrong direction, that I'm setting myself up for a much bigger failure down the road.

After 9/11, the Army reinvents and relaunches its 18 X-ray program, or 18X, in order to address the need for more Special Forces soldiers. The Army gets an influx of kids from all walks of life—many of them giving up lucrative, high-status positions in law or medicine or passing on athletic scholarships and professional sponsorships because they can get a first-time enlistment for 18X and become Green Berets. The Army calls these kids SF babies, which stands for Special Forces babies. It's kind of a disrespectful name, because these kids, for all intents and purposes, are babies. They don't even know what's in the box, and now they're supposed to start thinking outside the box.

I'm working for the Army's Special Warfare Training Group as an instructor in surgery and anesthesia when I go to the sergeant major of the medical training center and volunteer to train these kids. "Instead of complaining about this," I tell him, "I want to be there to try and make a difference for these guys." He grants my wish.

I'm really tough on my students.

It's very difficult to watch them go to war before me. I decide to talk to some people, and in August of 2006 I'm sent to Afghanistan. I see some of my former students. One guy runs up to me and says, "Sergeant Stube, we've got this crazy mission ahead of us. It looks like we're going to be going up against the Mongolian hordes and we really, really need you. Can you come with us? Can you get on this mission?"

You never know how many opportunities you're going to get to fight alongside the people you've trained. You never know how many mentorship chances you'll get, and I don't want to miss my chance to go out with these guys.

I go through the appropriate channels and then, finally, get the approval from Special Forces Command. I join the mission with the 3rd Group.

Three Special Forces teams are assigned to the mission called Operation Medusa. We'll provide a blocking force to help support the Canadian command. It's our job to go into the Panjwayi Valley and flush out the bad guys. As they flee, the Canadians will crush them.

We head to a hilltop called Sperwan Ghar. It's the nucleus of the Taliban—the birthplace of the Taliban. NATO had spent a lot of money developing the area, building resources like schools, and after NATO left the Taliban moved back in and reclaimed it. It's Taliban headquarters now and used as a training center. Our intel is very deficient, so we have no idea just how many Taliban fighters there are waiting for us.

We also have no idea how they're going to fight. From everything we've seen, they engage in guerilla warfare tactics: ambush, then disengage and disappear.

Our plan is to head south from Kandahar and move up through the desert along the border of Pakistan—a route that they would never anticipate. Our vehicles keep getting stuck in the soft red sand dunes. It takes us well over a day to travel those hundred miles through the desert. It's miserable, arduous work.

As soon as we get through the desert, we make contact.

The Taliban digs in and fights.

They aren't going anywhere.

During the first hour of fighting, as we're advancing on the hill, there's so much shooting that we go what we call black on ammo. We've got zero ammunition left. C-130s drop pallets of fresh ammo behind our position, and we have to leave our positions to go retrieve it.

As the fighting continues, we get intel from the air that says there are a thousand Taliban in our area.

And they've surrounded us.

There's so much gunfire going on, the noise so loud, I'm

desensitized to it. It's all the little noises that scare me: the sonic crack of a bullet going past me, rounds hitting my vehicle and the chicken plate on the fifth wheel.

Fear makes you feel small. I'm scared, and there's a moment when I have to wrestle with the frightened child inside me who keeps asking, *Do we really have to do this? Why would they want me to die? Do I really have to kill somebody to stop that from happening?* A part of me keeps wishing that we can all just sit down and talk. If we can do that, I know we can find stuff we have in common and not kill each other.

On day five, we're told we need to take the top of the hill.

Ten guys start to fight their way up to the hilltop. When they get to the other side of it, one of our Afghani counterparts steps on a mine. It blows off one of his legs and puts some holes in his chest. As I work to get him packaged up to be evacuated—if and when the fighting slows down—I hear the voices in my headset growing more urgent.

The gunfire suddenly gets even crazier. More intense. It seems as though our ten guys are about to be overrun. I'm ordered to get in the weapons truck, with its heavy machine gun, and drive it up to the top of the hill to provide covering fire so our guys can withdraw.

I manage to get to the truck. I drive up the hill.

There's an explosion.

I'm blown up, burned, and shot in a matter of moments. Yet I'm still conscious, so I can see what's happened.

I've lost half of my intestines. My right foot and ankle are missing, and I have major burns all over my body.

A bunch of guys rush over to me. One of them is a

medic—a guy I flunked in one of the courses I taught. His name is Riley Stevens, and he had to go all the way back through school a second time. I haven't been face-to-face with him since flunking him way back when.

"Hey," I say, my voice weak. "No hard feelings, right?"

I watch him go to work on me. "A remotely detonated IED got you," he says. "I've called in a medevac."

Two choppers arrive to clear the area for medevac. They're immediately attacked by RPGs. Luckily, they miss, but the choppers have to retreat because the fighting is too intense. It's too risky for them to stay.

An hour later, another pair of choppers—two Apaches—fly in and, like angry wasps, attack the bad guys. They work so hard—and risk so much—to kill them all. Later, I'll be told that these two brave Apache pilots, upon hearing that a Green Beret was down, decided to do whatever it took to wipe out the enemy.

Two hours from when I'm injured, I'm on a medevac. Behind the haze of morphine, before I go unconscious, my thoughts shift back to Riley Stevens, the man who just saved my life.

When I lay wounded on the battlefield and my teammates approached me to help, my first thought was, *There's no way these chuckleheads can save my life. They have no idea how to deal with this kind of trauma.* And whose fault was that? It was mine. I was the problem.

I wasn't able to see the greatness in Riley until there was something in it for me—and I'm tremendously disappointed in myself. That greatness was in him the whole time. I could have mentored him better. I could have brought him closer instead of stiff-arming him away, just allowing him to fail.

Later on, he'll be killed in Afghanistan.

I'm unconscious when I arrive at Kandahar.

Once the surgeons stabilize me, they spend eighteen hours doing vascular surgery to reattach my foot and ankle. Most of my intestines are already gone, but they manage to put my abdomen back together. I have to wear a colostomy bag.

Thirty percent of my body, I'm told, is covered with third-degree burns.

When the IED went off, the doctors explain, it pushed diesel fuel and rocket propellant and other stuff into me, and it just continued to burn, burn, burn. Because of the extensive damage from these full-thickness burns, I'm sent for treatment in Landstuhl, Germany.

After a three-day stay, I'm taken to Fort Sam Houston in Texas to do the "head down, butt up, shut up" routine. Because of the intestinal loss, I can't control my bowels. I have yellow diarrhea constantly running into my third-degree burns. Anywhere between fifteen to twenty times a day I have people I don't know coming into the room to wipe my ass for me.

This was never covered in my training. I'm not prepared for it.

These people take care of me in ways I've never taken care of anyone else. They say it's their job, but I can see the genuine love and compassion in their actions. These people teach me, on a daily basis, that true strength comes from this kind of love and compassion for others.

I begin to form a new opinion about the definition of the term "service."

The one thing people always told me to do was never surrender. But surrender is the one thing I'll have to do if I'm going to survive this. I have to surrender to this kind of service, to this kind of love and compassion, if I'm going to make it. Then I'm going to need to get to work developing the areas of my personality I know aren't tough enough to get me through whatever else life has in store for me.

When my recovery is complete, I fix up a uniform that I can close over my "wound vacuum"—the tubes, rods, and bars—and over the external fixation device I have on my bolted-together right leg.

The commander of the United States Army Special Operations Command, Lieutenant General Wagner, has an open-door policy. I walk unassisted into his office.

"Sir, I'm a patient at Brooke Army Medical Center. I know they're processing me for medical retirement. Sir, please don't let this happen to me. No disrespect, but there are people in this building who have never done as much as I can still do for this army."

He studies me for a moment.

"It's funny that you're here," he says, and picks up a folder. "This here's a request for you to go on Headline News for an hour-long live interview. Tell you what: if you can do this and not embarrass us, I'll give you a job in public affairs. How does that sound?"

It sounds like a lot of pressure. "Thank you, sir."

I wind up sitting down for an interview with Glenn Beck. I think it goes well.

Lieutenant General Wagner agrees and rewards me with a job as spokesman for USASOC.

The CEO of Burger King sees the Glenn Beck interview and calls the Army. He gets transferred to USASOC and asks about me. "We want him to come to our corporate retreat in Puerto Rico next week and speak to us," the CEO says.

Everyone says no. The request makes its way to Lieutenant General Wagner for final disapproval.

"Let him go," he tells everyone.

It's my first official job as spokesman.

What I was able to share with people was how I learned that we all need to serve something bigger than ourselves. And if we want to inspire, we need to make ourselves small, not large. Like mothers, for example. Moms can be exhausted and hungry, even injured, but they're wiping our butts throughout the night. Her success, though, is also *our* success. If we can all be servant leaders, then our teams will thrive and prevail.

None of us pictures the day when what we love to do suddenly ends, because we all see ourselves as being great. But it *does* end—a retirement that comes way too soon, maybe even a traumatic moment. Whether at home or at war, we soldiers need to be in the business of putting ourselves out of business. If the next generation isn't better than us, they might not be able to save us.

JENA STEWART

Jena Stewart grew up in South Florida. She served in the Army National Guard. Her job was 14 Juliet, which is Sentinel radar. She got out in 2007.

I want to drop out of high school," I tell my father. "I want to get my GED and join the Army National Guard."

I have no reason to drop out. I have good grades. It's not like I can't graduate. I'm just so done with high school. I don't understand cliques—the whole society of it. I've always been mature for my age, which explains why I feel like an adult stuck in a teenager's body.

My father shifts in his chair. He's a very, very tough and hardworking person. That's the way he raised me. He never questions whatever it is I want to do as long as I have a plan. *If you have a plan and know what you're doing,* he always tells me, *I'll back you up.*

I glance at my stepmother. She's a public school teacher. I

know it's going to be hard to convince her that I should drop out of high school.

I look back to my father, sitting next to the Army recruiter, and I tell him why I want to join the military.

I was at Booker High School in Sarasota, Florida, when 9/11 happened. President Bush was at Booker Elementary. We all watched his plane take off from Sarasota International Airport because it was the only plane in the sky at the time. Some of us were crying hysterically and others, like me, were simply overwhelmed. I called my mother to let her know I was okay, and later, as I was walking home, I had this eureka moment—one that felt like someone had just hit me across the face with a brick.

For the past sixteen years, I'd been thinking only about myself—about how I felt out of place in high school, how I was convinced something was wrong with me, yada yada yada. It was all me, me, me, I, I, I. For the first time in my life, I realized there was a world out there way bigger than me. When the school had a job fair, I talked to a recruiter at the Army table, and suddenly my life made sense. I had a direction. A purpose.

My father leans forward in his chair. Because I'm under seventeen, I need him to sign the paperwork.

To my surprise, my stepmother says, "No one really cares about a high school diploma. All they care about is a college diploma."

My father's gaze is pinned on me. "Do you really feel like you're done with high school?"

"I really want to do this."

"Then you have my blessing."

I drop out of high school and get my GED. The day I turn seventeen, I head to the local Military Entrance Processing Station and take the ASVAB—the Armed Services Vocational Aptitude Battery test. Afterward, I take myself to dinner. I order myself a dessert with a single candle, knowing where my life is going.

Basic is tough. They wake you up in the middle of the night and they're smoking you physically and mentally—they're doing anything they can to break you.

Everyone is freaking out, but I love it. I love the push of it all. Yes, it's physically and mentally exhausting, but I have this thought that gets me through it—one that I share with other soldiers who look like they're getting to the point of breaking.

"This is their *job*," I tell them. "These men go home and kiss their daughters and tuck them in bed. They go out to dinner with their wives. They're not monsters. They need to break us down to build us up."

It's the summer of 2002 and hot as hell. Midway through basic, I decide to shave my head. I don't want to fiddle with my hair, wash it, make sure I have shampoo. I'm not here to look pretty. I'm here for one reason, and one reason only: get through this as easily as possible.

The day we march to the range, I have my battle gear on, Kevlar, everything. We're standing in formation when the drill sergeant screams my name and says, *"Get the fuck up here."*

I walk up to him, wondering what I did wrong.

"Take off your fucking Kevlar."

I pull it off and then I'm standing there, in front of a ton of people, wondering what's going to happen to me.

"Now this—*this*," the drill sergeant hollers. "*This* is what I'm talking about. This right here—this is a motherfucking soldier. All you other chicks out there—'I've got to do my hair' and all that bullshit—take a good look at this…"

As he goes off, I can't hold back the smile. *Oh, yeah, I just scored major brownie points today.*

The US hasn't declared war yet, but we know we're going. The instructors keep telling us. I go to El Paso, Texas, to learn the specifics of my MOS training—14 Juliet, which is manning actual physical radar machines, identifying any unknown aircraft, and, if they're not friendly, calling up the Stinger missile boys to shoot them out of the sky. When I return home to Daytona, I'm told I'm going to deploy—and I'll be shipping out immediately.

I head to New Mexico for training. They stick us out in the middle of the desert and make us do everything we'll be doing overseas. We train hard for months.

The unit I'm attached to is terrible.

I'm young, pretty, and naive—and surrounded by men, most of whom are teenagers, too. The handful of women here are all spread out in different platoons. I'm the sole female in the unit, and the men delight in tormenting me—catcalls, sexually derogatory names, even spreading rumors like how I'm screwing guys in the maintenance room. It gets so bad, I'm not allowed to be within three hundred feet of a male barracks—because the men ganged up and said that *I'm* the problem.

A week before we're about to deploy, the US declares war. That same day, my unit is pulled out of formation.

To be honest, I'm relieved.

Happy.

Deep down, I know if I go over there, I won't be coming back home alive. I know this because not a single guy in my unit has my back. They've made that clear over these past few months. If we go over there, I'm certain they'd throw me under the bus any chance they got.

In 2003, around Christmastime, I'm told I'm going overseas on the first of the year. I know now not to get too overwhelmed because things can change—and they do. I'm not going overseas. I'm going to Washington, DC, to essentially make sure there isn't another 9/11.

There are roughly five Sentinel radars spread out all over DC. Our job is to watch the skies 24/7. For the next year, we work in shifts, checking for bad guys. I have to take different routes each day to make sure people aren't following me. I carry a weapon with me everywhere—not for self-protection, but to protect our equipment.

I love the work. And I feel such pride wearing the uniform. Every day, when I put it on, I feel a sense of purpose.

In 2005, when I return from DC, I start working hurricane relief. I'm sent to Florida to drive a convoy, through a hurricane, to Tallahassee.

We travel in Humvees with canvas tops and doors—and no AC. It's the middle of the night and raining like crazy—so incredibly *loud*—and the Humvees' headlights are terrible. We can't see shit.

We arrive in Tallahassee—and it's still raining like crazy. We unload at our quarters—a barn at a fairground—in calf-deep water. There's cow shit and cockroaches all over the barn floor, but we grab a couple of hours of sleep.

The next morning, we distribute clean water and ice. We drive all over the place, in five or six trucks. During a ride in what feels like the middle of nowhere, I see a really old man trying to clean up his property.

The entire convoy pulls over. We clean up his yard in fifteen minutes.

The old man is in tears. His wife is crying.

"Thank you," she says to us. "I thought my husband was going to die out here."

I know my job isn't huge—I'm not overseas and doing something that has a big global impact—but I'm still doing something important for the United States, and it gives me pride. I'm a soldier. This is what I was meant to do.

MIKE HANSEN

Mike Hansen joined the Army in 1993 as an officer. He got his commission in 1995, took the Infantry Basic Officer Leader Course, and then went on to the Army's Ranger school.

The most important day of my life is when I was eleven. I'm sitting on my dad's ugly green-and-black plaid couch, and I ask him about the big paratrooper tattoo covering his bicep and tricep. He tells me how he used to jump out of gliders back in Vietnam, how he was a cavalry scout and not a Ranger, and right then I decide I'm going to join the Army. I'm going to do what he did.

But I'm going to go a little further. I'm going to go to the infantry school and then Airborne School and then become a Ranger.

In high school, I'm the guy who shows up to class, barely pays attention, never studies or does homework, and still manages to get As and Bs. I carry this old recruiting manual that has a picture of a Ranger in green camo and a rolled patrol cap, and I flip through it every day, just staring at the picture, telling myself, *This is what I'm going to do. This is who I'm gonna be.* There is nothing I want more in life than this.

I want to go into the Army as an officer, so I decide to attend college at Marion Military Institute in Marion, Alabama. I was born in Chicago and raised in Bethlehem, Pennsylvania, and now here I am in the Deep South. Marion is this tiny little town near Selma, where Martin Luther King started his march. It's a culture shock, but I quickly fall in love with the South and the people.

The school structure is regimented—they have hall monitors and guards walking up and down the barracks to make sure every student is studying—and the academics are hardcore. I can't slack off anymore.

I go to Ranger school. It's pretty tough, but I love it. I love being out in the field. I'm assigned to an infantry unit in the Florida National Guard and attend Florida State. I start talking to the contacts I need to get where I want to go—the 82nd Airborne Division. That's my shot into a Ranger battalion. All I want to do is deploy, be an actual wartime officer. It's my life's dream.

And then here comes this girl from Florida State. I have zero plans to get married—but lo and behold, that's exactly what happens. She makes it crystal clear she's not going to be a military wife living either in Stewart or Benning—or, God forbid, Fort Lewis. I change my path to law enforcement and join the National Guard.

*　　*　　*

On Friday, September 7, 2001, I'm out to dinner with my wife and in-laws at TGI Fridays. Our conversation somehow turns to the subject of the Middle East. I tell them about an interview I heard the other day that the quickest way to shut down the American economy would be for terrorists to attack our airports.

"You're full of shit," my father-in-law scoffs. "They could never attack our airports."

On September 10, I work the midnight shift. I'm dead asleep the next morning when my wife calls.

"Turn on the TV," she says.

I look at what's going on and say, "I told you so."

My wife thinks I'm heartless, but she's wrong. It's just that I'm not surprised.

"I'm signing back up," I tell her. "I'm not gonna sit this fight out."

"Obviously."

I can tell by her tone that she's not okay with it, but she understands. She knew what she was getting into when she married me. When something like this comes along, a guy like me, with an extreme alpha personality, is not going to sit on the bench. Put me in, coach, I'm ready. I trained for this—went to Ranger school for this.

My wife gets pregnant right before my unit gets activated. On March 6, 2003, the day I deploy to Iraq, my wife is nine months pregnant with our daughter. It's weird thinking about how I'd spent the previous ten years wanting to go to war and now, at the last minute, I don't want to leave my wife or miss my daughter's birth. It's a kick in the balls, spending your entire life planning to go to war and when war finally comes saying, "I'm not ready."

My daughter is born on March 12, 2003. I miss her birth by six days. For the next year, I watch her grow up in pictures. For the next year, my wife raises our daughter by herself, as a single mother, while her husband is in a war zone.

We deploy from Fort Stewart into Jordan. Our mission is to leapfrog into Iraq from the western border and disable all the airfields. The US is afraid that Iraq, in a last-ditch effort, will launch a few SCUD missiles into Israel. If Israel responds and gets involved, every other Islamic Middle Eastern country is going to join the fight—which is exactly what Saddam Hussein wants, this coalition. I think the other Middle Eastern states are smart enough not to want any part of that, but once Israel's involved, all bets are off.

We're trying to figure out how to best take out the Iraqi airfields when a notice goes out that a SCUD has been launched. The gas alert blares as everyone scurries to get into mop suits and gas masks. It's the scariest moment of my life, sitting in this Conex, sweating my ass off in this suit, and unable to fight back. I'm a sitting target.

I just got over here to fight, and now I'm gonna die in a chemical attack? This sucks.

Ten hours later, we get the all clear—there's nothing here. The SCUD never made its way to Israel—a bad launch or something. It got about halfway out to the western desert.

I'm picked to represent the infantry on a recon. There's a

staff sergeant from 5th Group, a comms guy. The other guys are in jeans and T-shirts. They don't say where they're from, but I can tell they're the heavy hitters or the muscle of the group. I'm pretty sure they're CIA. Our job is to figure out a way to drive into Iraq from Jordan.

One of the CIA guys says, "Hansen, you pack any civvies in your gear?"

I nod and he tells me to go change. I come back wearing jeans, a T-shirt, and boots. "Hell, no," the CIA guy says. "No boots. I don't care if you have to beg, borrow, or steal. Go find a pair of running shoes or something."

The two white SUVs have TV duct-taped on the windows. That's our cover: we're going in as TV reporters. And because we're TV reporters, the only thing we're carrying is Berettas. The guy who I think is CIA is an American citizen, Iranian-born, and speaks Arabic. He's our interpreter, and our driver.

Jordanians stop us at a checkpoint right before we're getting ready to go into Iraq. Our interpreter does all the talking. One of the Jordanians starts screaming, and then they're screaming at each other. Our driver-interpreter is screaming back. They pull their M4s on us.

I look at the guy sitting with me in the back seat, the staff sergeant from 5th group, and I say, "Dude, I don't want to die in this car. You want to shoot our way out?"

"Yeah, you ready?"

I take out the Beretta, switch off the safety, and cock the hammer back. We're going to fling the doors open and basically try to shoot our way out of the situation.

"We'll go on three," I say.

He nods. My heart's pounding out of my ears as I start to count.

The Jordanians lower their weapons and wave us through.

Holy. Shit. I'm trembling all over as I stick the Beretta in my front waistband.

I'm trying to process what just went down when we start driving down bumpy roads.

"What just happened?" I ask the driver.

"They could hear my Farsi accent," he replies as we bounce in our seats. "They thought I was an Iranian spy."

When people think *desert,* they think *sand.* But here, in Jordan, it's old shale lava rock and there are these ravines that come up out of nowhere and drop thirty, forty, fifty feet.

The shale rock flattens our tires. We take out the spares, change the tires, get back into the SUV, drive, and flatten our tires again. It's not until then that I realize the whole time we've been driving across these bumpy roads, my Beretta's been pointed at my balls—and the hammer's still cocked. My balls could've blown off.

Instead of exchanging letters, my wife and I send cassette tapes to each other. During the middle of April, I'm at the airfield, trying to find a quiet place to make my tape, when a jet flies in and then quickly flies back out.

I start recording, giving my wife an update as to what's going on, when I hear another jet approaching. It lands, refuels, and then flies out.

This happens four times in a row.

I wake up the platoon sergeant and squad leader as another jet flies in.

"Get everyone's shit together," I tell them. "I'm pretty sure the invasion just started."

We start going over all the equipment. Sure enough, I find out jets are basically doing touch-and-goes—touching down, refueling, rearming, and taking off. This goes on for well over twenty-four hours. It's nonstop. All you hear are jet thrusters throughout the entire base.

For the next three days, we bomb the shit out of Baghdad.

Next comes the push into the city. Our battalion gets split. Some go to help support the 3rd Infantry Division (ID). I belong to the unit that comes in behind them. We take over a palace compound near the airport. The compound contains about five palaces, each one as huge and ornate as an upscale Las Vegas resort.

All the fighting positions are basically abandoned. As we clear the foxholes, we find bayonets, gas masks, AKs, even helmets and uniforms. It looks like these guys hauled ass right when we started rolling into town. Anytime we encounter the occasional sporadic gunfire, the Bradleys—troop carriers with heavy guns—make short work of the shooters.

That changes when we get to Ramadi, a city in central Iraq.

Hurricane Battalion confiscates a compound right on the Euphrates River. There are three palaces. One belongs to Saddam Hussein, and each son got his own palace. There's no indoor plumbing, so we have to make do with these makeshift portalets that have the fifty-five-gallon drums you cut in half. We take turns pulling 'em out, pouring in diesel, and stirring it all for a good hour before lighting it on fire. If you don't stir, it won't burn off, and you'll wind up with a big turd cake.

We swim, bathe, and do our laundry in the river's crystal

clear water. The chaplain says he'll baptize anyone in the Euphrates—which is pretty cool, given its Christian significance in the Bible. A lot of us do it.

The guys in Ramadi used to be military. Now they have no jobs and no prospects, and they decide to stay, dig in, and fight. They're more organized with their IED attacks, and they hit us with mortars—a lot of mortars. Every night, for forty-five days straight, they mortar the shit out of us. It gets to the point where we stop caring.

I'm not scared. The attacks don't get close because they're using 60mm mortars, and the insurgents really suck at targeting. Still, the chaplain regularly reads from the Bible, especially Psalm 124: "Had it not been the Lord who was on our side, when men rose up against us, then they would have swallowed us alive.... Blessed be the Lord, who has not given us to be torn by their teeth.... Our help is in the name of the Lord."

We sleep near the Euphrates. It's summer, unbearably hot. Most of us sleep naked. The flies and fleas—they're killing us. I'm getting eaten from head to toe. I can't take the sand fly bites anymore.

"That's it," I say. "I'm going to sleep on the roof."

"You can't sleep up there," one of my guys says. "We're getting mortared."

"Honestly, I don't care. I'd rather get hit by a mortar than bit by another flea."

I go up to the top of the palace with my M16 and set up my cot on the flat roof, next to a wall. In the distance I can hear some troops in contact. Anyone on the other side of the Euphrates right now could see me, but I don't care.

Then I hear it—the sound of a Spectre gunship, one of the deadliest aircrafts in the US Air Force. A moment later, the sky lights up from gunfire, and I witness the gunship's massive power as it helps the good guys on the ground.

It's one of the coolest things I've ever seen.

It's also psychologically motivating. The bad guys on the ground don't stand a chance. I install my bug net and go to sleep.

I'm woken up when an RPG hits the wall.

I'm pissed—not about getting attacked but about being woken up and knocked out of bed when I was getting my first good solid sleep in days. I jump up, grab my M16, and crank off a mag across the river, screaming, *"You missed me, assholes!"* I throw down my rifle and go back to sleep.

The next day, the guys who were sleeping down by the river say it was the funniest thing they've ever seen. Watching their skinny little naked lieutenant cranking off rounds and screaming and then throwing his rifle down and going back to bed—they were laughing so hard they were crying.

Nine months into deployment, and all we're doing is presence patrols. We're trying to turn the patrols over to the Iraqis, but these guys don't know their rear end from a hole in the ground.

One of my higher-ups says, "Hey, Hansen. You're a cop back home."

I nod, wondering where this is going.

"We've got eight, maybe nine guys in the battalion who're cops," he says. "We're gonna form this super squad. We want you guys to train these Iraqis, put together, like, a three-day in-service. You're gonna train them how to be cops and how to patrol."

I'm thinking that'll go over like a fart in church, but I keep it to myself. I go off and develop a training plan that will run in three-day cycles.

We end up training thousands in the Ramadi area. My super squad does so well, I'm told we're going to do training through the rest of central and northern Iraq. We'll be traveling on our own, too, without battalion support.

As we start driving to other places, especially in northern Iraq, where certain parts are still very tribal, I'm struck by the level of poverty. I've seen a lot of poverty back home—I've seen homeless people, and I've been in the ghettos—but the poorest of Americans have clean drinking water. They can get clothes at a Goodwill or a Salvation Army and, if needed, walk into an ER and get medical care. Here, a lot of really young poor kids—like between the ages of two and three—run around naked.

"I thought Muslims were supposed to be conservative and always wear clothes and stuff," I say to my interpreter.

"They don't wear clothes because they don't have clothes," he replies. "A lot of families are so poor they usually don't get hand-me-downs until they're four or five."

The IEDs get more serious the closer we get to Syria. On the highways, we begin to encounter ten-by-ten craters that are, like, three feet deep. Every time I see one of these craters, I say to myself, *You don't walk away from an IED like that.*

Instead of mortar attacks at the base, we get rockets launched at us.

Death starts to become real.

We roll into Fallujah to train the police. The colonel on the nearby patrol base insists we take the same route to Fallujah every time we leave.

"Sir, that's against basic infantry tactics," I tell him repeatedly. "You always leave the patrol base a different way. You enter and leave the wire a different way, every day."

And each time he says, "Don't deviate from the plans."

I'm a popular officer with the enlisted men, but I'm not popular with officers because I do something that most of them don't: I tell the truth. I tell the colonel, right to his face, several times, my assessment of the mission:

"This is stupid."

He doesn't care. He's more concerned about his officer evaluation reports than anything else. OERs are all about a business model, and for this guy (and a lot of other officers), this is a business.

I have no choice but to comply. We take the same route as we roll into Fallujah in our four vehicles—a pair of unarmored Humvees driving in front of me and behind me. My Humvee always stays in the middle since it's a soft-skin.

The bridge has a guardrail on both sides. I'm sitting in the passenger's seat, looking out the front window at a big mound of dirt on the guardrail near the driver's side. Then I'm staring at it and we're pulling up next to it and I see another mound of dirt on the guardrail near my side and I'm thinking, *That looks just like an IED—*

Boom.

The blast hits the forward and rear vehicles, which are unarmored. The second IED, the one near me and right outside my door, blows—*boom*—and I scream *"Stop!"* because I see someone running—or at least I think I do. I'm disoriented, so I'm not sure. All the oxygen has been blown out of the area. When I take a deep breath, I suck up a bunch of hot nitrogen gases and my lungs feel like they're on fire.

I get outside. Tony, a 249 gunner, says he sees the triggerman. I see him, too; the guy's a hundred yards away, running away from us. Even though I'm still disoriented, I lock down on the guy. Tony fires as I fire a couple of rounds. The triggerman keeps running and disappears.

Fortunately, no one is hurt. The IED on my side, the right side, was incorrectly tamped inside this big mound of dirt. The IED on the other side of the road was taped to the guardrail post. When it blew, the post acted as a deflector, and the blast blew out at forty-five-degree angles, away from my Humvee—and I know the triggerman was aiming specifically for my vehicle because it's the only soft-skin in the convoy.

We roll into town and pull into the police compound. The Iraqi police stare at us in disbelief—like we shouldn't be here. And that's when it hits me:

These motherfuckers were in on the bombing. And now they're looking at each other as if to say, *Holy shit, how did that go wrong?*

I can't trust any of these guys.

I'm done with you people, I want to say. *I want to go home to my wife and hold my daughter for the first time.* You want to feel like you're making a difference—and I know we do make a difference in a few of their lives—but it's the ones who don't care that make you jaded on why you're there.

*   *   *

The police find the triggerman at the hospital. Bullet went in the back of the guy's head, but it didn't penetrate the skull. Instead, it spun between the skull and the skin and ended up in the guy's nasal cavity. The police arrest him and bring the bullet back to the police station to show us.

The bullet isn't deformed. I can see the rifling marks and the green paint on the tip of the 5.56-round.

"That's my round," Tony says.

"Dude, it's my round. I took a headshot."

"Yeah, but I cranked off on him," he says. "Totally my round."

"Trust me, that was me."

And around and around we go, busting each other's balls while engaging in some much-needed gallows humor. It's a great distraction to keep me from thinking deeply about the IED attack. I should be dead. My vehicle was the target; I should be dead—we should *all* be dead. We shouldn't be standing here.

Days pass and my vision is still blurry, and I've got headaches and stuff. I'm sent to Baghdad to get checked out and dropped off at the green zone. I'm leaving the hospital, prepared to walk the couple of miles to the next place I need to go, when a Humvee pulls up next to me. The driver asks me if I want a ride. I jump in the back, next to another guy, and the driver turns on a little radio. I hear a pop song, one I recognize: Avril Lavigne's "Complicated."

I shut my eyes and the sun is beating down on me and there's this moment of normalcy. I feel like I'm back in

Florida chilling out to tunes with the ragtop down on my Jeep Wrangler, just riding around in a car with a group of guys listening to music.

And then it comes back to me: I should be dead from that blast. I think of the chaplain baptizing us in the Euphrates, and I think of that Bible verse he read about God's protection. Our battalion hasn't suffered a single fatality. I'm alive because God literally put His hands around my vehicle that day and protected me. I don't know how to describe it other than that.

MIGUEL FERRER

Miguel Ferrer had a really strong interest in the military from an early age. Growing up in Baltimore, he played with G.I. Joes and watched documentaries on the Discovery Channel and Military Channel. His grandfather served in World War II, and his uncle, a scout sniper with the Army, served in Afghanistan. Wanting to see the world and do something meaningful, Miguel bypassed college and entered the United States Navy. He's a hospital corpsman, second class.

I'm going to be a Navy SEAL. Today is the day. I walk into the Baltimore Military Entrance Processing Station (MEPS), stoked.

This is all I've ever wanted. I got hooked on a show on the Discovery Channel—a program that took you inside the Basic Underwater Demolition/SEAL school, or BUD/S. I watched it religiously. I thought it was the coolest thing ever.

But you have to be really physically fit. I've put in the

time these past few years—running, swimming at the pool, or working out nearly every single day. All my hard work has paid off. I did really well on the PFT, the physical fitness test for special operations. I blew them out of the water—high push-ups, high sit-ups, everything.

After I go through the MEPS process, I enter a room and sit across from a woman who is reviewing my file and test scores. It's the summer of 2008, and I'm feeling great. Confident. My dream is about to come true.

"Looks like you've completed all your paperwork," she says. "And you've had your physical. Your security stuff looks excellent." She shuts the folder and looks up at me. "But you can't be a SEAL."

My stomach drops.

"You have what's called color vision deficiency," she says. "It means you're unable to distinguish between certain colors, so being a SEAL is out of the question."

It hurts to breathe. This is all I've ever wanted, what I've been training for, and now I'm being told I can't do it. Because I'm color-blind.

My head is spinning and I'm feeling overwhelmed as she starts going down a roster of available Navy jobs. All of the ones that sound interesting to me—rescue swimmer, air-crew, explosive ordnance disposal—are out because I can't see certain shades of color.

"You could be a hospital corpsman," she says.

"I don't know what that is."

"Use my computer to look it up."

I go on Wikipedia and up pops a picture from 2002—a corpsman attached to a Marine Corps infantry unit. The corpsman is walking down some road in the mountains of Afghanistan.

My uncle was deployed to Afghanistan, and while he didn't talk much about what he saw and did over there, I kept up on all the news on TV. I watched the Towers fall on 9/11 and I watched Saddam's statue come down. I watched the invasion of Afghanistan and Iraq—and I know what's going on there right now, the battles in Ramadi and Fallujah.

Corpsmen, from what I'm reading, fly in and out of hot landing zones. They're on the ground, engaging in battle.

"Can I get into that?" I ask.

She nods. "We can get you into this, walk you into the job, and then we can try to send you off to boot camp as soon as possible."

When I get home, I tell my parents what happened. My mom reminds me of how, when I was a kid, I'd walk around with this toy medical bag, using a stethoscope to give everyone in the family medical exams. Apparently, I also did CPR on one of my sister's dolls.

"Hospital corps," my mom says, "sounds right up your alley."

The Navy doesn't have any slots open until next year, in March of 2009. I spend the entire time training, doing push-ups, and going to weekly meetings and weekly physical activity sessions. I talk to a couple of sailors and hear their stories. When the day to leave rolls around, I'm ready to go, get my life started.

Coming from Baltimore and playing lacrosse in a parochial school, I'm used to wearing preppy clothes. I put on a pair of yellow Ralph Lauren chinos and a Vineyard Vines polo shirt, board the bus, and immediately feel out of place. Everyone else is dressed in regular jeans and T-shirts.

I arrive at Chicago O'Hare airport with my yellow folder and backpack, which holds some toiletries and an extra T-shirt. I check in with the USO. Then I walk what feels like a couple of miles to a terminal where I see all these kids around my age sitting cross-legged, in perfectly aligned rows. They're all facing the glass windows. I'm told to go sit with them.

We can't get up. The moment anyone stands up, a sailor screams to sit back down. We all sit and wait.

For six hours.

Finally, we board a bus that will take us to the Naval Station Great Lakes, in Chicago. It's a solemn ride. The lights are off, and nobody talks. When we arrive at the gate, the bus is dead quiet. Outside the window, I can see the double doors leading into the recruit training center.

The first thing the Navy wants us to do is a urinalysis. Not a problem. I'm hydrated. I've been drinking Gatorade and water.

I can't pee.

This little Filipino chief who is running around cussing at everybody comes up to me. "There's one water fountain right here. The other is over there." He points across the big square room. "You drink from this water fountain. The one over there, you stand at attention. You're going to keep going in circles until you have to pee."

I spend two hours walking in a circle, drinking from one water fountain and standing at attention at the other.

"This recruit requests permission to use the bathroom," I say.

The Filipino chief blasts me. "*Head!* This recruit requests permission to use the *head!*"

In the normal world, when you go to take a leak, you use a stall or a urinal. The bathroom here contains only urinals—about twenty of them lined up against the walls. The Navy orders us to strip down and pee in a cup.

This is my first experience being completely naked in front of a bunch of other dudes. On top of that, I have to try to pee in a cup while a sailor stares at me. I want to ask him not to look at me, maybe turn the water on, so I can relax and get in the mood. I don't, so I stand there naked, straining to pee, trying to get out as many drips as possible to meet the marker line inside the cup.

They move us into another room to hand out uniforms. We're given a seabag and then, as we walk down an aisle, they throw our uniforms at us—two pairs of this, two pairs of that. Out of the corner of my eye I look down, expecting to see the "blueberries" the recruiters promised me—the blue camis that are so cool and so much better than the old Navy uniforms. What I see instead are these old-school prison dungarees straight out of *The Shawshank Redemption,* along with navy-blue dickies and a light-blue long-sleeve shirt. I'm holding a janitor outfit.

They lied to me. This is not the cool uniform I thought I would be rocking.

I'm used to wearing Patagonia, and now they hand me this watch cap and a borderline see-through ski mask and this scarf that's probably been in a Navy uniform locker since the 1800s. What did I get myself into?

*   *   *

They teach us how to fold, clean, and iron uniforms. Then we start learning basic seamanship, stuff like rope handling. When I arrived here, I thought I'd be running and gunning, and I'm learning how to fold towels and toilet paper, how to properly clean the head, all these menial tasks.

It's a really interesting mix of people, a real melting pot. I start finding these clichés. All the poor kids hang out together. You have kids who are here either to avoid jail or because they didn't have any other options. Then you have the group of dudes who have wanted to do this their whole lives. There are also some guys who are in their mid- to late twenties and early thirties who failed out of college. They have a ton of issues. This is their last chance to do something with their lives.

Everyone here is trying to talk a huge game, acting like they're hot shit. *Oh, I got hurt playing school football and decided to join* or *I got hurt my first year of college and couldn't go pro so that's why I'm here.* I'm here because I *want* to be here. This is my dream, serving my country. I'm proud to be an American. What these guys don't understand is that it doesn't matter if you're a *Fortune* 500 CEO or out of luck and out of work. Here, we're all E1s, the bottom of the barrel in the United States Navy. We're all in this together.

After boot camp, I'll have to learn some Marine Corps tactics and the fundamentals for shooting and patrolling. I become a sailor and begin to learn about medicine. There's a big emphasis on tactical combat casualty care. The instructors are fresh from Iraq—guys who flew casualty evacuation missions in Ramadi and Fallujah, ran in and out of burning cities all night long to pull out wounded Marines. I really respond to their passion and dedication. I want to be like them, do what they do. I want to qualify as a corpsman, be Fleet Marine Force.

The Navy, unfortunately, doesn't have any Fleet Marine Force orders at the moment, so I go to Sicily and spend two years working at the naval hospital. My leadership there—they're all Iraq combat veterans. I work on the multiservice ward, doing OB stuff, delivering babies. I'm happy to be there, but I'm chomping at the bit to get my chance to go with the Marines.

My opportunity comes in 2011, as my tour is winding down. I pick every Marine Corps infantry unit that I can. After a day on the beach, I come back to the barracks and find a Post-it note on my door: I'm going to 2nd Marine Division in August. I head to Camp Johnson in North Carolina and begin my field medical training to become a Fleet Marine corpsman.

I meet my chief, who is all of twenty. He can see how excited I am to deploy and answers my question before I ask it.

"January. That's when you'll deploy," he says. "First, you're heading to California, to Mojave Viper, to do your pre-deployment training. You're going to be a part of an embedded training team."

"What's that?"

"It means you're going to live with the Afghans and train them in combat medicine."

The classroom training is intensive. I learn Pashto and

Dari from Afghan linguists. I attend advanced medical classes and I undergo the same comprehensive combat training the Marines are learning at one of the Marine Corps' largest training centers. Advisor training requires a lot of reading case studies and books on American advisors and Marine Corps advisors in Vietnam. Little do I know it will have absolutely no correlation to the bullshit I'm about to find myself in.

I spend the holidays back home in Baltimore. I go to a New Year's Eve party with one of my best friends from high school, intending to have an awesome night out. Deep down, I can't stop thinking about what I'll be facing in Afghanistan.

What if this is my last New Year's Eve on earth?

I'm twenty-two years old and the corpsman for a twenty-man advisor team when I arrive in Afghanistan in 2012. As senior medical expert, my job is to teach an Afghan lieutenant commander, Farjaad, who is also a doctor, and his men how to treat casualties.

I come into the job with the mindset that we're partners. We'll share medical information and techniques. I'll help them learn their craft, and they'll help me learn mine. My pre-deployment training stressed the importance of having this attitude.

Farjaad, I soon discover, is absolutely worthless. He smokes opium all day long, every day. Sometimes he shows up to my classes, some days he doesn't. He's completely incapable of dealing with any negative feedback, no matter how I deliver it.

His men are the exact same way. Their attitude is, everybody is talented, and everyone's level of talent is on par. These Afghans don't want to learn. They don't want to improve. I try every which way I can to communicate information. They want no part of it.

At the end of my first week, I get my first experience as a corpsman.

I'm lying in my rack, trying to get a good night's sleep, when an explosion shakes the entire compound. I check my watch. It's two in the morning.

A Marine kicks open my door and screams, "Doc, everybody needs to get up. We have a couple of Afghan soldiers coming in who just hit an IED."

Holy shit. My eyes are wide-open, and my mind is racing. I have my medical bag and some medications sitting inside cabinets I made, that's it. No aid station or trauma center. The patrol base has a little open tent we can use for any mass casualties.

I throw on my kit and, Kevlar in hand, I run outside with my med bag.

Three Afghan rangers come blowing into the courtyard at the patrol base, but then they stand there, doing nothing. I start yelling up to the Marines to take action: retrieve the wounded, get them on the ground, and start stripping them. It's pitch-black out, so we put on headlamps.

I'm expecting to treat two very hurt Afghan soldiers. I get six.

Two of my Marines, Peter and Jeff, guys I've trained with basic combat lifesaving techniques, get to work and start calling out what's wrong with the wounded. Before Peter joined the Marine Corps, he was a volunteer firefighter from

Danville, Virginia. He loves medicine. Peter, like Jeff, is trust-worthy, a guy I can always rely on.

I work my way down the line and start triaging. The rest of the Marines leave to set up the cordon, sweep the LZ, and get it set up so the medevac bird can land.

The six Afghans are all suffering from directional fragmen-tation wounds—holes in multiple extremities, big chunks taken out. The worst one has dried blood all over his face. His hair is matted with it. He's barely breathing, and his eyes are closed. He's got a bunch of holes in his right arm and left leg.

I put on a tourniquet and pressure dressing and then I start stripping him down. He's got blood on his abdomen, it's all over the place, and he's making these agonal breathing sounds.

Farjaad comes out of nowhere holding this massive ten-milliliter syringe.

"What the fuck is that?" I bark at him.

"Morphine."

"No! No morphine, no morphine, no morphine!"

Farjaad's got this smirk on his face, like I have no clue what I'm talking about. The guy's a doctor; he should know you don't give morphine to anyone with head trauma or respiratory issues, because it will kill him.

A call comes over the radio that the medevac bird is ten minutes out.

I've got to move this guy now. We've got to haul ass. I start yelling at my interpreter to tell the Afghans to get moving, get this wounded soldier into one of their pickups since all of our gun trucks are already out. They pile the guy in the back.

As the idiot driver speeds across the desert in the middle of the night, hitting every rotten pothole you can imagine, Peter and I hold on to the cab with our butts resting up in the back of the pickup. Our butts keep coming off the seats, and we're flying up and down.

"Man," Peter says to me. "This is so fucked up."

We manage to get the guy on the bird.

Things get progressively worse from there.

Afghans seem to get hurt on a daily basis. They suffer mass casualties every single week, for months.

When I lose someone, it tears me up. Here I am pouring my blood, sweat, and tears into treating and saving guys who are wounded and dying, and these Afghanis are acting like they don't care about their own.

The little courtyard is the place where we hang out, listening to music, playing guitar and basketball. On a rare day off—no classes or patrols—I go to the courtyard to unwind. A bunch of Afghans run over and tell me they need a doctor.

I go grab my medical bag. When I come back, they take me to the Afghan side of the patrol base, into this little room, where I see a little girl no older than seven lying on one of the soldiers' cots. She has dark black hair and is wearing what looks like a red sequin dress. She's completely out.

I look to the tall, skinny Afghan with the white beard standing next to her. "Are you the father?"

He nods. He has an interpreter with him. A bunch of Marines have gathered outside the hooch.

There are religious customs that I have to adhere to, so I

say, "Sir, I would like to ask your permission before I touch your daughter. I want to be able to do an examination."

The man listens to the interpreter and then gives me his consent.

"If at any point you would like me to stop," I tell the father, "I will."

My Marine Peter is with me. I put on a pair of black latex gloves, and as I start doing my head to toe assessment, the father keeps calling out her name: Anja. Anja.

Her arm is broken. I open up her eyelids. One pupil is blown out, completely dark. The other one is a pinpoint.

"What happened?" I ask the group of Afghans gathered inside the hooch. Peter gently lifts up her head. Her hair is matted with blood. "How did she end up like this?"

One of the Afghans says, "She was playing in the road and someone hit her."

Bullshit. "Someone better explain to me what really happened, right now, because I'm starting to get mad. This girl's life is slipping away—"

"Fuck," Peter says behind me.

I look over to him. "What's going on?"

"Doc, you've got to look at this."

I move closer. He lifts up the hair on the back of her head. There's a massive crater in her skull.

"Someone needs to get me a radio, some kind of commo, right now," I call out, probing the wounded area with my gloved fingers. A few of the Marines standing outside start scrambling.

When I pull my hands away from her hair, my fingers are covered with brain matter.

"We need to call a medevac. She needs to go out immediately. She's dying."

A Marine comes in and says, "We set up a nine line. The Georgian Republic liaison team up north has priority on medevacs right now."

I start losing my mind. We can't fly her out, which means...what? Where can she go to get—

Delaram. It's the closest place with any kind of higher medical care. The Afghans can ground-medevac her there. I explain all of this to the father's interpreter as I throw a splint on the girl's arm. Then I try to gauze up and pad up her head as much as possible.

I stick an IV into her arm, carry her outside the hooch, and give her to her dad.

Her father's interpreter comes up to me and says, "He's going to take her back to the village."

"He can't take her back to the village! She'll die!"

I start screaming at the Afghans. *"Don't take her back to the village! Get her on that truck and take her to Delaram right now."*

Many of the Afghans don't speak English, have no idea what I'm talking about. I try speaking to them in their language, but no one is listening to me, and I start to lose my shit. A Marine tries to pull me aside, but I push him away.

My CO gets involved. "Doc, let it go. You have no control over this."

There's no way I'm going to let this go. I get into it with him, and he gets into it with me. We go back and forth and somehow, in the midst of all my cussing, I manage to persuade him to do something. He leaves me to speak to the Afghan Army.

They agree to drive her to Delaram.

When my deployment ends in August, I return to the US with mixed feelings.

I feel on top of the world, like a conquering hero returning home. I went to Afghanistan, did my job, survived, and came back. I'm confident in my abilities as a corpsman.

My experiences with the Afghan Army and the Afghan people, though, have left me feeling jaded. I wasted seven months of my life trying to train those guys in combat medicine. I poured my heart and soul into it, and then I ended up doing their fricking jobs for them. They screwed up at the most basic levels, and they didn't give a shit. They didn't give a shit about anything.

I keep asking myself if there was something I could have done better—should have done better. I keep wondering if I considered every possible option.

But I enjoy my time with the Marines. I enjoy medicine and I enjoy the Navy.

I'm never able to find out any information on Anja—how she got that head wound, if the Afghan Army did, in fact, take her to Delaram. When I think about her, as I often do, I wonder if there was something—anything—I could have done differently to help her. If there was something I screwed up.

Mostly, though, I like to think she got the critical medical care she needed. I like to think she survived.

ALEX

Alex's grandfather served in Korea, and his older brother joined the Marine Corps. Alex followed in their footsteps and entered the United States Naval Academy in Annapolis, Maryland, on June 27, 2013, and began his plebe year. During PROTRAMID, the professional training for midshipmen, he fell in love with aviation.

The night before first flight, my instructor calls me on the phone and says, "About 60 percent of students get airsick on their first flight, so plan accordingly. Pack Ziploc bags and stuff them in your flight suit. Keep 'em handy if you need to throw up tomorrow."

"Roger that, sir."

I immediately go and grab a pair of Ziploc one-gallon bags and shove them in my flight bag. The next morning, I throw it in the cargo compartment.

We're flying in a T-6 Bravo—a single-engine turboprop aircraft with a maximum speed of three hundred knots. It's a high-performance aircraft but not necessarily on the same scale as a jet fighter. Still, it's a big step up from the Cessna 172 I flew eighteen months ago.

I sit in the cockpit behind my instructor, wearing a helmet and oxygen mask with a hot mic that allows us to talk to each other. The mic picks up every breath, any sound I make.

After we take off, I realize that I left the Ziploc bags in my flight bag, which is about fifteen feet from where I'm sitting and inaccessible during the flight.

Things go well for the first forty-five minutes. I begin to relax. *This is no big deal,* I tell myself. *Clearly, I'm a natural at this.*

My instructor says we're going to perform a G awareness maneuver, which is where you roll perpendicular to the horizon at two hundred KIAS, then smoothly pull back on the stick to start a tight 360 while maintaining altitude in order to induce a g-force on the body. I've never done the maneuver before, and I've never had any g-load on my body.

My instructor performs the maneuver. My vision shrinks to the size of a quarter. It's awful. Not only that, but I feel like I'm going to throw up.

"All right," he says. "Let's get some landing practice in."

"Roger that, sir." I don't tell him I feel sick to my stomach.

We do touch-and-goes—landing and then immediately throwing max power and taking off before you leave the runway.

"How you feeling?" he asks.

"Still haven't thrown up, sir." *But I'm about to,* I add privately. There's no doubt in my mind.

"Okay," he says. "Let's head home."

We've got a twenty-minute flight ahead of us, and I've got about twenty seconds until I puke. There's no way I'm going to make it—and there's no way I'm going to throw up in the plane because if I do, I'll have to clean it up. Plus, if I throw up now, there's no place for it to go. I'm wearing an oxygen mask, and I left my Ziploc bags inside my flight bag and I can't get—

I throw up.

Clamp my lips together to prevent it from escaping.

Swallow it back down.

It's awful.

So, so awful.

Thankfully, though, my stomach settles.

I'm good. All I need to do now is make it back home and I can—

Suddenly, out of nowhere, I vomit inside my oxygen mask.

And I know my instructor heard it.

"Hey," he says. "What the heck was *that*?"

"It's nothing, sir."

"It sounded like—"

"I'm fine, sir. Let's get home."

When we finally land, I want to jump out of the plane and kiss the ground, I'm so happy. And I feel fine. I take off my helmet and then, very, very carefully, I remove my oxygen mask and, holding it like a bowl, place it inside the helmet so I can't spill it.

Now I have to unstrap myself from all the stuff inside the airplane. Because I'm strapped inside an ejection seat, I have to elevate my helmet above my head and place it on top

of the canopy—the sliding transparent enclosure—in order
to get out.

My helmet tips.

Falls inside the plane and splatters vomit everywhere.

My instructor pulls me aside.

"Don't feel bad," he says. "Happens to everybody."

JEFF MILLER

Jeff Miller grew up in Madison Heights, a suburb north of Detroit, Michigan. His father was a Marine, and his uncles served in the Navy, Army, and Air Force. Jeff joined the Air Force in April of 1994 and served as a master sergeant. He retired from the service, at forty-four, after twenty-four years of service.

An Army recruiter shows up at the house out of nowhere. I invite him inside and he shows me his portfolio of all the amazing and great things he did in Honduras and South America. He can tell I'm excited.

"So," he says. "What do you think?"

I think I need to get my life straight. I'm eighteen, and the sub-contracting job I had with General Motors, sewing leather products for their cars, went south of the border because of NAFTA. My friends are going down the wrong path, and I don't want to go with them. I think if I stay here in Detroit, my life is going to turn to shit. I think I need to get as far away from Michigan as possible.

"The Army looks great," I tell him.

When my father comes home from work, I tell him I'm going to join the Army.

"No, son. No Army."

"What about the Marines?"

The color drains from his face and he swallows several times—the same look he gets when fireworks go off during the Fourth of July.

My father was a Marine, served in Vietnam. Not that he—or my mother, for that matter—ever talked about it. The only reason I know is because I found an old photo album of his. He served four years, all of it pretty much on an aircraft carrier, the USS *Enterprise*.

My father takes a deep breath. He's a hard man. Growing up, me, my brother, and my sister—we couldn't do anything right in his eyes. I figured if I joined the military, he'd show me some respect, maybe even say, *Hey, I love you, son. I'm proud of you.*

"No," he says. "Absolutely not. No Marine Corps."

"I'm nineteen. I can do it."

"You're not going to join the Army, Navy, or the Marine Corps. If you're going to do it, you're going to do the Air Force."

"Why?"

"I've been to almost all the Army and Navy bases. The Air Force bases—the quality of life there is so much better. And you'll learn a trade, one you can take with you after the service. Besides, your mother made you soft, so the Air Force is perfect for you."

I think he's joking about me being soft. I hope he is.

*   *   *

Air Force basic training is the easiest thing in the universe. Once you get over the initial shock of someone yelling at you, it's like being back in parks and recs. Let's go on the monkey bars and climb across. Let's walk over this rope across a pool. You won't fall. No one is going to swing a rope at you.

My second week in, a career counselor asks me what I want to do. I tell him what I told my recruiter: I want to be a loadmaster. Fly with the aircraft, load 'em up.

The counselor consults his clipboard. "Closest thing I've got is air transportation. You'll like that. Says here you worked at a warehouse for a lot of your high school years. You'll load aircraft. It's pretty much the same thing as being a loadmaster."

It's not even close.

I don't fly with the aircraft or do any weights and balances. They have me load everything from explosives and tanks to refueling vehicles, helicopters, humanitarian supplies—just about everything.

Two months later, they send me to Elmendorf Air Force Base in Anchorage, Alaska. They put me on the graveyard shift. I don't see the sun for six months. Then the seasons change, and the daily allotment of five hours of dusk, no sunlight, becomes the northern lights. I discover that Alaska is beautiful—and covered in greenery.

The base is an aerial port, the focal point to get anything out of Anchorage by air. I love my job, which is primarily un-loading trucks and shipping everything on special air pallets called metal skids. The six of us stationed here become a close circle, do everything together—hunting and fishing, barhopping at night.

I have ambitions to be a hotshot entrepreneur and own a bar. The Montgomery G.I. Bill will pay for school, so I can go learn how to do it right. Four years later, though, when they ask me if I want to reenlist, I tell them yes. I like my job, my life. I like it very much.

On September 11, 2001, I'm married and working at the BWI Airport in Baltimore, Maryland. Air Mobility Command has a terminal there, and instead of moving cargo I'm moving passengers. Military personnel traveling to Europe or some other forward operating base, or FOB, fly out of BWI.

Before coming here, I worked in California, at the Travis Air Force Base, where I deployed to places like Saudi Arabia and helped open new Air Force bases and airfields. Sometimes we'd get fired at or shelled, but it was always far away, way outside the base. It was like going on a Boy Scout camping trip that might turn deadly. I never was in direct combat.

On 9/11, they shut down the airport. It's the first time that I actually feel, *Holy crap, I'm in the military. I actually may get the opportunity to defend the nation.*

This is going to be wonderful.

Then I remember I have a wife and three kids and I'm not so sure.

For the next six years, they send me all over the world. Then, in 2007, I'm deployed to Afghanistan. The Air Force puts me in charge of scheduling airlifts and putting soldiers on planes. No other country comes close to moving stuff like the US. We move foreign troops and equipment for Germany, France, even England.

I'm stationed on a German-led FOB with a team of eleven people. We're at the height of Operation Iraqi Freedom and Operation Enduring Freedom. A lot of American Special Forces are on base, as well as Air Force commercial and military cargo craft.

My job is forwarding Air Force property to the correct FOB while also coordinating troops for redeployment or sending them back home. I'm responsible for getting equipment, air certification letters, and people cleared through customs and for calculating the correct load plans for each aircraft to utilize space, which is critical. To fly a large military transport aircraft like a C-5 Galaxy to Afghanistan from the East Coast of the US is a little over a million dollars in fuel and flight costs. The work is mind-numbingly painful but also challenging and important.

Soldiers are getting killed and wounded in record numbers. My transportation group is placed in charge of finding aircraft for our fallen warriors and heroes and delivering them to the Dover Air Force Base in Delaware. I have seventy-two hours to get them home—and all the military aircraft are assigned to high-priority missions, Special Forces, and medevacs. Trying to reroute one of our aircraft to pick up the remains is a nearly impossible task, but fortunately I have a little bit more play with the civilian carriers, which normally start their mission in Dover. I enter the necessary information into our system, make sure that the funeral director who will collect the remains knows the state and condition of the body, which means I need to read the death certificates.

They're very difficult to look at.

And the deaths don't stop. I'm moving eighteen, twenty-two bodies at a time.

Then our timeline is cut from seventy-two hours to forty-eight. I can't get any additional equipment or manpower. My people and I have to figure out a way to do it on our own.

We work eighteen, twenty-two hours a day, and we sleep in our tents on the airfield. It's insanely hot and humid, flash flooding all the time, our computer systems crapping out, and we hunker down and make it happen because we're dealing with the human remains of warriors, and we've got to get them home.

I don't have, to my knowledge, PTSD or anything like that. When I deployed, I always found great people who made my time memorable even when we were living in a tent in the middle of winter and didn't have a working heater. But I won't lie to you: when I got back home, I wanted to go back overseas. I'm retired now, but if they asked me to put on the uniform and go back over there to support the mission, I would do it in a heartbeat.

JIM TAFT

Jim Taft grew up just outside Newport, Rhode Island. He joined the Army, then attended West Point and graduated in 2005. He served as a psyop officer before leaving the service.

One morning, in the summer of 1998, I wake up with an epiphany.

I get into my car, drive to Providence, Rhode Island, walk into an Army recruiter's office, and say, "Sign me up."

I never had any intention of joining the military until today.

I went to a Catholic all-male prep school in Newport, Rhode Island; played sports; did what my mom and dad told me. Then I went to a Catholic college in New York and figured out that I really, really liked beer and I really, really didn't like class. I left after one semester, came home, and went to a junior college. It felt like high school all over again, and I quit. My first bout of adulthood, and I failed miserably.

I'm eighteen years old and need to do something different

with my life. Clearly, I don't know how to be responsible. My thinking is maybe the military can teach me.

Two days later, I fly to Fort Benning, on the Alabama-Georgia border, for basic training.

It's a shock to the system.

I'm short, about five five, and the drill sergeant seems eight feet tall. He has his shirtsleeves rolled up, and I can see every single sinewy muscle and vein in his arms. He's got the perfect high and tight haircut and the perfect square jaw, and I'm pretty sure he has about half a can of Copenhagen packed in his cheek.

I have never been yelled at in my entire life. On top of that, the drill sergeant and all these other guys are using words and combinations of adjectives and adverbs and cusswords and made-up words that I didn't know could be put together. I hear the word *fuck* used as a comma.

I didn't know you could use *fuck* as a comma.

What the hell am I doing here? What is this?

I decide to give it some time. Slowly, my attitude changes from *I don't want to be here* to *Let's get this over with.*

I grew up in an extremely Irish Catholic family, in an Irish Catholic neighborhood. Here, I'm seeing all the colors in the crayon box. I'm being forced to interact with people from all different walks of life. And as hokey as it sounds, none of it matters because we're all here together to accomplish a mission. This doesn't happen in the real world. Even at my age, I know that in the real world you can't throw together a group of people who have no reason to be together and expect them to do anything successful.

After basic, I head to Fort Gordon and get advanced

individual training in communications. It's nearing the end of 1999, and I get word that I'm going to be joining a humanitarian mission called Operation Stabilize, in East Timor. We get issued timber boots, uniforms, and these cool boonie hats. I'm assuming we're leaving Georgia for someplace tropical. I've never heard of East Timor, but I'm assuming it's in Indonesia since that's our destination.

That's all we're told. That and we'll be providing UN standard communications so everyone can talk to each other.

I'm the youngest person on the deployment. I quickly find out that I'm surrounded by specialists and higher-up guys who have a proven track record of being great at what they do. I also find out that my team leader fought for me to deploy. He told the command that I'm a capable and good soldier. He thought this would be a great experience for me.

I've been the good private. Got the shiny boots, the tight haircut, and I do well at PT. I never cause any trouble. I wake up, go run a couple of miles, do some push-ups, go to work, go back to the barracks, and shine my boots. Up until this point, the Army has been easy for me.

Now I'm going to be put to the test, to prove my worth on an actual real-world mission.

The airport in Dili has been completely sacked by civil unrest. It's riddled with bullet holes and pockmarks left from an attack by some crude mortar systems. Some of the buildings have been mortared, maybe even bombed.

It's my first time seeing actual destruction—the kind of destruction that fighting causes—and I feel my fear kick in.

Oh, shit. This is actually real.

The University of Timor is about ten miles from the airport. We move there and set up our commo shop, build a hooch, and set up defensive positions.

About a week in, I'm pulling security eight hours a day, working another ten, and then sleeping and working out whenever I can. And then it hits me:

This is really fun. I'm chilling out in some crazy, beautiful, foreign, tropical country with a loaded weapon. It's fantastic.

I'm working out by myself in the crude little gym we've set up when the task force commander, Colonel Yarney, enters.

"Why are you here, Private?" he asks.

"I've got to stay in shape to do good on my PT test, sir."

His smile says *Good answer.* "Are you enjoying your time here?"

"Yes, sir, I'm having a blast."

"Working hard?"

"Yes, sir."

We work out for a bit. Then, out of nowhere, he says, "Did you graduate from high school?"

"Yes, sir. I graduated with a 4.0 from a prep school."

"And did you take the SAT?"

"Yes, sir."

"Did you do well on it?"

"Yes, sir. I went to a small Catholic college on a full academic scholarship." Which is true. I leave out the part about how much I enjoyed beer more than class.

"Have you ever thought about becoming an officer?" he asks.

"Well, sir, I like money, so yes, I've thought about it."

We finish working out. We eat some chow, shower up, put on our uniforms.

"Come to my office after lunch," he says. "I'd like to talk to you."

When I arrive, Colonel Yarney is there with one of his captains. They tell me they're both graduates of West Point. The military academy, they say, tries to get two hundred active soldiers a year to matriculate. I can go to West Point, they tell me, but since I haven't done any academic work for a good amount of time, first I have to go to their military prep school for a year.

"Think about it," the colonel says.

I don't have to think about it all that long. I like the Army. West Point is a great college, and I won't have to pay anything, which is cool.

I head back to the colonel's office before dinner.

"Sir, about your offer," I say. "Where do I sign up?"

Five months later, when I arrive at Fort Huachuca, in Arizona, Colonel Yarney takes me to the officers' club for a little celebration. I have lunch with him and five lieutenants who graduated from West Point.

Then, in 2000, I head to Monmouth County, New Jersey, for prep school. I get right back into the swing of academic life.

Showing up at West Point in the middle of summer—my first day, like the Grateful Dead say, is a trip, man. I see Gothic buildings that look as though they were plucked out of eighteenth-century Europe and placed down along the

Hudson River. I eat lunch served family style with roughly four thousand people.

Cadets run the training, called beast barracks. It's my plebe year, but I'm the same age as the juniors and seniors. In my private first-class head, since I've actually deployed, I have infinitely more military experience and knowledge than any of them. My beast roommate is a recruited swimmer, the first in his family to go to college, no military experience whatsoever.

When the cadets in my room scream at me like the drill sergeant did on my first day of basic, it's hard to take them seriously. But my roommate does. He breaks down in tears.

"Dude," I say, shocked. "What are you doing? You can't cry."

"I just . . . Why were they yelling at me? I just wanted to pick up my bag and they wouldn't let me pick up my bag."

"Calm down. No one's gonna die today. Nothing's going to blow up. This isn't the end of the world. You're going to be okay."

Later, when no one else is around, my beast barracks squad leader approaches me and asks, "What did you do in the Army?"

"I was a signal guy."

"Really? I want to branch signal."

"That's great, Sergeant."

"Can you tell me what it's like?"

You're supposed to tell me what the Army is like, I want to say. *Not the other way around.*

Then it occurs to me that the guys here have accomplished something I haven't: making it through freshman year. They're on track to graduate, and more important, they're in charge, so I reconnect with the attitude that got me through basic: *Let's get this over with.*

Two weeks into the academic year, 9/11 happens. *The country is going to war* is all we hear from the active-duty officers who are our teachers.

West Point has a lunchtime tradition of announcing the names of graduates who have died. Those first few months, during the initial invasion into Afghanistan, are rough. Cadets who know the names of the dead—some of them can't handle it. Some of them say, "I can't do this," and quit.

The older I get in cadet years, the more people I get to know, and the more names of the dead I start to recognize.

Alumni who have served in Afghanistan and Iraq return to talk with us about the war. They share combat stories from the battlefield. The way they speak, I can tell they're trying to mold the students into good leaders.

Graduating West Point cadets get to pick their first post. Much like the NFL draft, the lineup is by branch, in order of merit. When it's my turn in 2005, I pick infantry. I want to be on the front lines. I want to go to Afghanistan and have my revenge on what they did to us.

RON SILVERMAN

Ronald Silverman grew up in Philadelphia, Pennsylvania. His father, a World War II veteran who served in the Army, was a dentist and General Patton's senior medical officer. Ron went to college at the University of Wisconsin during the height of the Vietnam era, and in 1967, he joined a two-year ROTC program, wanting to be an officer in the Army. The military was more interested in physicians and dentists, and after Ron was commissioned in 1969, he went to Temple University's school of dentistry, in Philadelphia. As a brigadier general, he was in charge of all medical assets in New England. His final command, as a major general, was commander of the 3rd MEDCOM—the US Army Medical Command—located out of Fort Gillem, in Georgia. From 2004 to 2008, Ron was in command of all medical assets in Iraq. He retired in 2008, after serving forty-one years.

I'm in Florida, getting ready to retire after thirty years in the reserves, when a two-star general I've never heard of calls me at home.

"Congratulations," he says. "You're going to be the commander of the 804th Medical Brigade."

This is the furthest thing from my mind.

After I graduated from dental school, I served as a dentist at Fort Belvoir, in Virginia. After four years, the Vietnam War was winding down very quickly, and the Army was shrinking in size. I chose to leave the active Army and opened up a private practice in dentistry in Alexandria, Virginia. My father, being a reservist, kept saying that I should join the reserves. I did, and then I ended up joining an Individual Mobilization Augmentee unit that was attached to the deputy chief of staff for logistics. I got to see how the Army organizes things on such a large scale. I got promoted to lieutenant colonel. It worked out great. Twelve years later, I got another job doing the exact same thing for the dental corps within the surgeon general's office.

In the reserves, to become a general you have to apply for the job. You're given a list of twenty generalships that are vacant, and another list of ones that aren't currently vacant in case somebody drops out or retires early.

There was no dental general job. But there were what they call medical brigade commands, where you command all reserve medical troops in a geographic area. They've never had anyone but a physician hold that job, but there was no law that said I couldn't apply for it, so I did. I applied for six jobs. I didn't get selected for any of them, went back to working at the surgeon general's office, and got my mind set on retiring.

And now this guy on the other end of the line is telling me I'm going to be a general.

"What are you talking about?"

"The guy who's currently in command has to leave the re-serves," he replies. "You were the next person on the list."

Next thing I know I'm the commander of the 804th Medical Brigade at Fort Devens, in Massachusetts. It controls all the medical assets in New England. As general, I'll be on active duty for about six months a year.

And I'll be traveling. A lot.

Besides holding my primary job, I'm put in charge of New Horizons, a humanitarian mission in Central and South America. We send down engineering and medical assets to Honduras, El Salvador, and Guatemala to help rebuild some of the areas destroyed, in 1998, by Hurricane Mitch. I know all the medical parts, not so much about engineering. I need to learn that.

We always have problems finding translators, so I ask the Peace Corps to help us.

"No way," they tell me. "We don't want to be associated with the military in any way. The locals view the military as the bad guys. And if our people are associated with the military, we would be viewed as not being the peace workers that we should be."

When we end up in Paraguay, the Peace Corps changes its mind and gives us translators because the military is well liked by the locals. The locals also like us, so the Peace Corps workers won't be contaminated or compromised, so to speak.

We set up these little day clinics in this small town out in the middle of nowhere. The Peace Corps workers—about thirty of them, all Americans—translate while we work on patients. They're all young and roughly the same age as my men: between eighteen and twenty-five. The Paraguay military puts us up in a school gym and some other places. They want to put the Peace Corps workers in separate buildings.

"No way," I tell them.

Generally speaking, Peace Corps workers are much more liberal, and military guys are much more conservative. But I make them work together and sleep in the same facility every single day.

"They can't be separated," I say. "We all work together. We're all Americans. They sleep in the same quarters as we do—and they eat with us at every meal. I want every table to have a Peace Corps worker and a military guy."

When I leave, I get a letter from one of the Peace Corps workers: *I never realized the military could be so human. I never realized that the military could be so caring. Your guys are so enthusiastic about their work and what they do.*

After my four years are up, I apply, in 2003, for a vacant position: commander of the 3rd MEDCOM, the US Army Medical Command, at Fort Gillem, in Georgia. The following year, I'm offered the position. It's the first time a dental officer is given a two-star command.

The 3rd MEDCOM is a headquarters of maybe 120 people. I have a war team. I have to go overseas three times to get the lay of the land, see what's there, what the tempo is like.

The unit gets mobilized six months prior to our departure date. We spend four months training at Fort McCoy, in Wisconsin, and two months at Fort Hood, in Texas. We go back to Fort McCoy and take a charter plane to Kuwait.

It's summer, unbearably hot. I like heat, but I'm also wearing fifty-seven pounds of body armor. I'm not a big guy—about five six and 140-some-odd pounds—and this stuff weighs a ton.

I'm going to travel with the troops. At least that's my plan. Headquarters says I'm being flown by helicopter—a Sea Stallion (CH-53), the biggest bird the Navy has—because this is my first time going into combat, and because I'm a general in charge of all medical assets, hospitals, and clinics. I'll also have a gunship accompanying me because I am, effectively, in charge of the largest trauma facilities in the world. We provide care for everybody—military personnel and civilians.

The helicopter is noisy, and we fly with the back door dropped down. The loadmaster sees me looking outside, at the terrain, and says, "We're over Kuwait. You can hang over the side and look down, if you want. Put this harness on. We don't want to drop you."

I'm hanging out there on the back, having a great time. When we cross over into Iraq, the loadmaster says, "You've got to come back in a little bit. We've got to make sure we're safe—"

The helicopter's hydraulics system breaks and sprays fire-hot fluid into the cargo area and the next thing I know the helicopter's going down fast—and the pilot is losing control.

He executes a hard landing in the sand near Camp Bucca. Nobody gets hurt, but the guys in the back are covered in hydraulic fluid. The gunship circles, waiting for the Black Hawk to come and pick us up and take us to Bucca, where we'll get another flight to Camp Victory, the headquarters of the US military in Iraq.

This is all so new to me.

*　　*　　*

I soon learn that I've been targeted for assassination.

The attack happens when I travel to a place called Korean Village in Anbar Province, where the North Koreans built roads for Saddam. I am inspecting a little clinic there. As I'm walking away from the helicopter, it gets hit by an incoming rocket.

Although I get blown down, I'm not injured.

We remove the pilot from the wreckage to treat his injuries. He's a kid, not much older than my son Matthew, who is also serving in Iraq right now. My heart sinks when I see that the pilot is eviscerated, his femoral artery cut. There's nothing I can do to save him.

The gunner has a bad leg wound. I save him, and we get him a medevac out.

When I'm in Baghdad, if the military hospital downtown is very busy, I help out with triage whenever I can. I do a lot of interviews. The first question I'm always asked is, "You're a dentist. What are you doing here?"

First of all, most of my work is administrative. Second, the CEO of Ford isn't necessarily an engineer. The CEO of American Airlines isn't a pilot. I look at dentistry as a subspecialty of medicine. I deal with the head and neck. No different than if I was a dermatologist, I'd deal with just skin. Or if I was an ophthalmologist, I would deal with eyes. I think I have enough medical background to make the necessary decisions.

Being a general, I soon realize, allows me to make command decisions that save lives.

My senior medical staff officer comes to me and says, "There's a kid who got badly burned in an explosion. We've got to get him to San Antonio in a hurry."

San Antonio, Texas, is the world center for burns. Cost isn't an issue. Moneywise, I can have anything I want. When I have staff meetings with General Petraeus and tell him what I need, his answer is always the same: "Okay, you got it."

"Do it," I tell my medical staff officer.

"No, you've got to do it, because if we do it through proper channels, it will take six, seven hours to get a plane here."

I call up an Air Force guy, a one-star general. "Where's your closest C-17?"

"I actually have one flying right over your head."

"Tell him to land," I say, and then explain what's happening.

"No problem."

When the C-17 lands, it takes less than twenty minutes to convert into a cargo plane—a hospital plane, with all the necessary medical equipment. We get the kid to Texas.

He lives.

Other days, I'm not so lucky.

My son Matthew is a signal officer with the 82nd Airborne. He lives in Sadr City, in a combat outpost—a disgusting old police station. When I visit him, I have to come in by helicopter.

One day Brian, an orthopedic surgeon, calls me and says, "Do you want to go visit your son?"

"Sure. Why do you want to go?"

"Well, I need a helicopter ride. If I go with you, I get a helicopter right away."

"Okay."

When I hang up, my aide says, "For God's sake, leave that kid alone. You just saw him last week."

My aide has a point. When I go to visit someone—anyone—it's a big deal. Matthew doesn't like people to know that his father is a two-star general. He doesn't like the fuss that comes when I visit him. I pick up the phone and call Brian back.

"Listen, Brian, I can't go. But I'll get you the helicopter."

Brian takes the helicopter. It gets shot down, and Brian is killed.

After the invasion of Iraq, the US military took over Saddam Hussein's sprawling complex of ostentatious palaces and artificial lakes and gave it the name Camp Victory. The main palace is now our military headquarters. When Saddam is captured, he's brought to one of his son's houses out in the middle of a lake. I have corpsmen stationed there around the clock.

Saddam has significant medical issues: heart disease and lung problems from smoking Cuban cigars. "Your job," General Petraeus tells me, "is to make sure he stays alive."

Every morning, one of my physicians checks him over. I also send a psychiatrist. Saddam, he tells me, believes he's going to be released and take over the country, go back to being who he was.

"I think he's a little depressed," the psychiatrist says.

"What do you mean you 'think'? I'd be depressed, too."

The head of the prisons calls me and says, "Saddam broke a tooth. Can you send over one of your dentists?"

"I'll do it."

He laughs. "Can you send someone over?"

"I just told you, I'll do it. I'm a dentist."

"Stop kidding around. I really need a—"

"Do you want me to send you a photocopy of my license?"

"Just bring your equipment out," he finally says.

"I'm not bringing my equipment out there. We've got clinics all over Victory. There's a small one-man clinic—bring him to that one. At night. You can have all the security you want, as many guards as you want, but within that room, it's only me and him, and maybe a translator and an assistant, if I want one."

"Okay."

The general in charge of the prison gets very nervous when he finds out what's happening. "Don't talk about anything," he tells me repeatedly. "And do it real fast."

"It's fine. I know what I'm doing."

The dental smock I'm wearing doesn't show my name or rank. When Saddam comes in, I'm surprised at how short he is—five eight, maybe. He's well groomed and holding a Koran.

"Hello," Saddam says.

I have a translator with me. Fortunately, I know a little Arabic. When Saddam asks a question in Arabic, I answer it before my translator translates it—which surprises Saddam.

"You know Arabic?" he says.

It's clear he knows English. "Why don't we get rid of the translator, and we'll speak English because your English is better than my Arabic?"

After the translator leaves, I check his tooth. He needs a crown.

"I can do this fast, have you out of here in half an hour," I tell him. "Or we can spread it out over a couple of appointments."

"Oh, spread it out."

Which isn't a surprise, as I'm sure he wants to get away.

He's relatively friendly but a bit aloof in the beginning. I speak to him very matter-of-factly—none of this "sir" stuff. He starts talking about the history of the Middle East, how Iraq was won, the king before him. It's not so much a discussion as a lecture.

When I was an undergraduate at the University of Wisconsin, my major was ancient history. I know a lot about the Middle East. When Saddam says something that's wrong, I tell him he's wrong.

"How do you know?" he asks.

"I studied this stuff." I quote him books and authors.

He realizes I know what I'm talking about and stops lecturing me.

"You have a mistress?" he asks.

"What?"

"A woman."

"I'm married."

"You're too happy," he says. "You must have a mistress someplace."

"I don't."

"When I get out of here, I'm going to get myself a new wife, another wife. A younger one."

We talk about that for a bit.

"What's with the Koran?" I ask. "You're not religious."

"Yeah, I know. But it's good for show."

The next day, Saddam and I get into a discussion about Camp Victory. I tell him that I live in a nice home in a palace. I tell him which one and ask if he lived there. He says he did, but it didn't mean anything to him.

Then he blurts out, "Do you think I killed a lot of people?"

"Yes, you did."

He pauses for a moment.

"You're right, I did," he says. "But if you want to control this country, you have to kill a lot of people."

We start talking about current events. I ask him, "What's the story about weapons of mass destruction?"

"I wanted them."

"Did you get them?"

"No."

"So why did you kind of lead everybody on that you had weapons of mass destruction?"

"Well, that was for the Iranians. I never thought you, the Americans, would believe it."

It's the last conversation I have with him. He doesn't come back for the next appointment because the Iraqis hang him.

Contrary to popular belief, we treat our prisoners well— treat them to the same level of medical care given to our own soldiers. When the International Committee of the Red Cross comes to me and says I have to provide cataract surgery for a guy who's incarcerated, I tell them no.

"We don't do cataract surgery," I say. "By law, we have to do everything we would do for our soldiers, in country."

"But he needs it."

"We don't do it. Nobody gets it. And we're not going to medevac him to Germany."

A group from the UN comes to see me, wanting to inspect

our hospitals in Baghdad. The UN had an office there that was bombed, and the bombing killed a lot of people. The UN left Iraq, and before they come back, they want to evaluate the hospitals to see if they meet the UN's standard of care for their staff.

"We're the US Army," I tell them. "Our military hospital system is the best."

"Well, we have to check."

"You're not checking. If you don't want to come to us, feel free to go to the Iraqi hospital. We're happy to treat you, whatever you want, but I'm not being critiqued by you."

They go to our hospitals.

The general in charge of the prison rotates out and is replaced by another guy. I have him over at my house for dinner one night and tell him the story about Saddam.

"Oh, my God," he says. "Did you take notes? Write everything down?"

"No."

"You could have got more information out of him than anybody else."

"I would have, but the guy before you kept calling me all the time, telling me to hurry up."

The general sighs, looking dejected. "I could have given you great questions to ask."

"Too late now," I say. "It's over."

This is what happens when command changes: so do policies.

My sleeping habits in Iraq were horrendous. We worked 24/7, literally. We had to monitor all area hospitals and all the helicopter traffic, including Kuwait and Qatar. I had a total of about five thousand people working for me. Although I was stationed at Victory, I was on the move four to five days a week. I would sleep no more than three hours at a time. When I would wake up in the middle of the night, most times in the bed in my office, I would walk into the operation center and check out what was going on.

When I finally get back home, to Palm Beach, I often find myself wide-awake at two o'clock in the morning. I do a lot of walking on the beach.

I was the first Army Medical Department major general to ever deploy in combat in the history of US warfare. During my command in Iraq, I had the highest survival rate in the history of warfare—93 percent. My rank helped. It allowed me to make decisions on the ground. The trauma board we conducted, where we reviewed what worked, what didn't, the best ways to care for a patient, the drugs we were using—all these decisions were implemented immediately in theater. Because of my rank, I had the authority to directly implement changes.

Tonight, as I'm walking along the beach, the sky is beautiful and clear, the moon glistening over the calm, still waters. It's very serene. I think about how, for over a year, I couldn't go anywhere alone—I certainly couldn't walk anywhere by myself at night.

And here I am outside, walking along this beach in freedom, and it brings tears to my eyes. Most people don't recognize or understand what we have here, in the United States.

PART THREE:

IN COUNTRY

STEVEN DOMOKOS

Steven Domokos grew up in Rochester, New York. He and his sister were raised by their grandparents and were the first in their family to get college educations. He joined the Army in 2004 and served for thirteen years. He left the service as a sergeant first class.

My first night in country and we're lost in Iraq.

Fifteen trucks, about half of which are tractor trailers, are stuck at a dead-end road. I get out of my vehicle, remembering all the security training I got beforehand—looking at your five meters, looking at your ten meters, and then looking at your thirty meters because the last thing you want to do is get out of your vehicle and walk onto a roadside bomb.

It's pitch-black outside. I've got my M249 light machine gun locked and loaded. I've got no idea what's going on. The only thing I *do* know is that there are ten-story buildings on either side of us. There are a lot of windows in those buildings, a lot of places for the bad guys to hide.

If you want to ambush an American convoy, what better opportunity than right now, when we're stuck at a dead end?

I've got my weapon trained on the windows, waiting to hear the snaps and cracks of gunshots.

Then I start thinking about that blown-up tanker we saw on the side of the road, on our way here. It sat there, destroyed, smoldering. If someone here shoots an RPG at the convoy, we're screwed.

I'm twenty years old and absolutely terrified.

We're there for a total of maybe two minutes. It feels like two hours. We drive on to Abu Ghraib without incident.

Three days later, I'm standing in the chow line at our forward operating base when I hear something tumbling rapidly toward us. I look up and maybe fifteen, twenty feet above my head is a stream of smoke.

Then I hear this deafening explosion.

It doesn't take long to find out what happened: an RPG hit a storage area packed with ridiculously large and heavy US government shipping containers holding various equipment and supplies we need to deliver all over Iraq. If that RPG exploded five feet short of its destination, it would have killed me and everyone else standing in the chow line.

That's when I realize that I may not be going back home. That there are things here that are out of my control. Random. For all I know, I could die while taking a shit in a porta-john. If that happens, what will they tell my family? *Your kid died in combat. Well, sort of. Not really.*

But it's a reminder of something I thought a lot about right before I left, which is that I need to be safe. Precautious.

That's why when I wake up to take a leak at 0130 in the morning, I don't leave the hooch without my flak vest, Kevlar, and weapon.

We start getting mortared. Then we receive word that a group of Al-Qaeda fighters is approaching our base. I'm ordered to go with Sergeant Heath Jewitt to a designated tower.

Our FOB is roughly the length of one and a half football fields and probably just as wide. The towers, about twenty-five feet tall, are on the corresponding corners of the base. I run, dressed in full battle rattle, and I'm carrying three hundred rounds of ammo—and I'm all of a whopping 160 pounds. By the time I reach the tower, I'm tired.

We start receiving gunfire.

We get a call on the radio that there's a firefight between the local police and Al-Qaeda. I can see it; the firefight is happening about fifty meters from our location. Our quick reaction force, we're told, is responding.

We start receiving gunfire.

We don't return it. We haven't been given the green light yet. It's 2006, and at this point in the war, we're under strict protocols when it comes to the rules of engagement.

The bad guys keep shooting at us.

I can see the muzzle flashes. I know exactly where the gunfire is coming from.

"Sergeant Jewitt, I'm locked and loaded. What do you want me to do?"

"We have to wait," he replies.

We don't want to do the wrong thing, so we wait.

For an hour.

Sitting there as it turns dark, unable to return fire and waiting for one of these freaking AK bullets to go through my head because we're all wearing these bullcrap helmets—it's the scariest moment of my life.

Holy shit. I've just got here, and I've got a year of this.

MIKE EVANS

Mike Evans grew up on the South Side of Chicago. In 1987, during his junior year in high school, he dropped out, wanting to join the Army. Because he was seventeen, his mother had to sign enlistment paperwork. Mike served in the Army as an 11 Bravo infantryman and left the service as a staff sergeant. He now works in law enforcement.

Captain Flowers is doing paperwork when I enter his office. He's got a TV on top of his filing cabinet, and it's turned to the news, to the civil unrest unfolding in Mogadishu, the capital city of Somalia. It's 1992, and the country is gripped by famine and conflict.

While two warlords fight each other for the role of dictator, dozens and dozens of smaller factions are thwarting the United Nations' humanitarian efforts, hijacking and looting food convoys. The pictures of the starving Somalis—I've never seen anything that horrible. It's like the worst nightmare courtesy of *National Geographic*.

I'm watching a Somali manning a weapon mounted in the back of a pickup truck when the captain says, "We're going to wind up over there."

He's probably right. In fact, I know he is.

I've been trained to fight a conventional ground war against the Russians. During training, we shot at plastic targets dressed in green uniforms and green helmets with a red star on the front. If I'm sent to Somalia, I'll be fighting guys dressed in civilian clothing and running around with guns and guys firing guns mounted in pickup trucks.

"Sergeant," he says, leaning back in his chair, "I've got an anti-tank section that I want to turn into a reconnaissance section, for my company. The battalion commander has already signed off on it."

That last part doesn't come as much of a surprise. Gordy Flowers, Alpha Company, 2/87 company commander, is a fireball of energy and charisma. Whenever you debate him on a topic, you best be squared away because he'll find a chink in your armor and crush you. He wins a lot of arguments.

"I want you," he says, "to take it over."

That surprises me—and not in a good way. His anti-tank section has got a bad reputation as a dumping ground for problem soldiers or those who are struggling. I have a good reputation, and it comes from the best platoon in the battalion.

And now he wants to send me there?

"So," he says, smiling. "Can you fix this thing for me?"

"Yes, sir."

I'm barely twenty-two years old.

*　　*　　*

I grew up on the southwest side of Chicago in this very, very tight-knit Irish community where young people were expected to be able to handle themselves. Dad wasn't around much, Mom was struggling to raise three kids. I wasn't a good student. I had problems focusing in class; I daydreamed a lot, fought even more. I knew the college life wasn't for me—one of several reasons why I dropped out of my junior year in high school.

I needed to do something real—in the *real* world. Something as far away from my past, my neighborhood—and from Chicago—as possible.

From a young age, my dad introduced me to military movies and documentaries. I'd watched a story on *60 Minutes* about the Army's Ranger school and thought, *Now* that *is real courage. That is a real challenge*. And the guys, how they carried themselves, looking larger than life and sharp in their perfect uniforms—something about that personality type, that life, attracted me.

So I joined the Army. That day on the bus, driving away from home, I was scared to death, but I also realized that this was my chance to start over, turn myself into the person I wanted to become.

After basic training, I decided to go out for one of the riskiest jobs in the Army: a scout platoon in a light infantry company. These were the guys who acted as the eyes and ears of a battalion commander. You went out in five-man squads, anywhere from three to five klicks, and reported back. Out there on your own on the battlefield, you had to be extremely resourceful. Nobody was coming to help you.

I went out for it, got it, then got assigned to the scout platoon 2nd Battalion, 87th Infantry. I was seventeen.

And I still felt I had something to prove. The Army sent me to Ranger school, and I graduated at nineteen. Now I'm twenty-two, a doggone staff sergeant, and I've been asked to turn around thirteen men, whip them into shape.

I have no idea how to do it.

I seek out a previous leader of mine, a guy who is one of the hardest people I've ever worked for: Archie Spinner. I tell him about the section I'm about to take over and ask him what I should do.

"What you've got to be," he says, "is a Bic lighter. You've got to be able to light these guys up and then shut it off. You've got to ask them how their day is going and how things are at home and really care. You go in there with standards so high they can't possibly reach them, and then you slowly lower them until they do. Then watch how their pride changes."

A week later, in early December, we receive word that we're going to deploy to Somalia. I'm given some early intel—aerial photography from satellites showing a bunch of bandits setting up roadblocks in an African town called Wanlaweyn. Hardly anyone can pronounce it, so we call it Wally World.

"Roadblocks aren't uncommon there," Captain Flowers says, surveying the photos. "As to whether or not they're preparing for our arrival, we don't know."

I nod, studying the roadblocks and the bandit patrols and the fortified positions the Somalis have set up in Wally

World. My unit will be flying into an airfield southeast of Mogadishu called Baledogle. We're told that Somalia's most powerful warlord, General Mohamed Farrah Aidid, is using the airfield to supply his troops with weapons and plants called khat. The leaves contain a stimulant that causes excitement and, supposedly, euphoria. Aidid's soldiers chew on them to stay awake and alert.

"We've gotta get your boys on the ground first," Flowers tells me. "We need to scout all this stuff here, to figure out what's going on in the city."

For the next two weeks, I train my men and plan and prep recon missions. We don't know what the topography is like, and we don't know how we're going to infiltrate this town after we land our C-130 on the airstrip ten miles away.

The day we fly out, Lieutenant Colonel James Sikes, 2/87 Battalion commander, delivers his speech. "This isn't some humanitarian mission like you boys did in southern Florida after Hurricane Andrew. This is a combat deployment. You're watching the news, you see what's going on—you know there's a recipe for something bad happening here. We've got to be on our toes."

My men are lined up and dressed in what we call battle rattle—they're wearing their full gear. As I do pre-combat inspections, I remind them to take the humanitarian stuff out of the mission because the news is reporting more and more violence. I've got to get them in the right mindset because we're going in hot.

I climb aboard the C-130, feeling anxious. *Showtime,* I think. *If you've got something to prove, this is where you prove it.*

*   *   *

We hit the airfield really hot. The back gate drops before the plane even stops, and we haul ass outside.

The heat is stifling—it's as if someone covered my face with Saran Wrap—and there's dust everywhere, the plane kicking it up from the old and barely used airfield. I have no idea where the enemy is, what they have planned for us.

They're not in the airfield tower. We clear it within minutes. We set up a perimeter and then begin to clear the rest of the airfield.

I don't know much about the history of Somalia, so I'm surprised to discover, inside the old barracks, that the Russians had been here at one point. They left recruiting posters hanging on the walls, filing cabinets.

Only their stuff is still here. No people.

The airfield secured, we set up our leadership command post. Captain Flowers puts out the order to get American flags on the buildings.

"Sergeant," he tells me, "I want you and your scout teams doing roving patrols outside this air base."

I've endured four years of some of the hardest, most grueling training, and it's all been preparation for this moment: going out and looking for the bad guy.

Wally World is ten klicks away. We slowly make our way through the high desert scrub. We don't have any solid intel. We don't know if the enemy is setting up on us or if they're waiting for us. I've got guys that are locked and loaded with live ammo for the first time in their lives, and we're expecting contact at any moment.

We don't encounter a single soul along the way.

We reach Wally World, undetected, and start our recon.

Almost immediately I notice that all the women are working—and I mean doing everything.

The men are armed. Not just a handful but, like, every single one of them. It doesn't seem right, seeing them all walking around smoking Sportsman cigarettes and carrying AK-47s, and there's no way to tell the bad guys from the good guys. The village is small, but it has stores, and I don't see a single person who is starving. One Somali woman, large and overweight, is carrying a basket on her head. It's full of bread. The whole thing is surreal to me, just surreal.

The Marine Corps arrives two days later. They secure the airfield and relieve us. We're getting pushed over to this coastal town called Merca. It's a port city, like Mogadishu, and the aid shipments being sent by Oxfam and other independent charitable organizations—things like flour, grain, cooking oil, and little boxes of Kilimanjaro water—are being raided by powerful clans. They're controlling the country by holding the food hostage. Our mission now is to secure the city and the food shipments and get rid of the bandits and drive them out of Merca.

On our way to the city, we take on fire—errant shots, but still, *guys are shooting at us*. I'm jacked with adrenaline, super focused and alert. This isn't a training exercise; this is the real deal.

Game on.

I've been told there's a sweet spot where you're able to

perform your job while also being able to think clearly and make good, solid decisions. That's the place I find myself in right now as I engage the enemy.

By the time we reach the city, which is covered in clan graffiti, we're all geeked up. We take on fire again—this time from Somalis in concealed positions—as we seize the port.

That's our job for the next two months: defend the ports and defend the convoys so they can get the aid into the smaller cities where there are people who are really starving. These warring clans are starving these people to death.

Near the end of February, Flowers comes to me with new orders. "We're heading down to a place south of here called Kismayo. Colonel Jess is head of one clan, Colonel Morgan the other. They were both trained by the US, back when the country had an actual government and was a strategic location. We trained a lot of them then."

Big archways greet us on our way into Kismayo. I can tell they were probably beautiful at one time, but now they're in near ruin, pockmarked with bullet holes.

No contact on arrival, though Flowers told me that Bravo Company had been ambushed here the week before. We get to work and declare martial law, send everyone home by 10:00 p.m. to keep these clans from battling it out on the streets. It's a fairly big city, so we have to use a lot of patrols to enforce the curfew.

The terrain is going to make our job tricky. The city isn't a perfect grid. You have a couple of major roads, but mostly a maze of alleyways that run between huts, some of which have compounds around them. You can get lost very easily, and there's not a lot of room to maneuver in the event we get attacked. We break the city down into sectors.

Captain Flowers wakes me up my third night in Kismayo. He's all smiles.

"Got an intel brief on Morgan and Jess," he says. "The two clans have agreed on a temporary truce to come together and fight us. They're going to hit our compound tonight. We're going to find them and hit them first."

I'm up and on my feet.

"All right, Sarge," he says, "we're gonna see what your boys are made of. We'll break down into teams. I'm gonna take half your sections, you're gonna take the other half, and we're gonna go out and find some bad guys."

Flowers is a warrior, a born fighter and leader. I just love the guy, and like so many others, I find the man inspirational. I want to please him.

Flowers leads us to the sector he wants to clear. He takes one of my sections. I take the other half, about six men each. We're making our way through the night-black alleys, trying to parallel each other in case something goes down, when I hear his section light up.

In that environment, gunshots are loud as hell. The gunfire stops by the time I rendezvous with Flowers.

"What's going on, sir?"

"Made contact," he says. "Engaged two guys, ran right into them—I mean face-to-face. One guy got away. We're going after this one." He points to a trail of blood.

We follow it to a residence.

"Our bad guy's in here," Flowers says. "Everyone: set up."

We get the home surrounded very tactfully, very stealthily.

Flowers radios in our coordinates and location while I'm kneeling down, a gun pointed at the front door. He comes over to me and says, "Hey, Sarge, you ain't got that building cleared yet?"

"I didn't know what we were doing, sir. You want me to clear it?"

"Yeah. Let's clear it."

I take Kevin Smith, one of the guys from my old scout platoon, with me. We're crammed into this little area that can't be more than five meters in diameter. The door is to my twelve; Smith and a couple of other guys are at my two and four; and Flowers, my seven, is at my due left.

This door isn't like the ones back home. It's about the same size but it's cut down the middle so you can open one half or the other. I kick it as hard as I can and hear it splinter.

The guy in there lights it up. I see a muzzle flash.

Start to fall backward.

Start shooting as Captain Flowers, to my left, charges his weapon.

I've got thirty rounds in the magazine, a full combat load. By the time I hit the ground I've put the butt of my weapon right into the center of my chest and I'm firing off as many rounds as I can into the doorway. Everyone is around me lighting it up, too, except Kevin Smith. He grabs me by the flak vest and pulls me out and through our guys who are firing and firing.

I'm lying on my back, thinking about the muzzle flash, how close it was, when Flowers orders a cease-fire. I barely hear him say it. My ears are ringing from all the gunshots. I hear someone nearby yelling for a medevac.

I'm hit. Oh, my God, I'm hit.

Only I don't feel like I've been shot.

Holy shit, am I already dead?

Kevin is kneeling next to me, working on removing my vest.

"I feel good," I tell him. "Nothing hurts."

"That's the adrenaline."

I've taken a round in the chest. The shooter was right there; I could've touched that muzzle blast. There's no way he missed—and I'm wearing a really old vest. Those vests don't stop anything.

Kevin rips open my shirt.

Freezes.

"Shit," he says.

"How bad is it? Tell me."

Kevin looks at me. His face is pale. It must be bad.

"You're fine," he says. "You're fine," he says again, like he can't believe it.

I can't believe it. I touch my chest and feel skin—*solid* skin. No gunshot wound. It *has* to be there, I tell myself, and keep checking my body. The guy was less than five feet away and I saw the muzzle flash. There's no way he could have missed.

But he did. He did miss.

Flowers and his section have finished clearing the house. They come out with the shooter. Our interpreter talks to him first, then to us.

"He says he's not a bandit—he's not a bad guy. He didn't know who you guys were."

But I'm not really listening or caring because I'm staring at the shooter. The guy doesn't have a scratch on him.

How I missed him—how *we* missed him—I don't know. It's unbelievable. We were the same distance apart.

Flowers thinks the guy dumped into a corner. Probably wasn't his first battle, probably not his first firefight, probably not the first time he shot at somebody. He probably dumped into a corner and waited for us to finish lighting it up.

"The compound is big, with these little rooms," Flowers tells me. He seems unfazed by everything that just went down.

Inside we find weapons—and women and children.

Nobody got shot.

Later that night, we go back to our command post—an old schoolhouse. I sit on my cot, still geeked up, trying to figure out how that guy missed me. I keep turning it over in my head, and I can't come up with an answer.

Flowers comes into the room. He still seems unfazed. This was his first combat deployment, and nothing seems to bother the guy.

That's why he's a warrior.

"Boys," he says, pointing at me. "That's the luckiest man in Somalia right there."

He's right—I *am* lucky to be alive—but hearing him say it—hearing someone say the words out loud, maybe—wakes up something in me. Wakes me up to *life*. I'm the luckiest man in Somalia. I'm not gonna die in this country. I just got a second chance at life—and I've got a lot more to do in my life than this. It's really profound, this feeling, and it stays with me for a long, long time.

JASON BURKE

Jason Burke grew up in Philadelphia and served as an officer in the Navy. He retired, in 2013, as a Navy captain. During his last tour, he was stationed at the Naval War College as an associate professor of national security affairs. His grandfather served in the Army and fought in World War I.

The governor of Ghazni Province lives in a compound secured by wire fencing and armed guards that constantly patrol the area, day and night, on the lookout for attacks from the Taliban—who live right here in the city. When I step inside the man's home and see chairs, lights, and walls, an actual *floor*, I feel as though I've stepped through a portal, back into the modern world.

I've spent my day traveling the rural areas, along with my savvy interpreter, speaking to Afghan tribal leaders and elders about the US-backed construction projects—everything from a thirty-million-dollar paved road to smaller but equally

critical projects like women's literacy programs and building more chicken coops. As part of the counterinsurgency
mission, I need to secure the leaders' support so their people
will assist in helping rebuild their country.

Our western culture is based on municipalities and local
and national government. Here, in the Islamic Republic of
Afghanistan, government is very low on their list, if it's on
their list at all. Living their lives as Muslims is their top
priority. After religion, they have family, their tribe, and then
regional tribes.

When the elders and leaders invite me into their homes,
it's imperative that I show respect. I take off my helmet, body
armor, and shoes. In more rural areas, the meetings usually
include a small meal. We eat sitting on the floor, sometimes
nothing more than hardened dirt covered by a few decorative
rugs. The rugs get lined with plastic to protect them from
food stains as we pass around bowls of rice and mutton,
everyone sticking their ragged hands into the meal. I do that,
too, without hesitation.

This is all profoundly different from my previous career as
a naval aviator.

However, meetings with the governor are "off the floor."
After I wash up, I head to the dining room to eat with him,
his staff, and my comrades with the US Army's maneuver
battalion. The governor is a good guy. Solid. He's also vastly
different from the first governor, who lasted only three
months. The tribal leaders didn't like him because he was too
secular and wore western-style suits and spoke a little too
much English in the rural areas. I liked him because he was
easy to work with and he tried to reduce corruption within

his constituency. This point made him unpopular with the other Afghan leaders who thought it "okay" to earn "extra" money. Ultimately, he was going to be ineffective with peers and subordinates, and therefore ineffective for our mission in Ghazni Province.

That's the other part of my job: trying to reduce corruption. It's a difficult and, at times, impossible task. Afghanistan in 2008 is like the Wild West—maybe even more primitive. The level of poverty here—people can't imagine it. In some of these areas, you see groups of kids running around without shoes in forty-degree weather, dirty from head to toe, hair in dreadlocks, snot in their noses. But as a whole, they smiled and played like children anywhere else on the planet. They had hope.

The maneuver commander, the governor, and I are discussing the strategy for Afghanistan's upcoming voter registration when the door opens. An Afghan police officer enters, flanked by the governor's security guards. The officer speaks a few words in either Dari or Pashto, the two local dialects, and then the governor stands.

"Please excuse me for a moment," he says to me, and leaves the room.

Has to be the Taliban, I think. The Taliban are actively disrupting and sabotaging all our projects. Earlier today, they kidnapped a dump truck and the driver of one of our funded health clinic projects. Now they're holding them for ransom.

The Taliban has also started booby-trapping the province's culverts with IEDs. In late winter of 2007, heavy snow on the mountains surrounding Ghazni Province had a very rapid snowmelt, causing the city to flood, killing dozens and washing out many of the dirt and paved roads. Since then, we've installed new culverts to prevent the roads from being washed out. The Taliban are intent on destroying them—and anyone who drives over them.

The governor returns an hour later. He looks troubled.

"The police have arrested a woman," he explains. "They found her and a young boy—her adopted son, she told the police—outside the governor's compound. She says she's from here, but she speaks neither Dari nor Pashto."

"Why was she arrested?"

"A shopkeeper noticed a woman in a burqa drawing a map and decided to alert the police."

I understand the shopkeeper's suspicions. Pashtun women in Afghanistan rarely travel without a male relative and are largely illiterate.

"When the police approached her," the governor says, "they saw her crouching against the ground while holding two shopping bags. They thought she might be hiding a bomb underneath her burqa. Upon further inspection, the local police officer found she was carrying a large quantity of plastic explosives, some powdered poison, and a written manifesto of her hatred for America."

His eyes cloud in thought. "The police found a considerable number of handwritten notes listing various US landmarks. They may be potential targets. I need to inform President Karzai."

We agree. As we watch the governor call President Karzai on his cell, the battalion commander and I recall a recent report about a woman and a young boy traveling together through Afghanistan, trying to recruit women for suicide bombings.

Could this be the same woman?

The governor doesn't need to explain the situation to the president. Karzai has already been informed.

"Has any harm come to her?" Karzai asks the governor.

"No."

"That is probably a good thing. This woman—Aafia Siddiqui is her name. She's a terrorist. The American FBI has her on their most-wanted list."

And that's when I make the connection. Aafia Siddiqui, a woman born in Pakistan to a Muslim family, is rumored to be a carrier for Al-Qaeda. She is the only female to have made the FBI's list of most-wanted terrorists. The CIA, FBI, and Interpol have been actively looking for her—put her on their "kill or capture" list back in 2003. They call her Lady Al-Qaeda.

Then, as if this were a movie, the office door opens and in comes a group of American guys—bearded, dusty, and stinky. They look like Special Forces, either Delta Force or SEALs. Their lead officer introduces himself, says he's with the FBI's counterterrorism team. He has a few documents.

In the file he shows us there's a photograph of a young dark-skinned woman with doe eyes, black hair, and an incredibly open, innocent-looking face.

"Why did she come here, to the compound?" I ask. "Was she going to try to assassinate the governor?"

The FBI agent shakes his head. "He wasn't the only target."

"Who else was?"

"The battalion CO and you," he says.

I'm still registering his words when he informs us that he's here to take Siddiqui into custody and fly her back to the US, to stand trial for attempting to kill Americans in Afghanistan. That snaps me back to the present. The battalion CO and I talk for a brief moment.

"You'll have her," the battalion CO says to the FBI agent. "But not right now."

The fed shakes his head. "All due respect, this isn't up for debate. The FBI—"

"We need to think of the larger picture here."

The agent doesn't try to hide his annoyance. "What're you talking about?"

"The Afghans are proud that they've captured her. Let them have this victory—it's theirs. It will help our efforts here, what we're trying to build. Just a little bit of press for the governor, and then he'll turn her over to your team."

What we're suggesting is a smart move—and the FBI agent knows it. We see our tactical point hit home.

"Okay," he says. "In the meantime, we're going to speak to her."

When a small cadre of US Army forces arrive at the Afghan National Police facility in Ghanzi Province, the battalion intelligence officer positions himself in the meeting room, which has a small portion partitioned off by a black curtain. Several Afghan police, two federal agents, a military interpreter, a US Army captain, and a warrants officer file into the room and gather around the table.

The US team hasn't been briefed by the Afghan police and doesn't know that the prisoner is behind the curtain in the meeting room.

The curtain is suddenly drawn back. We see a dark-skinned, disheveled woman without a burqa or handcuffs holding an M4 rifle. Later, we'll find out that she got the weapon from someone who leaned his weapon next to the part of the table near the curtain.

The woman is Aafia Siddiqui. I recognize her face from the picture.

She lurches forward. Everyone in the room scrambles for cover and reaches for their weapons.

She aims the M4 at the closest soldier—an intel officer.

The interpreter standing nearby pushes her as her M4 goes off.

The round barely misses the intel officer's head.

The interpreter is wrestling with her, trying to disarm her, when she fires again. One of the FBI guys returns fire with his 9mm, hits her twice in the midsection. The interpreter manages to disarm her but she's still struggling, kicking and screaming until she eventually passes out.

In the following days, while Aafia Siddiqui is recovering from her wounds at a nearby military hospital, I'll learn more about the infamous woman who wanted to kill me. Things like how she was carrying sodium cyanide and a thumb drive containing manuals on bomb making, documents on how to weaponize Ebola, and thousands of electronic communications between terrorist cells operating in the US.

But the most unbelievable part, what I keep coming back to over and over again, is her connection to the United States. She left Pakistan and went to Texas on a student visa and attended the University of Houston. Massachusetts Institute of Technology took notice of her and offered her a full scholarship. After she graduated from MIT, she went to Brandeis University and earned a PhD in cognitive neuroscience.

While our country educated her, she studied ways to destroy America. While she lived in our country, she went to work for Al-Qaeda, first helping operatives renew US travel papers and open post office boxes; graduated to laundering money; and then, following the terrorist attack we would later call 9/11, engaged in assault with firearms on US officers.

LYNNE O'DONNELL

Lynne O'Donnell grew up in Melbourne, Australia. When she was six-teen, she received a scholarship to study in Japan. She worked for the Melbourne Sun News Pictorial, then Australia's biggest newspaper.

When my phone wakes me up at 9:00 a.m., I'm lying on the top bunk of my sleeper car, traveling on a train going from Urumqi, the capital of Xinjiang Province in northwest China, down to an oasis town on the Pakistan border called Kashgar. I'm heading there to cover a story.

The person on the other end of the line is a woman who works for me at the *Australian*. I'm the paper's Beijing correspondent. I cover the entire country of China, as well as North Korea, Mongolia, Hong Kong, and Macau.

"I'm just calling to say hi," she says.

"You never call anyone, anytime, to say hi. What's going on?"

"I thought you might like to know what's going on in the United States."

"Yes?"

"Thirty thousand are dead in New York, and the president is missing."

The line goes dead.

I check my phone. My signal has dropped, which isn't all that surprising. I'm literally in the middle of nowhere, crossing the Taklimakan Desert, near the China-Pakistan border.

I put the phone on the table between the bunk beds and then sit there, waiting for the signal to come back. I stare out the window, at the black gravel desert. Every now and then I see what looks like a little old man in a turban riding a donkey.

My phone rings two hours later. The caller is a friend of mine, an American who lives in Beijing. He's able to fill me in on what's going on in the US. Three thousand people, not thirty thousand, have died, and the president isn't missing.

"I saw the second plane go into the tower," he says.

Oh, my God. This is Al-Qaeda.

And I'm traveling on a train taking me to Kashgar, an ancient Silk Road trading town and one of China's biggest and most contentious Muslim cities.

It's September 11, 2001.

When I arrive, I head straight to a café. The TV is on, but the Chinese state propaganda machine is in full swing, so I can't see any news or footage of what's happening in the US.

The Muslim people of Kashgar are very worried because riots have broken out in the streets of the Pakistani towns just over the China border. Everyone I speak to seems to know the hunt is on for the Muslim Islamist perpetrators of the US attacks.

I'm a front-page reporter. The big story I came down here for is no longer a big story, no longer front-page material. Now I've got to find a way to work myself into what is going to be the biggest story in the world.

The border crossing into Pakistan is still open. I can get a visa at the border, but no one at the paper has time for me because the news is now focused on the United States and the reaction to the attacks. I was in the middle of nowhere geographically and professionally. I'd gone from covering the biggest story in the world, China, to...nowhere.

I go back to Beijing and talk my editors into putting me on the story. I get on a plane and travel to Tashkent, in Uzbekistan. There I make my way down to this tiny and hard border town called Termez, where I'll wait for the Uzbeks to allow me over the border, into Afghanistan, in time for the invasion.

The only other reporter there is a Moscow-based guy for the Associated Press. The only place where foreigners are allowed to stay is this sad little horrid hotel. My bed is a Russian cot. That night, when I wake up to use the loo, I push the door open and feel something fall on my arm. I turn on the light and find the door covered in cockroaches.

Over the course of the next two weeks, the number of journalists showing up at the hotel keeps growing and growing. People play football in the courtyard, and we drink a beer called #9 because it comes in different strengths—nine being the strongest, I think. The hotel runs out of food. The conditions are so bad many people get sick.

The Uzbek authorities show up dressed in uniforms and set up a visa table by the port. As they issue us exit visas, they warn us that we have exactly one week. If we're not back by then, they won't allow us back into the country.

We're put on a barge carrying grain, freight, and some other stuff. The barge will take us down the Amu Darya, the river that forms the border between Afghanistan and the central Asian states, and into Mazar-i-Sharif. Two days before 9/11, Al-Qaeda sent people disguised as television journalists into Mazar-i-Sharif to kill Ahmad Shah Massoud, the general for the Northern Alliance, the anti-Taliban group.

From the barge, I see what appears to be an elderly man standing with his arms behind his back on the banks of the river. When he looks in my direction, I wave to him.

He puts a hand up and waves back at me, this woman with red hair, as if he's saying *Welcome*. As if seeing people like me is a sign that things are finally going to change for him in Afghanistan.

It's a really moving moment.

We arrive at Mazar-i-Sharif just in time for the siege and my baptism into war reporting.

The Qala-i-Jangi fort is the base for Uzbek warlord Rashid Dostum. It's made of mud and surrounded by high crenelated walls; it looks positively medieval. The fort is fifteen kilometers away from the hotel. I can see it from the north-facing floor-length windows in my room, this big old mud fort from the nineteenth century that, as I arrived in Mazar, was being taken over by Taliban prisoners. And they can stay there for a hundred years and never run out of weapons or ammunition because Rashid Dostum has turned the fort's basement into his personal arms cache.

Like Afghanistan, the hotel, once nice, has gone through tough times because of the Taliban. The Russian military-style cots in the room—every movement makes me feel as though I'm bouncing around on a rough ocean. I take my mattress off the bed and put it on the floor.

Every morning at five, I break curfew and go to the roof to get a signal on my Uzbek-based mobile phone so I can call in my copy to the typist waiting to file my story in Sydney. Through a male Afghan interpreter I have with me, I've been talking to a lot of locals about what it's been like living under the Taliban and what they hope for now. I talk to women who believe that they may finally be able to go back to work and send their daughters to school. I report back on everything I do, see, and hear in order to build a picture of what's happening in Afghanistan.

I'm a one-woman news and photography team. It's just me, my camera, my notebooks and pens, and a pair of Soviet military field glasses I picked up in a market.

Every day is a learning experience—and a steep learning curve.

On the morning of my third day in Mazar-i-Sharif, I awake at dawn and sit upright. From the north-facing windows I can see a mushroom-shaped cloud rising above Dostum's fort.

The Americans, I discover, fired an ICBM from the Gulf into the middle of the fort to stop the siege.

"It's over," the Afghans tell me. "It's all cleared."

The man running the hotel urges me not to go down there. He also reminds me, again, to cover my hair. Again I don't. Dressed in my jeans and boots, I head down on foot to the fort. My interpreter accompanies me.

Half a mile from the fort, shots start coming in our direction.

We hide behind a low-rise mud wall while bullets fly over our heads. I'm afraid but I don't move, thinking that would be a stupid thing to do.

Fear, I believe, is a sign of intelligent life. As a military friend of mine once told me, "Fear keeps you alive."

I chain-smoke cigarettes with my Afghan companion, waiting for the firing to stop.

It takes two hours.

Enough time for journalists, Afghans, and members of the Northern Alliance to gather. I see a bunch of heavily armed Afghans sitting in the back of a truck, RPGs on their backs, bandoliers packed with ammunition slung across their chests. It looks Wild West picturesque, and I want to capture it. I raise my camera.

One of the armed men stands up, looking at me.

Oh, shit. He doesn't want his picture taken.

He raises his automatic weapon. I think for a heart-stopping second that he is going to shoot me. Then he strikes a pose, himself with his weapon. Very dashing.

My time spent war reporting in Afghanistan got under my skin. I enjoyed the raw nature of the reporting—I decided where I went, who I talked to, what I did—as well as doing the analysis. I start planning how to get to Iraq. At the end of 2002, I move from Beijing to Istanbul. Turkey shares a small border with Iraq, where I believe the US is going to lead an invasion.

I'm not alone in my thinking. Very senior-level newspaper

and media executives across the world were being told as early as September 13 that the endgame is Iraq.

I go to Iraq and get to know the physical landscape and all the players. The week before the actual invasion, I travel to Tehran to do some reporting. Two days before the invasion, I go over the border, into Iraqi Kurdistan, and find out the Americans and the Allies are trying to talk Turkey, a NATO member, into allowing them to use their bases near the border. The Turkish government polls their people. Roughly 98 percent won't support an American military presence on Turkish soil, so the government denies the US's request.

I go to Mosul. I'm one of the first people there to see the chaos as it unfolds in real time.

The Iraqi military left, and now there's a void. People are terrified. Banks are on fire, and no one knows what's going to happen to their money. Businesses and government offices are being looted.

The Americans arrive and take over the airport.

I'm standing with thousands of people around the quad-rangle of crossroads around the governor's office when I see the American soldiers. Boots crunching over gravel and glass, I follow them, watch as they head straight to the governor's office to set up their headquarters.

We start taking fire from snipers on the roofs of nearby buildings.

As the war continues, I'll find myself lying in a hole in the ground with missiles flying over my head. Years later, from 2009 to 2016, when I wind up back in Afghanistan with the Associated Press in Kabul, with forty Afghan men working for me—some of whom are extremely anti-foreigner and anti-woman—I'll receive death threats signed by ISIS that are traced to people inside my news bureau. I reluctantly decide to leave because I'm a sitting duck to be seriously injured or, because I'm worth money, kidnapped, sold to a Taliban gang, and thrown in some hole in the ground in Pakistan.

People always ask me what it's like being in a war zone. The only thing I can say is "Intense." Then they ask why the people in Iraq and Afghanistan continue to live in a war zone. The idea is shocking to us but normal for them.

What choice do they have? When a huge bomb goes off in the busy center of Kabul, the whole city will go quiet for a couple of hours, and then life resumes. People have to buy food and pick up their kids from school. They're completely and utterly traumatized every second of the day, but they don't have a choice.

Now we've got this ridiculous situation where the Americans are leading an effort to negotiate a surrender so that they pull out and leave an ungoverned space again to the Taliban. I think it's absolutely shameful. It's not being covered enough because reporters and TV news editors favor the bangs and the bombs and military failures over showing what the country of Afghanistan is really about. All the metrics there—education, health, mortality, media, women's rights—are in positive territory compared to before 2001, under the Taliban.

If we pull out now and surrender, all these positive gains for the Afghan people could and probably will be lost. Life will go back to the way it was because the Taliban think they have impunity. If that happens, it will be South Vietnam all over again.

TORIE

Torie started her military career in the Army, in 2003, as a 31 Romero—a multichannel transmission operator/installer/ maintainer. She left the active Army and then, in 2007, joined the New Jersey National Guard and became a crew chief.

G ood news," the rear detachment first sergeant tells me. "You're going to deploy to Iraq."

I keep the fear from reaching my face. "When?"

"Tomorrow."

I knew we were at war when I joined the Army. I had already made the decision to join in high school, well before 9/11. When that happened, I knew I'd be heading off to either Iraq or Afghanistan, and I went ahead with enlisting— was excited about it.

Still, I'm frightened hearing the rear detachment first sergeant say the words out loud.

I head out and exercise my right to drink as an eighteen-year-old. Across the street from the US base in Germany is a bar. The guys deploying with me tomorrow and I buy as much liquor as we can because come tomorrow morning, we're going to war.

I *think* I want to go to Iraq. Every soldier wants to deploy. My job will be setting up line-of-sight antennas and maintaining communications, so I shouldn't be seeing much, if any, combat. But I can't wrap my mind around the reality of the danger I'll be facing.

I get drunk, and the reality that I'm leaving, the fear— everything hits me. I leave the bar and go back to the barracks to use a pay phone.

My dad, who was in the Army, is a hard-core military man. As a kid, my punishments would be things like push-ups and chopping wood. On major military holidays, he would ask me if I knew the significance of the day, and if I didn't know he would send me off to go read until I figured it out. He was very gung ho about me joining the Army because the Army could give me a future.

He gave me a lot of pep talks right before I left for basic training, drilled in me the importance of never giving up. *There are going to be moments when everything sucks—when you think you can't do that last push-up or run that last mile,* he told me. *But you have to do that last push-up and run that last mile, or you'll be a failure. You have to push through it because success is right around the corner.*

And I did. I made it through basic.

I call my dad and tell him the truth.

"I don't want to go," I say, and start crying.

"You don't have anything to worry about. You're a woman," he says. "You're not gonna be on the front lines."

When my dad served, women were all in support operations. Now, in 2004, there are *no* front lines. Women are exposed to combat regardless of their job.

The next morning, we take a commercial flight to Kuwait. We're in full battle rattle, holding our weapons. I've gotten it into my head that the moment we land we're going to have to run off the plane. It will be like the first scene in *Saving Private Ryan,* the enemy shooting at us, everyone dying.

When we land, the flight attendant welcomes everyone to Kuwait and tells us to enjoy our stay.

When my training in Kuwait comes to an end, they start telling everyone what individual companies they'll be joining. I'm heading to Alpha Company.

"They're at the tunnel of death," someone tells me.

First Sergeant Lester shows up and takes me to an arms room. He's this giant mountain of a man who ends every sentence with "airborne" or "killer."

I'm given a shitty weapon—a giant dirty A2. I follow him to a Humvee with canvas doors and sandbags on the floor for armor and I sit behind him, in the right rear passenger seat. I'm holding a weapon and ammunition, and I'm not on the range.

As we roll out the gate in our unarmored Humvee, I suddenly feel as though I'm so in tune with my environment that I can actually *see* everything around me.

First Sergeant Lester looks at me and says, "Are you gonna load that thing or what, airborne?"

I load my weapon. As we drive to Baghdad, I'm pretty sure I'm going to die.

Forty minutes later, we arrive at our destination in downtown Baghdad: Martyr's Monument. The entire building is made of marble, and the exterior is unique, designed to resemble two giant blue teardrops.

Underneath the building is a museum shaped like a big circle. There's a wall containing the names of all the Iraqi soldiers who died in the Iran conflict, which is why, I come to find out, the Iraqis built the monument to resemble teardrops. I also find out why this place is called the tunnel of death. The wall, similar to our Vietnam memorial, is inside a tunnel. Saddam, when he was in power, let only a handful of prestigious, powerful people see it—never the general public.

The enemy starts to mortar us multiple times during the night and during the day, when I'm out setting up antennas around the monument. When we're not maintaining the antennas and radios for when guys are going out on actual combat missions, we're the communications support for those missions.

We're also going out on convoys.

It's confusing, these convoys, because our lead changes day to day—who we're supposed to shoot, who we're not supposed to shoot. When we go through cities and get to areas of congestion, we have to dismount and walk alongside the truck.

One time I'm walking and, without warning, everyone is jumping back on the trucks. Before I can figure out what's going on, the trucks take off. I'm standing there watching the taillights and suddenly realize I'm surrounded by hostile people glaring at me.

I'm dead, I tell myself. *I'm dead, I am so fucking dead.*

The fear is intense, like nothing I've ever experienced.

I see the trucks stop. I catch up to them and jump in.

It isn't the fear of taking a bullet. It's the fear of being taken.

Right before I leave Iraq, I see this big, heavily decorated Iraqi soldier standing inside the tunnel of death. I'm curious and go up to him and talk. He speaks English.

"This name here is my uncle," he says. He's a little teary-eyed as he points to another name. "This one is my brother."

"Have you been inside here before?"

"No. This is the first time I've seen this."

Shortly thereafter, they open up the gates to the Iraqi people, so they can come in and see the names of their dead fathers and sons written on the wall.

DAVE KINSLER

Dave Kinsler grew up in Morristown, Tennessee, a small town east of Knoxville. He graduated from high school in 1999 and, after playing college baseball for a couple of years, joined the Army because he wanted to go out into the world and make a difference. He completed five deployments in Iraq and Afghanistan—a total of fifty-seven months spent overseas. He's a staff sergeant, 11 Bravo Infantry.

In late 2002, after Airborne School, I'm assigned to a mech unit in Friedberg, Germany. In-processing is going to be a two-week deal because of all you have to learn—the culture and some of the language, how to use the train system.

When I arrive, I'm asked if I'm ready to go to Iraq.

"Don't you mean Afghanistan?" I ask. We've been over there only seven, maybe eight months.

"You're going to Iraq. We have our DCUs in now."

"What the hell are DCUs?"

"Desert combat uniforms, Private."

I head to Iraq for a six-month deployment, nervous as shit. President Bush has been talking a lot about how the US is going to invade this, that, and the other. I'm being told the attack plan is for 1st Armored Division to come into Iraq through Turkey. The 3rd Infantry Division (ID) is going to push their way into Baghdad, which is roughly located in the middle of the country.

My unit, the 1st Brigade, 1st Armored Division, is a good three to four weeks behind 3rd ID. When we finally link up with them in Baghdad, in late April of 2003, some feel like the war is over. A couple of weeks later, President Bush delivers a televised speech aboard an aircraft carrier, the USS *Abraham Lincoln*. Behind him is a banner that reads MISSION ACCOMPLISHED.

We soon find out that the war is far from over.

Five months into my six-month deployment, we're told we're going to be there for nine months. The Iraqi Shia cleric and militia leader, al-Sadr, shows his ass and starts creating all sorts of havoc and problems. Then nine months gets extended to twelve, and then fifteen, so we head down to the city of Karbala, located southwest of Baghdad.

It's an absolute shit show down there. Al-Sadr is holed up in mosques. The military drops leaflets that basically say, "If you're innocent, get out of the city now, because we're going to come in and destroy it." Our mission is to go into Karbala and kill al-Sadr.

We're two hours from executing our kill mission when al-Sadr decides he wants to negotiate. The military, from my understanding, ends up doing a big deal with him—trading arms for money. The Iraqis turn in enough arms and munitions to fill a bus. We give them a little money.

IEDs aren't a thing in 2002. They don't exist yet. That year, we roll through Baghdad in Humvees with no doors, our feet hanging out.

That changes in 2007 and 2008. We learn a lot about IEDs—what to look for, what to do when we think we encounter one. The problem is, the Iraqis are so good at disguising them.

IEDs change the whole spectrum of the war.

I'm on a resupply mission to a very small town called Jurf al-Sakhar. I'm driving in a convoy, on an elevated road, when the enemy fires an RPG. Fortunately, the road levels out, and an RPG misses my vehicle and ends up exploding against the tree beside me.

On the way back, they go at us again. We're about to take a right-hand turn into an intersection when the whole median to my left blows up. The explosion rocks our truck, and we can't see shit through the thick blackish-grayish cloud outside.

"*Push it,*" I tell the driver. The standard operating procedure at the time is to keep moving through a kill zone because it could be an ambush. "*Push it,*" I tell him again.

Later, I find out that when the IED blew, it blew the wrong way, which is why no one got hurt or killed. We got lucky—real lucky.

When the enemy isn't attacking our little outpost in Jurf al-Sakhar, trying to overrun our base, they're coming up with ingenious ways to blow us up. One of my guys, a gunner, gets out of a Bradley to move the coiled concertina wire, or C-wire, away from the road so the convoy can leave our outpost and go out on patrol. This kid looks down and sees a heavy plastic US MRE food pouch. He moves the C-wire back, not knowing the pouch has explosives in it.

It blows up and he bleeds out before we can medevac him out.

The enemy runs an IED wire across a river and connects it to a pressure plate. One of our trucks rolls over it. Everyone inside the truck is killed.

On Father's Day, we go out on a three-day mission to clear villages. It's all desert. A minefield of IEDs is buried deep in the ground.

We lose four tanks and two Bradleys.

The Bradley I'm in drives over an IED. It blows up right underneath the driver's seat. This kid gets out and starts running. He's so pumped with adrenaline he doesn't realize chunks of his leg and arm are missing. We have to tackle him in order to patch him up.

The commander tells us to halt movement. We've lost too many vehicles.

The Explosive Ordnance Disposal (EOD) guys have to come in and clear a path for the Black Hawk that will be coming to airlift us out.

I look across the desert, thinking about all these deep-buried IEDs that have been strategically placed out there. They're buried so deep that when we roll through with our tanks and Bradleys, the IEDs respond to the pressure and explode. But we can walk across them because our bodies don't apply enough pressure to make them explode. These guys can take a simple AAA battery and make it into a lethal weapon. They hide it in trash because in Iraq there is trash everywhere.

The enemy is smart.

JUSTIN BROG

Justin Brog bounced around quite a bit as a kid before his family settled in Eugene, Oregon. He joined the Army at twenty-six. He's a master sergeant and a 68 Whiskey, a combat medic.

I quit college after two years and start working at a local pizza parlor. Gradually, I become a manager because I need a full-time job. I'm unhappy and unfulfilled even though I'm paying the bills. I explore the idea of becoming a cop.

One early morning at work, I open up the back door for the delivery guy. He comes in every week and I barely say more than two words to him. This morning, though, he's very talkative.

"You hear what happened?" he asks.

"No. What are you talking about?"

"A couple of planes crashed into the World Trade Center."

I turn on the radio and learn about what happened in New

York. It upsets me, but I also have an epiphany. I now know what I want to do with my life. I'm twenty-six years old.

I visit a recruiting station. Shortly thereafter, I sign a contract.

I go to the Military Entrance Processing Station (MEPS) and take the ASVAB—the Armed Services Vocational Aptitude Battery placement test. I get a high score. The recruiter tells me I can do pretty much any job I want.

I'm thinking either military police or maybe counter-intelligence, because that sounds really cool. I'm thinking I can be Jack Bauer from 24, running around and fighting terrorists. When I move to the next testing station, I'm shown these wheels of color with numbers written inside them. I can see only half.

I fail the test. They make me take a different one.

"Remember when I said you can do pretty much any job you want?" the recruiter tells me. "Now you're qualified to do maybe nine, because you're color-blind."

She tells me about these jobs. Only two sound interesting: signal—a communication specialist—or medic. I choose medic because it's the closest you can get to being on the line. That's where I want to be—helping people.

Six months after 9/11, in March of 2002, I head to Fort Hood, in Texas, for basic training.

Basic is tough. I'm skinny and not strong, and it's nothing but constant exercise. I feel permanently smoked and get pneumonia about halfway through.

The docs want me to stay in the infirmary. But if I do that, I'll get recycled—and there's no way in hell I'm going to recycle. I decide to embrace the physical challenge and go forward. I tell myself it's all a game—the worst mental game imaginable. But I graduate, and then I'm off to Fort Sam Houston for advanced individual training.

The following year, in April of 2003, I'm sent to Kuwait. The scheduled six-month rotation turns into a deployment as a medic for Charlie Company, 1st Battalion, 22nd Infantry Regiment. We're heading straight to Iraq.

As soon as we cross the border in our Humvees, I see berms and wire—and people. They're crowded here in the middle of nowhere because they want the soldiers to throw them an MRE or trade a US dollar for an Iraqi *denar*. A kid reaches inside my window and tries to snatch my sunglasses.

It's pure chaos.

Charlie Company has a little checkpoint on a busy road outside Tikrit. As we head there, coming up through the road marsh, I see all the destruction along the highway—abandoned fighting positions and abandoned vehicles engulfed in flames. Saddam is still on the loose, but his army has been crushed. Defeated.

For the next three weeks we do these twenty-four-hour ops—stop vehicles on the road toward the city and do quick investigations. The Iraqis are always asking for a doctor to examine their sick kids, so I'm not surprised when the guys in my squad call for me, sounding alarmed and frantic.

I find a parent holding a baby with a hospital IV still in his head—a common practice for starting IVs on very young infants. The child is nearly naked, wearing only a makeshift diaper.

"American doctor," the parents say, over and over again.

The Iraqis see American medicine as the gold standard. What they don't understand is that if they've been treated and released from one of the local treatment facilities, then there's nothing more I can do for them. I'm carrying only a basic aid bag, the contents of which are primarily used for managing trauma.

I evaluate the child and don't find any signs of trauma. We don't have a translator, so I do my best to try to find out the medical reason for why the kid has an IV in his head—and fail because of the language barrier. I keep telling the family to take the child back to the hospital. They finally leave, clearly frustrated. I stand there, feeling helpless.

We stop a small pickup holding eight people. There's a goat and three kids in the truck bed. We have everyone get out. I open the glove box, see what's inside, and shut it.

"Sergeant," I say.

He hustles over, looking alarmed.

"Look in the glove compartment," I say.

He does. His eyes narrow.

"The hell's a chicken doing in the glove box?" he says, more to himself than me.

The enemy engages in a lot of guerilla warfare–type stuff—pop a shot or fire an RPG and then go run and hide. IEDs are everywhere. Identifying the difference between the enemy and a friendly civilian is difficult. The guy who's smiling at you and acting real nice, wanting to be your friend, is probably the same guy who, at night, is taking shots at you or firing rockets or indirect fire into our little compound.

One day we get a call and go to full alert—to REDCON-1, which means the unit needs to get ready to move out and fight.

A Black Hawk was shot out of the sky by an RPG. When word comes down for us to move out, we hop into the BFVs—Bradley Fighting Vehicles—and drive out to the location. The ground is on fire, and I can see pieces of the helicopter—and body parts. We secure the perimeter and get out.

The area the Black Hawk is in is big, bushy, and overgrown. Guys are busy trying to police the crash site. We head toward it and smell burning flesh, stopping to gather the downed soldiers' personal effects, anything we can find.

I find a charred torso missing an arm and a leg. As I check the body, I see an NCO staring that blank, thousand-yard stare. I walk up to him.

"What are you looking at?"

He doesn't answer—doesn't even appear to have heard me. I follow his gaze, to the cockpit of the Black Hawk. There I see the pilot and copilot buckled in their seats, their bodies on fire. The copilot looks female.

I look back at the NCO. He's clearly rattled. Shaken. I've got to get him to focus.

"Shouldn't you be pulling security?" I ask, trying to get his mind off what he's seeing and doing something else.

He doesn't answer. I wait.

"Yeah," he says finally. "I'm going to go check over there and then pull security."

There are men and women here who in training could handle anything, but when they get into a stressful situation like this, they shut down. I have a whole platoon counting on me. I can't afford to shut down. I have to turn off my feelings in order to function and do my job.

The aftermath of the explosion is a nightmare. I find a guy

with both arms and both legs blown off, along with half his head. One of my battle buddies shows up carrying a leg.

It's ugly stuff.

I'm not overly emotional or affected by emotional things, so maybe that's why I'm able to flip the switch.

I just don't know how to flip it back.

When I arrive home a year later, in March of 2004, my folks are at Fort Hood to welcome me back. We're all on buses, and they drive us into the gym while playing "Eye of the Tiger." All the families cheer and rally us. It's a pretty cool homecoming.

When it comes time for me to reenlist, I do, and I go to Fort Lewis to work at the hospital. I want to see the other side of the medical field. I work in the emergency department for a year. I end up meeting Carla, who is on active duty.

We marry.

Have a daughter.

Move to Hawaii.

There, in April of 2011, I find out I'll be heading out to Afghanistan. A platoon sergeant who crashed his motorcycle and broke his leg can't go, so I'm going to be the platoon sergeant for basically an entire company, at FOB Fenty, in Jalalabad. I'll be gone for one year.

"Look," Carla says to me. "We're not both going to stay in the Army, because that's hard, especially with kids. You're either on the same deployment cycle and need someone to watch your kids for a year or you're on opposite deployment cycles, and you don't see each other for two years." She tells me she's going to get out and go to school.

My son is born one month before I deploy.

Afghanistan is built-up now. FOB Fenty is the complete opposite of my time in Iraq. It has all the creature comforts of home: a Green Beans coffee store, a barber, dining facilities, and a shopping area. I have a room with a mattress, and I have electricity. We get indirect fire and rockets once in a while, but I'm way safer than I was in Iraq.

I spend pretty much my whole deployment on the FOB. If a helicopter pilot comes in nice and cool, deliberate, it's pretty much a standard casualty. But if a pilot is flying like a bat out of hell, I know I'm dealing with a really urgent casualty. In a case like that, we need to go out and grab the wounded, drop them in the ambulance, and drive them straight to the forward surgical team.

One morning, at around six, I come awake to one of the loudest, biggest explosions and shock waves I've ever experienced. As I hop out of bed, I know the building right next to me was destroyed. I just know it in my heart.

I quickly find out what happened: a vehicle-borne IED drove up to the front gate. The explosion, about three-quarters of a mile from where I was sleeping, was powerful enough for me to feel it.

We end up with sixteen casualties. About six were KIA, all Afghans who were on the outskirts of the gate. The injured American soldiers, fortunately, were farther inside, away from the gate, when the explosion happened.

I'm not good at keeping in touch with people back home, including my wife. Sometimes—long periods of time, actually—when I get so caught up in what I'm doing, I don't notice I haven't called or emailed. It creates some problems with my wife and family.

It's difficult for me to maintain my family life while maintaining my deployment life. Maybe it's because I'm trying to keep them separate. Or maybe it's because since I don't connect emotionally when I see people dead, burned, or being blown up, I can't then go connect emotionally with my family.

But as tough as it is overseas, the Army, as much as it takes from me, has also given me everything. It's given me my wife, and it's given me my children. The medical support has been really fantastic. My wife's second pregnancy was more complicated, and we had to see a specialist every week. I would never have been able to pay for that stuff—or my degree. And I've met a lot of great people and made a lot of great friends along the way. If I had never joined the Army, I couldn't tell you where I would be today. I have no idea.

JEDDAH DELORIA

Jeddah Deloria was born in the Philippines. When he was three months old, he immigrated with his parents to Southern California. As he was pursuing a nursing degree at a community college, his older brother urged him to join the Army. Jeddah went to the recruiter's office at the mall and joined that day. He was a sergeant and his MOS was 11 Bravo. He served with an airborne infantry unit. Before dawn on August 22, 2007, nearly eighty Taliban tried to overrun the forward operating base called Ranch House, in Nuristan Province, Afghanistan. On December 20, 2007, while Jeddah was recovering at the Walter Reed Army Medical Center, President George W. Bush presented him with the Purple Heart.

The problem," the Army recruiter tells me, "is you're way too big."

He's right. At five eight and 280 pounds, I'm definitely a chunker. Just a big round ball.

"For me to even take you," he says, "you've got to be no more than 240."

For the next five months, I work out, trying to drop the weight. I want to be a soldier like my friend Mike, who is a Marine infantryman. He was part of the Fallujah invasion, and when he came home, we had a big party for him.

Mike and the movies are my only frames of reference when it comes to soldiers. In every movie you see soldiers going in and kicking ass, doing really cool shit. In real life, Mike did the same thing—flew in and killed the bad guys—but I'm also fascinated by all the other stuff he did in between his moments of glory.

I manage to drop the weight. I skirt through and go to basic, where I'm immediately put on the fat boy diet: cottage cheese and hard-boiled egg whites twice a day.

The Army has us run a mile out and then run back. I can't keep up with anyone. The guys make it back before I do. A couple of my battle buddies are sent out to retrieve me. They walk next to me while I try to run. It's so frustrating. When I finally get back, a drill sergeant says, "Deloria, you are the slowest person we've ever had here."

I feel horrible.

When basic is over, I weigh 175. In less than a year, I've dropped a hundred pounds.

Next stop: Airborne School. After that, I'll be going to war.

In May of 2007, I fly out of Aviano, the air base in Italy, on a C-17 cargo plane going directly to Bagram, Afghanistan.

A C-17 isn't like a commercial plane: it's loud, cold, and bumpy. I don't have a window. I can hear the pilot talking to someone up front: "It sounds like they're getting rocketed down there, so we're going to do a combat drop for you guys. We'll drop the tailgate, and you guys run off."

Wait, the plane isn't going to stop? *We're going to have to run—*

The plane goes nose down.

In my mind, I'm thinking *Rockets*. I don't have a gun or ammo, and I'm just supposed to run off the plane into combat? At least we'll be in the shit.

The plane lands and drops the tailgate. We all run into . . . nothing.

It's the most anticlimactic moment ever.

We're taken to a collection area where we wait for some other guys to show up. When they do, we'll all fly together to Camp Blessing. From there, we'll be flown north by helicopter to our final destination, Ranch House, which is about an hour away.

Bagram is *massive*. The place has got actual street signs. I can't see the wires, so I have no idea where the perimeters are. My battle buddy and I walk past a Dairy Queen. I see a billboard advertising Salsa Night at the base. *Salsa Night?*

There's a busy shopping area on Main Street. You can get your hair cut and you can buy books, magazines, and Cuban cigars. I pass by souvenir shops selling jewelry. There's a place where you can buy Harley-Davidson bikes and other luxury vehicles and have them delivered back home. The base even has a food hall that's open twenty-four hours. It has Burger King, Popeyes, Pizza Hut, and more, and it's all right here in the middle of Afghanistan.

I turn to my battle buddy and say, "What is going on here?"

Later in the day, we board a Black Hawk and fly to

Blessing. As we approach, I hear guns going off—big guns, like howitzers. A mountainside is on fire.

Blessing has refrigerators and electricity. I have no idea that this is the last time I'll ever have a cold drink in Afghanistan.

This is also my last opportunity to make a phone call. There's a big line, and I don't feel like waiting in it.

There's no need to call my parents, I tell myself. *I'll be fine.*

Ranch House is a remote outpost located in the Hindu Kush mountains in Afghanistan's Nuristan Province. The building looks like something from a Western—small, the front half made of wood, its backside built into the mountain. The ground is rock and smaller rocks. No dirt. I have no idea how trees can grow out here, but they do.

A guy named Baldwin says, "Deloria, you and Dell are at Post Three. That's up at the top, about three hundred meters away." He points to a trail. "You can go straight up this way or you can do the switchbacks. I suggest you use the switchbacks."

We head up the steep mountain, following the switchback trail as we lug our heavy bags and equipment. The higher altitude starts to get to us. Dell starts throwing up. *This is going to be way different from what I had planned in my mind,* I think.

Post Three faces the top of the mountain. It consists of a guard tower, and underneath it is our fifteen by fifteen sleeping quarters. The front half of the guard shack looks up the mountain and is level to the ground. The back half provides a small lookout to the north. Two other guys, Dogs and

Tennon, who are new to the platoon, will also be sleeping here with us.

There are twenty-two of us here at Ranch House. One squad stays behind while the other goes out on patrol.

The nearby village has no electricity, just donkeys and women slaves. I don't know what else to call them. Women do all the work while the men sit with each other and smoke what I'm pretty sure is opium.

Before our platoon arrived, some Army engineers built a hydroelectric dam, but it doesn't power anything because there's nothing here *to* power. Besides, these people don't want or care about electricity or our money or equality. The men are in charge, and they don't want equal rights because they don't want to ruin the lives they already have.

It's our job to persuade everyone we encounter, using our interpreters, to not support the Taliban and to help us. We promise to give them safety. Their question to us is always the same: Are you guys going to be here for the long haul? This is Afghanistan. War is constant, and people are constantly at war.

Over the next two months, I feel like we're making strides. The village elders are starting to warm up to us. Still, there's no way to know if they're telling us the truth or feeding us bullshit.

Everything changes the following month, when propaganda leaflets produced by Hazrat Umar, the one-eyed head of the Taliban, the man who sheltered Osama bin Laden before the 9/11 attacks, flood the village. Al-Qaeda promises to kill anyone in the village seen talking to us.

We go to the village and put on a show to convince

everyone that we'll protect them, keep everyone safe. Kids are walking around grabbing at our shit and asking for stuff. I'm trying to deal with them while paying attention to my sectors of fire when an explosion pops off. I get covered in sand and dirt.

Did we almost get hit by an RPG? What happened?

Our battle damage assessment crew figures out that the explosion was caused by what appears to be a timed explosive device. We soon discover that it was planted the day before by Al-Qaeda—and the entire village was purposely holding us here so this bomb could target somebody.

They refuse to answer our questions.

ASG, the Afghan Security Group, is a local security militia. "This is getting bad," they tell us. "All the intel we're getting says there's a huge Taliban crew coming this way, and they're going to attack."

He's referring to Hazrat Umar's guys.

The Afghanis in the ASG and the ANA, the Afghan National Army, are used to dealing with primarily white American soldiers. I don't know if they're racist or not, but over the past three months I've discovered that, because I'm a brown guy, they often open up to me.

One day on a patrol, the ASG commander says to me, "Look, our guys want to leave. I want to leave, too. I want to get my family out of here."

He's made it crystal clear he's not going to fight for this village.

"This is my job. I'm not going anywhere," I say. "You guys do whatever you gotta do."

The next day, half of the ASG is gone. The guys who have

stayed behind are from the village—and the worst of their fighters.

That leaves us with the ANA. The problem is, those guys aren't from this area. They don't give a fuck about the village at all.

Whatever. When the bad guys come, I'm going to shoot them all down. I feel invincible.

We work in four-guard shifts. I take the 2:00 to 6:00 a.m. shift at Post Three while the two other guys sleep. Normally, there are four of us here, but yesterday we had an opportunity to send some guys back to base. Tennon didn't want to go do laundry—no one does; everyone wants to stay here and be a part of whatever is about to go down—so Tennon and I rolled the dice. I won and Tennon had to go.

I'm sitting by myself, on top of some ammo cans, in the middle of the guard shack, my back up against a wooden pole. I'm wearing my NVG—night vision goggles. I can see, to my left, our Mark 19. It's a big, big weapon—a grenade-launching automatic machine gun. My favorite weapon is on the right side of the tower: the M240, a belt-fed machine gun. It's mounted on a heavy metal tripod. It has a traversing and elevation mechanism, or T&E, which allows you to raise or lower the barrel, move it left and right. My assault weapon, an M4 carbine, is behind me.

Dawn breaks, the light glaring across my night vision. I remove my NVG and put them back into my rack—the vest where you carry all your gear—and I hear what I'm pretty sure is a gunshot.

It's just the locals, I tell myself, *getting up early to work.* They are trying to build a road around us, so the sound I heard was probably from their digging equipment.

I turn around and face the mountain, hear two more shots.

The sandbags in front of me burst open.

Oh, shit.

I grab the mic. *"Ranch House, Post Three making contact. Brigade, get us on the map."*

Brigade is one of our staff sergeants. He replies, "Say again, Post Three."

"Ranch House, Post Three is making contact."

"Roger, over."

I clip the mic onto my Interceptor Body Armor (IBA) and start shooting.

Post Two starts engaging the enemy. I can hear the SAW machine gun going off, and then I hear the 240 roaring from Post Four.

I spot a couple of Taliban guys about fifty feet away—half the length of a football field. I hold down the trigger of the 240 and let it rock. The great thing about the 240 is that you don't need to be super accurate; all you have to do is keep the shooting tight and you'll hit them with a wall of lead, keep them pinned down.

I'm shifting the gun to my right, laughing and yelling at them, firing and thinking I'm going to kill them all, I'm going to—

The next thing I know I'm on my back and somehow the roof of the guard shack has collapsed and, instead of crushing me to death, is now hovering eight inches above my face.

What the fuck? What just happened? I didn't even hear a bang, an explosion—nothing.

I can't hear, but I can move my hands and feet. I look down at my right hand, and in the early morning light I can see it's torn to shit. I can see the white meat when I move my fingers. *Oh, shit. This is not good.* I see white meat on either side of my right arm. *This is not what I thought was going to happen.* I wiggle a little bit and manage to catch a peek at what happened to the guard shack.

When I was on the 240, the wood post to my right that was holding up the roof—it's now gone. *They must have hit it with an RPG. Maybe even more than one.*

The post gets slammed by two more RPGs.

When my hearing finally comes back, I can make out gun-shots. They're getting louder, closer, which means the Taliban is moving closer. I'm thinking about the guys here with me at Post Three. Where are they?

They must be at the regress position we made. They're probably there right now, fighting—

"Deloria, are you alive?"

I recognize the voice: it's Sullivan, one of my guys. I can't see him—he's somewhere on the other side of the roof.

"I'm fine," I say.

"I need the radio."

"The *radio*? Help me get out of here."

"I need the radio."

"Okay, fine." I remove the mic from my vest. My feet are hanging outside the roof; it's the only space available—my only way out of here. Using my boots, I try to kick the radio off to the left because there's some light on that side. Maybe there's a spot there where he can grab it.

"The radio's not working," Sullivan says.

"Dude, you need to help—"

"Shit, they're coming through the wire. I've gotta go."

"What?"

"The enemy's come through the wire. I gotta go."

In movies and on TV, you see soldiers risking their lives to help a fallen brother or sister. In real life, when you're in the fight—when you're in the thick of it—you're on the objective until the enemy is either dead or pushed out. *Then you go back and mop up the pieces.* I don't want Sullivan to leave, but I understand why he does.

Now it's just me up here.

At least you're not dead, an inner voice says. *Now find a way out of this.*

Bullets splinter the plywood roof above me and skip off the plate armor just below my chin. The Taliban is shooting down at me from the mountain.

The floor of the post is covered with sandbags, which isn't the smoothest surface. When I try to slide forward, my armor gets stuck on something and I can't move.

I get shot in the shoulder.

Well, shit. I guess the vest isn't doing its job anymore.

My armor is useless. If I keep it on, it's going to weigh me down, so I decide to take it off. I need to get out of here. Now.

After I undo the Velcro straps and slip out of the armor, I shimmy toward my only escape route: the small hole where my feet are.

I take a grazing wound on my ass.

I wiggle out from underneath the roof. I move toward the left side of the post.

Take a round to my thigh.

The bullets don't hurt, but as I crouch in the corner and watch the bad guys shoot my vest, rounds pelting off my armor and ricocheting off the ammo cans, I'm aware that I have holes in my body, that I'm bleeding.

I see my M4. It's nearly buried in rubble. I go to it and pull it out.

Can't.

It's stuck.

I touch the places where I've been shot. They're wet. My hands come back covered in blood. It triggers a memory of something my squad leader once told me: *If you get shot in the arm, you have another arm. If you get shot in the leg, you've got another leg. Don't stop because you're hurt, because the enemy is not going to stop until you're dead.*

I've got to keep moving forward. I've got to keep doing shit.

I find the radio I gave to Sullivan. As I try to fix it, I can hear the enemy behind me and in front of me. The bullets keep on coming. *If I don't get this radio up and running, these guys will take me, bring me in, and torture me—or just kill me if I piss them off enough.*

I can't get the radio to work. It's useless, and my right arm is useless. I've got holes in me and I'm bleeding, and I don't have my first aid kit.

My arm is clearly the worst. There's meat flapping everywhere. I take off my jacket and wrap up my arm and, with gunshots and explosions going off all around me, I wait to bleed out.

They say your whole life flashes before your eyes. I don't have any of that. I see more of a slideshow of things I'll never be able to do and things I'll never be able to do again because I'm going to die.

And I am going to die, right here. I'm bleeding out pretty good.

I'm not religious, but I was raised Catholic. I don't have anything more to do at this point, so I begin to say some Hail Marys.

Let's see what happens with that.

As I pray, things seem to be quieting down around me. But I can hear fighting in the not-too-far distance. I'm in a real shit situation, but I know my brothers are in way more shit than I am.

I hear explosions caused by missiles—*our* missiles, from our A-10 fighter planes.

It gets real quiet after that.

I bet that pushed the Taliban back, I think.

I'm dozing off when I hear helicopters.

That's good. Helicopters fly in to help people who are alive. Pilots are here to pick up the casualties. I move to the edge of the shack and sit there, watching a Black Hawk hovering a little bit out. I try to wave at it, try to say something. I try to wave the guys down.

Nothing happens.

Sometime later, I see people moving, coming up from the bottom.

I don't have a gun. If this is a bad guy, there's nothing I can do. If it's a good guy, then great.

I check my watch. Three hours have passed since I was attacked.

I see Staff Sergeant Phillips, our mortar platoon sergeant,

followed by Baldwin and Longman. Phillips is super professional; he secures the area, tasks everyone out. I see Longman staring at me from a secondary position. He looks concerned.

Then I see Baldwin below me. "What's wrong?" he asks.

"I got hit by a fucking rocket," I say.

"Then why are you smiling?"

"I smile all the time. What do you want from me right now, man?"

Longman says, "Baldwin ended up shooting Hazrat Umar. We got their leader."

"How did they advance so quickly?" I ask.

Baldwin answers the question. "The ASG and ANA completely abandoned their posts five minutes into the fight. Once that happened, they started ripping through us."

Phillips comes up to me. With him is an Army guy I've never met. Phillips hands me an M9 handgun.

"Take that shit back," I say.

"No. You want a gun. We—"

"No. No guns. I can't see right, and I don't want to shoot you guys."

They prop me up. Phillips tries to carry me down the mountain. I stop him.

"If you slip, we'll both fall and die," I say. "I'll walk."

I brace up on him. He's on my left, and the Army guy is on my right. We slowly go down the mountain. I look to the Army guy and apologize.

"What are you apologizing for?" he asks.

"I got blood all over your uniform."

"Dude, don't worry about it. It's fine."

I get bandaged up by one of the brigade medics and put on a bird. I'm able to sit in one of the jump seats. There are people lying at my feet. I stare at them, trying to take in everything that happened, while we fly to Asadabad. It's hot as fuck when we arrive.

I'm starting to feel pain.

They start cutting my clothes off. I'm buck naked, being carried on a litter through the desert sun. Next thing I know I've got four or five doctors working on me. They're all talking, asking me questions.

One guy says, "This is going to sting."

I'm given a catheter.

It's the most painful thing I've felt that day.

One doctor works on my arm, one on my shoulder, one on my leg, and the fourth is carefully at work removing debris and chunks of metal from my head.

I black out.

When I wake up, I'm in Germany.

A doctor comes in and runs down a list of my injuries.

I have permanent blindness along the right side of my eye. Both of my eardrums were ruptured and had to be reconstructed. I have some shrapnel up and down the right side of my body. It's not life threatening. My body, the doctor tells me, will eventually push the shrapnel to the surface, and then it can be surgically removed.

I'm told a six-millimeter fragment from an RPG is just chilling somewhere on the right side of my brain, right next to my motor movements—which explains why I'm having a hard time moving the left side of my body. I'm no longer in control of my body; it's in control of me.

To get that control back, I'm going to have to fight like hell.

Someone comes into my room and gives me a phone. My mom and brother are on the other end of the line, crying. I'm still out of it.

I tell them I'm fine and hang up.

I want to go back to Afghanistan.

I've got to get back.

LIZA VICTORIA

Master Sergeant Liza Victoria was born in Panama. Her MOS is 68 Whiskey, which is a health care specialist. She is still on active duty.

When we arrive at the village, all the female medics file into a building. The rules of Iraqi culture dictate that male medics can't treat the local women, and we have to follow the rules. The husbands will wait outside while we treat their wives.

We have security all around us.

Because I have a bit of a Middle Eastern look, the women all try to talk to me. I try to explain to them that I'm Spanish, not Middle Eastern, and I don't speak Arabic. Most of them want medication. We can give them Tylenol, Motrin—stuff like that.

They're nice to me and grateful. So, so grateful.

I respect them because they're human beings. It's hard at

times because while they're so nice, I know some of these women want to hurt us—the American soldiers.

The children have beautiful brown eyes and long lashes. One boy has a big scar from, I'm guessing, a recent surgery. The scar goes all the way around his head and across his face from a wound likely caused by an IED.

Seeing the boy reminds me of growing up in Panama.

I was a young girl when the Just Cause invasion happened in mid-December of 1989. Someone came into my room in the middle of the night, woke me up, and said, "We've been invaded by the United States. Go look out the window."

I did. The sky looked like it was on fire.

I lived with my family on the fifth floor of a building. Every time we had a war or an invasion, people would start breaking into houses and businesses to steal things. The security guard made everyone go to the stairs. Then he barred the door.

Panama is very hot. The next morning, in the middle of the city, with airplanes and helicopters flying across the sky, I saw American soldiers wearing ghillie suits that made them look like walking bushes. I was convinced that these huge men were there to hurt us—to take over our country.

Then I found out the truth: the Americans had come to get General Noriega, who was hiding.

Everyone in Panama knew he was a dictator. A bad, bad person who had his hands in a lot of awful and dirty stuff. But it was a lot easier to ignore him rather than go against him. Everyone knew Noriega had people killed or made them disappear.

I moved to Houston, Texas, in 1992. While I was at

Houston Community College, I met an Army recruiter who asked me if I was interested in learning a new skill and getting money for college. I joined.

And now here I am, an American soldier, in Iraq.

I feel so close to God.

I ask Him to protect me.

I don't want to go, but if you want it to happen, I'm ready. I say it every night.

I hope and pray it's not my time.

ANDY BRASOSKY

Andy Brasosky grew up in Flint, Michigan. His father served four years as a Navy corpsman during Vietnam. After attending Western Michigan University on a football scholarship, Andy enlisted in the Marine Corps. He served from June of 1997 to May of 2008.

A lot of people hear *Iraq* and they think mountains and caves and villages. But there are a lot of built-up areas that, while not Manhattan, have a large civilian population. You go into a place like that, you're dealing with a three-dimensional battlefield—which is exactly what we're facing right now, out on the wire, doing a routine patrol on foot in this shithole. An army battalion came through here not that long ago and laid waste to the area, but it's still dangerous.

There are two fights going on in Iraq. First, you have Al-Qaeda being Al-Qaeda, blowing shit up, disrupting everything. Then you've got sectarian violence—Sunni fighting Shia—which is pretty brutal. Al-Qaeda, the insurgents—they're always watching us, tracking where we go and what we do. We can't move undetected.

It's February of 2005 here in Iraq, the middle of the day, sunny, hot as balls. I'm sweating like a pig and carrying more ammunition, more batteries—more shit than we could even possibly imagine using. Little kids follow along, begging us for the pencils and chocolates we carry in our pockets.

All of a sudden there's no one around.

I know what's coming. We all do. We don't know where or what.

Then I've got all these faces—these kid soldiers—looking to me for direction. I'm their captain. I lead the way, knowing I'm never going to make it home, back to my wife, my family.

And I'm completely fine with it. I've made peace with God. I don't care about me, only my Marines.

Our patrol ends once we reach the remains of an abandoned ice factory. I'm literally walking inside when I hear it—an RPG shot. I drop to the ground, but I know the RPG's gonna hit me and there's not a damn thing I can do about it.

But it doesn't hit me. Instead, the RPG hits a nearby building. I'm lying on my side, shivering, my mind telling me not to move for cover, just stay down.

My squad is scrambling. We've got sandbags on the top of the ice factory; our scout snipers are up there, other Marines. We also have another threat: the nearby mosque we bombed. Al-Qaeda sets up in there so they can fire down at us.

I get to my feet, weapon in hand. Somewhere nearby, another explosion. It rumbles under my feet, dirt, dust, and soot raining down on me from what's left of the ceiling.

IED? Mortar attack?

People are firing at us. Some of my guys are returning fire. Some are good-naturedly bitching and moaning, and there are a couple of others, like this eighteen-year-old kid, John Smith, who is trying not to lose his shit. I'm often a complete prick to this private first class, but he needs toughening up—needs to face the grim reality of what life is like here in Iraq, what the enemy is capable of.

I can't be a prick to him now. I move to him and lean in close so he can hear me over the gunfire. "John, look at me."

He does, his face pale and eyes wide with fear, looking at me the way a kid looks at an adult: *Make this shit stop. Make it go away. Please.*

I cup my hand around his neck. "I know you're scared as shit right now. I get it. But you're not alone in this, okay? I've got you—*we've* got you. Now: you want to make it out of here in one piece?"

"Yes, sir."

"Good. So do I. Now focus. Focus on doing your job. Do that and we'll get through this together. Understood?"

"Yes, sir!"

When the fighting dies down, I get word over the radio that a mobile car bomb—what we call a vehicle-borne IED, or VBIED—hit an adjacent platoon. We're ordered to provide support and help secure the area.

The area is in chaos—debris everywhere. Thick black smoke twists from the blackened remains of a car. The area is quiet, but not for long. I see a car on the horizon, and it's heading straight for us.

Won't slow or stop.

Could be another VBIED, I think, and give the order to the sniper. He shoots one of the tires.

The car doesn't slow, continues straight at us. We shoot at the engine block and the car is still coming and we hammer the front windshield with rounds and the car finally stops.

An Iraqi gets out, screaming at us, no visible weapon. We're all over him. We drag him away and then wait for the explosive ordnance disposal technicians to take a closer look at the vehicle.

EOD tells me it's safe to approach. I see the blood first and then, when I get closer, I see a woman in the passenger's seat and, in the back, a kid.

They're both dead.

The driver is still screaming his head off. I look to our interpreter.

"He wants to know who's going to replace his vehicle," he tells me.

It takes every bit of leadership ability and restraint not to shove my pistol in the driver's mouth and pull the trigger.

The next day, I get a visit from a JAG officer.

"The judge advocate general has opened an investigation into the shooting," he tells me. He's a Marine, a lawyer, and a major, which means he's probably been in the Corps all of eighteen months. "I want you to take me back to the area where it happened."

Is he for real?

He can't be for real.

The JAG officer looks at me, wondering why I'm not up and moving. I take a deep breath.

"Sir, with all due respect, going back there is a phenomenally bad idea—a tragically bad idea."

I patiently list off all the reasons why it's dangerous, but he's adamant. We're going back out.

We drive to the location in a caravan of trucks—a total of seven. I'm in the far back, driving with the JAG officer, and we can hear it in the distance—*boom*. We keep driving. *Boom. Boom. BOOM*. Louder, closer, too goddamn close. I've been counting them—*boom*; number seven this time—and I see the front truck in our caravan roll onto its side.

Road bomb. Truck could have run over a trip wire and triggered it, or there could be a triggerman lurking somewhere nearby, watching and waiting for the right moment to light us up.

We come to a jarring stop.

Debris rains down on us.

The truck is engulfed in flames and I am fucking *pissed*. This didn't have to happen. The JAG officer's face is pale, he's horrified—and he's completely worthless.

We get out and get down. The enemy is trying to engage us with small arms fire. As we deal with the situation, I receive word on our casualties: one dead Marine, twelve wounded. I call in medevac and then ask for the name of the Marine KIA.

I hear the name and it's chilling.

I know this kid.

By the time the medevac helicopter arrives, the enemy

has retreated. I watch as they load the kid's body onto the stretcher.

Back home, people ask what death is like. You can't explain it. It's not dramatic, there's no music, it's sudden, it's violent, it's reality.

CRISTIN MICHAEL MCKENZIE

Cristin Michael McKenzie's family has a history with the Army. His father served in Vietnam and he had two great-uncles who served: one as a transporter during D-Day, the other as a soldier who stormed the beaches of Normandy. Cristin joined the Army in 1995 and served as an 88 Mike throughout his whole career. He's a sergeant first class and his last assignment was at the US Army Transportation School, as an instructor.

I've seen and faced death before when I jumped out of airplanes during training, but this is the first time I'm going into battle, and I'm feeling like I might not come back.

Once I get settled on the plane taking me to Iraq, I start writing a death letter to my wife and our almost two-year-old son, in case something happens to me. I want them to know how proud I am of them, and how things in life happen for a reason.

When I joined the Army in 1995, it was a peacetime Army.

My first job was truck driver for the 82nd Airborne Division, one of the most storied, outstanding units in all of military history. General Petraeus was the brigade commander at the time. Because I was attached to an infantry unit, I had to be fit to fight. My squad leader, my platoon sergeant, and my platoon leader were all infantry, so I got trained on infantry tactics more than on driving. I did jump training with them in Panama.

In 2001, twelve of us from the transportation unit based out of Fort Campbell, in Kentucky, were sent to Fort Polk, in Louisiana, to support an MRE, which is a mission readiness exercise, for the 10th Mountain Division. We were sent there to help them get ready to go to Kosovo.

On the morning of September 11, when I delivered water to one of the little bases set up in the training area, a contractor from KBR, a company that did a lot of work for the military, came out of his trailer and said to me, "Hey. Come and take a look at this shit."

I walked into the trailer. The news was on the guy's TV. I watched the second plane hit the tower.

Oh, my God, I thought. *We're under attack.*

Training was shut down immediately. We all got recalled to the barracks. One of the guys had a radio. We sat around it and listened to the play-by-play on what was happening in New York. We heard President Bush's speech condemning the terrorist attack.

There was talk about units leaving right away for Afghanistan. Our unit, the 541st Transportation Company, had five-thousand-gallon fuel tankers, but we were soon told that there wasn't a real need for bulk fuel in Afghanistan per se, so we got put on hold.

And then Iraq happened.

Now it's April of 2003, and I'm going to war.

When the plane lands, an Air Force guy comes aboard and says, "Welcome to the war." The way he says it makes it sound like we're going to get shot at as soon as we get off.

We get on a bus and head over to Camp Wolf. The gate guard is dressed head to toe in a chemical suit: protective mask, gloves, boots, the whole nine yards. Someone yells *"Gas, gas, gas!"* and there's a moment of sheer terror inside the bus. We're all thinking the same thing: *Oh, my gosh, this is really happening.*

Everyone panics. We rush to grab our gas masks, to get them on within nine seconds, as we've been trained to do.

It turns out to be a false alarm.

This is our first introduction to the war.

From Camp Wolf we head to Camp New York, another staging ground in Kuwait. We train and practice shooting on the ranges until we get the call that it's time to leave. We're going to take all our equipment up north. I board a vehicle that's part of a massive convoy of four to five battalions of support vehicles crossing the border into Iraq.

The idea of crossing the border is scary. On top of that, we have to deal with a new threat: Bedouins—people who were shunned by the Iraqi government and pushed out into the desert.

I see the Bedouins when we cross. They live in tents and most of them are shoeless. They remind me of the sand people from the first *Star Wars* movie—the Tusken Raiders that scavenge the Tatooine desert for scrap metal.

The Bedouins are aggressive and immediately jump on our vehicles, looking to steal food, water, sunglasses—anything they can make a dollar on.

Our vehicles don't have any armor on them, and we're not wearing any armor, either. We're wearing old frag vests, which are worthless. It's like wearing a pillow, basically. We eventually shake off the Bedouins and continue driving.

We stop in the middle of the desert, off Route Jackson. It's well after midnight, and we can't get a good view of the entire area. After we build camp, we pull half security and take turns sleeping.

The next morning, someone sees a piece of rebar sticking out of the ground. Everyone's Spidey sense starts kicking in. The thinking is it's an anti-tank mine.

A closer examination reveals that it is, in fact, just a piece of rebar. Command, in its infinite wisdom, says, "All right. We're going to probe for mines." Literally, in the middle of the desert. Us middle management guys think, *Man, these people are dumb.*

We end up staying there for three days, probing for mines.

And we're still ten hours away from our primary destination: Baghdad.

One of my first refueling missions is for a couple of vehicles on Route Tampa. We go out in a convoy of ten fuel trucks and a pair of gun trucks, which are old-style Humvees with guns mounted in the back beds. One has a forty-millimeter automatic grenade launcher, the other a modified turret with a .50 caliber machine gun. When we arrive, we pull off the highway, park, and wait. There's a little village nearby.

We start hearing gunfire.

My blood pressure goes up a little bit, but there's a comfort that comes from training. I start maneuvering my people into the necessary fighting positions.

We hear two explosions. Two Humvees come flying up over the side of the road. They're following each other pretty closely.

The first Humvee has a screaming eagle on the front of it. It slows down, revealing its passenger, General Petraeus. He gives us a thumbs-up and takes off. Right behind him is his deputy commanding general, Lieutenant General Freakley, who offers his own thumbs-up before rolling on.

The vehicles that need refueling never show up. We end up turning around and going back to the base.

I have female soldiers. They're serious fighters, these women, and they embrace the warrior spirit. Neither I nor the other soldiers look at them or treat them any differently. The same is not true of the enemy. As time goes on, I'll discover that the insurgents go out of their way to attack our female soldiers. They pinpoint the truck carrying female soldiers and try to hit them.

Our mission is to deliver fuel out to the Al Asad area, which is over past Ramadi and Fallujah. What we do is run down Route Tampa and get on another route called Golden, which is at a market area. You take a right there and it takes you through some back roads out to Route Mobile, the major highway in Iraq. Route Mobile takes you all the way out to Al Asad.

Fuel is a commodity. Every time I go out on a mission, the insurgents try to take out our trucks and steal our fuel.

The majority of attacks involve IEDs. When you're carrying bulk fuel and get hit, you don't stop to do a BDA, which is a battle damage assessment. You just keep going, get to your destination, and then do a BDA.

The attacks get more frequent.

Become more planned.

It's like the Wild West out there when we're driving.

Each time I go out, I take with me a light machine gun called a SAW. I want the most firepower with me while I'm out on the wire because we're getting hit every day. Command doesn't believe we're getting hit every day and refuses to change our driving route. It's only a matter of time before someone gets hurt.

Inside the truck, we have a CD player set up with portable speakers so we can blast music, keep us amped up and occupied. I'm sitting next to my driver, changing out the CD, and glance in the side-view mirror and see a motorcycle with two gentlemen on it. The gentleman on the back has his hands in tight behind the other guy's back, and right then I know something's going to happen.

I look to my driver and say, "Keep your eyes peeled."

She nods.

The road explodes.

I feel like the air is sucked out of my lungs. Something hits me in the face, and I feel some stuff hit me in back of the vest. Thankfully, because I anticipated the blast, I was able to turn sideways in my seat, so I don't take everything straight to the front of my face. But the blow still glances off my side.

I black out.

When I come to, the truck is stopped. I don't know how

long I was out. The trucks that were driving behind me have stopped. I go into checklist mode. I'm checking to make sure I have all my bits and pieces when I hear gunfire.

We take multiple rounds.

I hear more explosions. Right then I know we're in a complex, coordinated attack with multiple IEDs.

The next step on my checklist is to identify a target and eliminate the threat. I scan the area and see three hundred, maybe four hundred meters away a white truck sitting between two berms. Normally, Iraqis don't sit around: they take off. This truck, an SUV, is creeping toward us.

In a situation like this, if you're sticking around to watch, you're pretty much gonna be a bad guy. You're a threat. I target the SUV with my SAW, start throwing rounds at it. In between firing, I yell over to my driver to get the truck moving.

She doesn't respond.

We don't move.

I look back over at her. She's seriously dazed. She has all her limbs and stuff, but I can see she's been hit—and we're still taking fire.

I hear an LMTV horn—the Light Medium Tactical Vehicle horn, this little *meep-meep* sound, which is comical coming from such a big truck. The horn means the rest of the convoy is coming around the contact side. I check my fire real quick so I won't blast the people driving by. They all go around me, except the rear gunner truck. It pulls up next to me.

My truck still isn't moving, and my driver is in shock, so I jump out. The enemy takes shots at me as I run around to the other side of the truck and throw open the door. I quickly check out her injury, see that she's taken a piece of shrapnel a little bit bigger than the size of a quarter to her knee. There's not a whole lot of blood, but the wound is severe, and there's no way she can walk.

I see a guy, one of my buddies, in the gun truck trying to get my attention. He cups his hands over his mouth and yells, *"Bring her over to me,"* just as one of our helicopters, a Kiowa, swoops down to the road in front of me, to about driver level, and lets the enemy SUV know that, hey, if you go any further, I'm going to launch one of these Hellfire missiles.

There's a lull in the gunfire. I take her out. As I carry her over to the gun truck, I hear another explosion. It's followed by more gunfire. I get her inside and my buddy goes to work on her, providing aid. I hear someone call in for a medevac as I run back to my truck to get it moving.

The air lines, I discover, are severed. I grab some duct tape, get underneath the vehicle, hear another explosion. I duct-tape the lines. When I get back into the truck, I can't get any air pressure. My truck is disabled.

We don't have a wrecker on this mission, so the convoy brings up a 1088 tractor (bobtail) with a tow bar to use as our wrecker/recovery vehicle. My platoon sergeant and my buddy come and tell me they have the firefight contained. All threats have been contained, and they've captured the guy from the SUV. Inside, they found a cache of weapons, ammo, and IEDs.

The medevac shows up while the recovery vehicle is caging the brakes on my truck. I help carry my driver to the bird. She's got a worried look on her face.

"Hey, you're gonna be okay," I tell her. "They're gonna take real good care of you." Then, to lighten things up a little, I add, "You may not be dancing anytime soon, but it's okay."

When a vehicle is disabled, the standard operating procedure is you destroy it. You put an incendiary grenade, which is a thermal grenade that burns super, super hot white phosphorous, on the engine block. It burns through any type of metal. You burn the vehicle and you take all the sensitive items out of it and you burn them, too.

The colonel has another idea. "That truck," he tells me, "is going back."

I don't want to drive the truck back. I want to go with my unit, continue on mission to Al Asad. That said, I really feel like it's my responsibility to take the vehicle back, so I volunteer to do it. When I get into the bobtail, I find out it doesn't have working brakes. I drive it all by myself in the convoy, nursing my anger. I'm pissed off at command. We told them we were getting hit every day on this route, and they didn't believe us and refused to change it.

On the way back I see a couple of farmers out in a field. They flip us off as we drive by. I'm thankful the truck doesn't have brakes, because I want to stop, get out, and shoot them, I'm so pissed.

When I arrive at the base, I go get checked out at the medical clinic. They say I have some hearing issues and took some glass to the face. The cuts are so fine they had all mostly healed up during the hour and a half drive back. I've also got a bruise on my back from the piece of shrapnel hitting my vest. There really isn't anything wrong with me, which is a surprise, given the amount of shrapnel that entered the cab.

I'm told the battalion commander is going to talk to the

company later on that evening about what went down earlier. I'm told I don't have to attend, but I'm going. There's no way I'm going to miss it.

I go to take a quick nap. When I lay the side of my head on the pillow, I feel something sharp poke me in the face.

It's a piece of shrapnel.

That fuels my anger even more.

The battalion commander stands on an elevated sidewalk and talks to us about the attack. We all stand there, listening to him brief us.

"Are there any questions?" he asks.

I know I shouldn't be here because I'm still super amped about how everything went down, but I've got some things I want to say. I raise my hand.

"Sir," I say, "it's really fucked up that we're going down these routes every day and there's no route clearance."

My first sergeant gives me a look that says *You better shut the hell up.*

"We're getting hit every single day," I tell the battalion commander, "and you guys are doing shit to ensure the safety of the convoy."

I have no business talking to a lieutenant colonel this way. I'm not saying he's stupid; I am saying that the higher-ups are making tactical mistakes force-feeding us these routes despite our continued protest. We need to be seen and our voices need to be heard.

"Sergeant McKenzie," the battalion commander says, "today is your day to say whatever you want. After what you've been through, I totally understand."

After the meeting, my first sergeant pulls me off to the side and cusses my ass out. It's worth it. It's the last time we ever go down that route.

During my four deployments, there are multiple times when I have to be brutally honest with the chain of command to the point where they take great offense. But I always do it. The welfare, safety, and morale of my soldiers is way more important than officers' feelings.

JOHN KNITTEL

After graduating from the University of Akron in 2002, John Knittel worked a series of law enforcement and security jobs before deciding to join the Army, in 2005. He was a lieutenant and served as a platoon leader when he was deployed to Baghdad, Iraq. John left the service as a captain.

H ere's the issue," the operations officer tells me. "Lieutenant Martinez is transferring soon to another unit, which means Alpha Company needs a new platoon leader. Problem is, we have two lieutenants, you and this other guy, and only one spot."

It's 2008, my first morning in Baghdad. I'm half awake, my nerves raw. Last night, as I flew into FOB Loyalty by helicopter from Kuwait, flares lit up the sky. I didn't know if someone was shooting at us or attacking the base. It was completely overwhelming.

"So," the operations officer says, "whoever does the

better job painting the battalion commander's office gets the platoon."

Is he serious? It's hard to say, given his deadpan expression. But if he wants me to enter a painting contest, okay, fine. I'll go all HGTV, do an accent wall, whatever it takes to get Alpha Company. I'm going to be here a year, possibly longer, and I'm sure as hell not going to spend it in an admin office, working as a personnel guy, helping sort out pay problems.

I'm given a cheap roller and local paint that probably has a bunch of lead in it. The concrete here in Baghdad is made of shitty materials, so as I paint the cement walls, little rocks get stuck in the roller. Still, my painting project turns out really, really good for an Iraqi building.

I end up getting the platoon.

I meet Alpha Company later that day, at Combat Outpost 762, for their evening platoon. Lieutenant Martinez is with them. He introduces me and then says, "Lieutenant Knittel would like to say a few words."

I wasn't expecting to speak. I see these kids sizing me up, looking at me like I'm an old man—which to them I am, since I'm twenty-six. After I graduated from the University of Akron in 2002, with my degree in political science/criminal justice, I bounced all over Ohio, working law enforcement jobs—first for a private company that did undercover narcotics investigations, then as a private investigator, and, finally, as an investigator of insurance fraud. When my dad got cancer, I moved back home, and I started reevaluating what I wanted to do with my life. That was when I decided to join the Army. After basic training, I went the officer route, going to Officer Candidate School.

This is my first deployment, my first time in country. I look at this melting pot of kids, from all walks of life, waiting for me to say something profound.

When in doubt, stick to the truth.

"I deployed late because of an injury," I say, "so I've probably missed out on a lot of essential training. I'm probably going to mess up a lot, so bear with me while I get up to speed."

As we head out to do our patrol, Martinez points to a girl standing beyond the gates of the combat outpost, or COP. "That's Najima," he tells me. "She lives nearby, so you'll see her around here a lot, selling food. Does a pretty good business, too, because who wants to eat MREs all the time?"

He's right about that. I grab a falafel and then go off with Martinez, do what we call left seat/right seat—the transition period where you do ride-alongs with someone already experienced with the battlefield.

"What's the deal with your rifle?" he asks.

"When I was at Fort Polk, all the M4s had already been deployed. I had to do my weapons qualification, and they gave me this off-brand M16 that was probably used back in Vietnam." I don't have to tell him what a pain in the ass the rifle is, how after every single shot you have to pull back the charging handle. It's like firing a musket. "When I got to Kuwait and did my two weeks of training, they gave me my vest, all the equipment I needed—"

"Except an M4."

I nod. "They were all accounted for. Same here."

"That thing's a piece of shit. We've got to get you a proper weapon."

"Good luck finding one."

"I'll give you mine when I leave."

We're beating the streets, about to end the patrol, when we see ten, maybe twenty yards away one of our mine-resistant, ambush-protected (MRAP) vehicles sitting at an intersection. All of a sudden I hear that *psshhh* sound an RPG makes.

We see it coming from a nearby building.

The RPG hits the MRAP's roof. By some miracle of God, the RPG doesn't explode, and as it skids down the street, it doesn't go off. We take position and start shooting at the building where the RPG came from. I manage to get off three shots with my musket.

A couple of hours later, on the way back to COP 762, I start getting super sick. I'm throwing up in front of my new platoon—and shitting my pants.

"I've got to lie down," I tell Martinez.

I get back to base and hit the rack. I'm still throwing up, and of course the shitters are two hundred yards away from me. Throughout the night, I'm running over there when I'm not puking.

The next morning, I'm still sick—and I have to do patrols. After each one, I return to the COP and get an IV because I'm so dehydrated.

This goes on for two days.

On day three, Alpha Company is ordered to go out and do an overwatch position. I'm still feeling terrible, unable to keep anything down, as I head out to a three-story house, a rarity in Baghdad.

The family who owns it is kept on the bottom floor. From the top floor, we watch for a patrol that's getting ready to come up. Nature is calling again, the bathrooms are outside, and I can't go out there because that will give away our position.

The bedroom, I notice, has an armoire big enough to step inside.

Screw it. I drop my drawers and do what I need to do. I'm dying, making all sorts of sounds. One of my soldiers enters the room.

"Sir, are you okay?"

"I'm shitting inside someone's closet," I say. "How do you think I'm doing right now?"

The fighting is intense the first three months. It doesn't let up even when I return to my new base, the joint security station (JSS) called Camp Marlboro, located on the premises of an abandoned cigarette factory in Sadr City. We're constantly getting hit with mortars and IEDs.

We can shoot into Sadr City, but we can't patrol it. The people there are constantly placing IEDs, especially on Route Predators, our main supply route and possibly the most dangerous place in Baghdad. Small bombs called explosively formed projectiles (EFPs) are hidden inside the roadside mountains of rubber tires, scrap metal, and rusted vehicles. Manufactured in Iran, an EFP bomb is the size of a coffee can and, when detonated, forms a projectile that can penetrate our armored vehicles. EFPs are showing up in alarming numbers, and they're being smuggled in by city residents paid fifty dollars to place the weapons. They do it so they can feed their starving families.

We live inside the cigarette factory, which is on the city grid, so we have power maybe half the time. We walk around a lot with headlamps and flashlights. We sleep in the basement. There are no showers. To keep morale up, we have video games going in one of the big rooms. After patrol, I'll sit down with the guys and play college football and talk smack about their teams sucking and vice versa. The practical jokes are constant. One of my guys duct-tapes my vest and helmet to the ceiling.

I keep in contact with the woman I met right before I deployed. I told her I would be gone for about a year and promised to stay in touch. I brought a deck of cards with me, and I write a message on a card and mail it to her once a week.

To resupply, we have to go down to FOB Loyalty, which means driving Route Predators. We always go in a convoy of thirty to forty vehicles. One day, at the start of our supply run, we're hit by sixteen IEDs.

My ears are ringing, and I'm thanking God that there aren't any casualties, when I get a radio call about another possible IED up ahead. They give me the grid coordinates. I radio them to our engineering unit. They drive ahead to investigate, and we wait along Route Predators.

We're sitting ducks.

Finally, an engineer radios me. "We just don't have . . ."

"What?"

"I don't know what we're going to do about this."

He's saying he can't clear it. The problem is, we can't take any other routes. We have nearly forty vehicles in our convoy—and most of them are too damaged at this point. We can't take another IED. I radio that up to the battalion.

"Look, you guys have just got to get through it," battalion says. "Figure a way out. Charlie Mike."

Continue mission.

We reach the grid location. The convoy stops. We can't go around the bomb, only through it.

I've given what I'm about to do next a lot of thought.

I order the MRAP to go first. It's designed to withstand attacks from IEDs, but that doesn't mean the people inside are safe. Soldiers still get injured and die. The IED up ahead could—

A thundering, earsplitting explosion shakes the ground—an EFP hits the MRAP and pierces its armor.

The vehicle catches fire. We're attacked. Troops in contact.

We start doing everything we're trained to do, everyone getting into a fighting position while we figure out how to corner off the vehicle, get the fire out, and assess any casualties. Only I can't get any reports because my radio is down. I jump to a nearby vehicle, get the same result.

A kid from another platoon gets hit in the leg. We can't get an IV in him because we can't find a vein, and if we don't get fluids in him he'll die. I've got to call in a nine line for medevac. I jump from vehicle to vehicle as gunfire goes off, trying to find comms.

Not a single radio is working.

I need to get that wounded kid medical attention because he's bad. I know there's a medic unit at FOB Loyalty, so I order four vehicles to take the kid there for treatment or he's not going to make it. The vehicles take off and the rest of us stay behind to try to defeat the enemy and put the fire out in the MRAP.

We tow the MRAP back to base. There's a terrible feeling we all get looking at the blood and scorch marks, where the EFPs penetrated the armor. The feeling worsens when I receive news about the wounded kid: he died while on the way to FOB Loyalty. It's the first time I've experienced a loss.

Morale reaches a low point when convoys stop delivering our food. They can't. Route Predators has become so bad no one will drive it. We end up getting airdrops of food, water, and ammunition. A lot of the MREs go bad because it's 130 degrees. When we go out on patrol, we search for food at homes and shops. We buy chickens.

Months later, a kid named Matt Taylor goes out on foot patrol. A van pulls alongside him, its side doors opening to men armed with M16s. A round hits Matt in his left arm, and the shrapnel goes up his shoulder and into his heart. I break the news to Alpha. This one hits us especially hard. Matt was a beloved individual. Everyone loved the guy. Great personality.

We lose another soldier shortly thereafter, in a firefight that lasts over twenty-four hours. Everyone's emotional, exhausted and dragging ass, sick of the shitty living conditions. But we still have to drive on. We still have months to go on our deployment, and as their leader I've got to get my team through this while also knowing when to kick ass to get everyone performing at their optimum levels.

That means doing drills after long patrols. We can't be complacent. Whatever the crucible experience, you've got to go out tonight, tomorrow, and the next day. Maybe you won't come back or maybe it will be someone else. The unit is what matters. The unit needs to keep going and going because war doesn't stop.

RED

Red grew up in Gastonia, North Carolina. His father served in the Navy. Red joined the Army at seventeen, shortly after high school. Two days before he graduated from basic training, 9/11 happened. He served for thirteen years. He was a noncommissioned officer and worked as a human intelligence collector, MOS 35 Mike.

In 2006, I'm coming off my shift when I step outside the prison and see the bus. Normally, it carries one, maybe two of what we call high-value individuals. This afternoon, the bus is packed with Iraqis. They're being led into the prison.

I walk up to Chief, the warrant officer in charge of the prison, and ask what's going on.

"Someone got intel about an HVI [High-Value Individual] at a café," he says. "Don't know who the guy is or what he looks like, so we rolled up the whole café."

"If you need help screening people, I'll help you screen."

Chief knows I've learned Arabic and can speak it pretty decently—which irritates the locals, having some white guy come in and start asking them questions in their language.

I've always had a knack for languages. At fifteen, I learned Spanish because I liked a Mexican girl. Then, after I joined the Army, I was sent to the Defense Language Institute, where I studied Korean for fifteen months. I won their annual speech competition and went on to compete against other colleges in California and won the state title. Not bad for a kid from Gastonia, North Carolina.

Chief also knows I'm an interrogator. "Okay," he says. "Get to it."

The Iraqis go first to medical, where they get screened. There they trade their long white robes, called *dishdashas,* for jumpsuits, and then they're brought straight to the interrogation booths. I go in without an interpreter and start having basic conversations: "Hey, what's your name?" "Where are you from?" "Why'd you get captured?" I love asking that last question because it always gets them pissed off. When people get angry, sometimes they let things slip. Valuable things.

One of the guards comes up to me while I'm screening a prisoner. He pulls me aside and hands me a folded piece of paper.

"I found that note inside a guy's *dishdasha,*" he tells me. "We don't know what it says—it's in Arabic."

I can make out some of the Arabic but not all of it. I leave to go find our interpreter. He reads the piece of paper several times.

"This isn't a note," he says. "It's a letter addressed to the leader of the Jaysh al-Mahdi militia."

I'm familiar with the militia. We all are. JAM, as it's called, is a lesser-known extremist group in the area. Everyone back home in the States thinks all we deal with is Al-Qaeda, but there are a ton of extremist groups operating in Iraq, and for different reasons they don't always work together.

"This unit," the interpreter says, "is called the Army of the Messiah. It seems to operate like an Army platoon—company, battalion, brigade, division—but the letter is mainly an inventory of a weapons cache somewhere here in the city."

My blood is pumping. "And the person the letter is addressed to?"

I'm floored when he tells me the guy's name.

This JAM battalion commander is an extremely high-level HVI. We've been looking for his ass for a long, long time. And someone right here in the prison was carrying a letter addressed to this guy. I leave the interpreter, find the guard, and have him bring me to the letter holder.

I go into the booth, find one of my young soldiers talking to this old man sitting at a table. I kick out the soldier and look the old guy over. He is dressed in a jumpsuit, handcuffed, shaking.

"Why are you shaking?" I ask in English.

"I need a cigarette."

I pull out a cigarette and a lighter and sit down. "How many you smoke a day?"

He holds up three fingers.

"Three cigarettes? That's it?"

He shakes his head. "Three packs."

Most Iraqis look older than they are because of the sun.

This guy also smokes three packs a day. No wonder he looks seventy even though I was told he's forty.

I light a cigarette.

Blow smoke in his face as I remove the folded letter from my pocket.

"You want a pack of cigarettes?" I ask. "Don't tell me a single fucking lie about what's on that piece of paper, and you'll get all the cigarettes you want, bud."

"I don't know what the fuck the paper even is!"

Okay, cool. Here we go.

I smoke one cigarette after another as I ask him questions. He won't answer them. He throws his hands around, cussing me out in Arabic, thinking I don't know what he's saying. I don't react, either, which is critical.

The man keeps insisting he knows nothing about the letter. I keep chain-smoking to the point where I've got a headache, maybe even nicotine poisoning. My goal is to keep the whole room filled with smoke. I'm a smoker, so I know what it's like to not be able to have a cigarette.

I sit there, waiting, smoking. This isn't some crazy technique I learned back at the schoolhouse during my advanced intelligence training days. I'm just playing the game that's coming to me. I keep at this guy, keep asking him about the letter, and he keeps telling me he doesn't know anything.

This goes on for hours.

And then he says, "I do remember that letter."

I wait.

He says, "I found it on the ground of the bus, and I was gonna give it to you guys."

Which is pretty clever of him to say, since he knows we pay people to turn in IEDs, even other insurgents. What we're doing is paying the Iraqis to protect their own neighborhoods. We're putting security in their hands—and it's working. Significant attacks have started to decrease.

"I was gonna give it to you guys," the man says again.

"Bullshit."

"No, not bullshit! That was my plan, to give—"

"If that were true, you would have started off with that. But you started off with the whole 'I don't know what the fuck that letter is.' Why did you change your story?"

"I can't think. I need a cigarette."

"Why did you change your story?"

"Give me a cigarette. I can't think."

"I'll give you a cigarette when you tell me why you changed your story."

We keep going around and around, keep going at it, keep going at it.

Chow time rolls around, so I leave the cell to get him a plate. My head is pounding, and I feel woozy. I check my watch. I've been at it for six hours.

I bring him his food. He slaps it off the table.

"I want a cigarette!"

I decide to step up my game a little. "You know what? I'm gonna help you think," I say, and hand him a cigarette.

He's handcuffed, so he has to take the cigarette with both hands. He mutters "Thank you, thank you" over and over again as he brings it up to his mouth. Then he leans forward, obviously wanting me to light it for him.

"You asked for a cigarette," I tell him. "I've given you

what you asked for, and you haven't given me a single thing I asked for. Now you want a cigarette *and* a lighter? Fuck no."

The guy isn't happy about this. He breaks the cigarette in half and immediately regrets his decision. He tries to put it back together, sees that he can't, knows he can't, and his nicotine withdrawal grabs him by the balls and breaks him. I can see it in his eyes.

I light another cigarette.

I blow smoke in his face.

He starts to cry genuine, real-life tears. He's a defeated man. He crosses his arms and stares at the broken cigarette.

He says, "I wrote the letter."

"Oh, you did?"

"Yes."

"Well, that's wonderful," I say. "Now listen. I'm gonna start asking you some questions. I need you to understand that I don't believe a goddamn word you're saying, so make sure you answer these questions appropriately." I take a drag off my cigarette and blow smoke in his face. "Why'd you write the letter?"

He starts talking, and it becomes very clear to me that he's telling me the truth. He says he's the personal assistant, for lack of a better word, to this brigade commander. The man was asked to write the letter because he has very good handwriting. His job was to deliver the letter, which contains a detailed inventory of a weapons cache. He gives me the location.

After I finish writing down what he's told me, I get up and leave to check out his information. Before I go to my computer, I send one of my junior interrogators into the booth and do what's called map tracking: I trace the weapon cache's location using satellite imagery.

The guy's information checks out on my computer. On my way back, I see my junior interrogator coming out of the booth. He's smiling.

"We've got the location," he says, and starts laughing.

"What?"

"He told me to see if Master needs anything else. That's what he's calling you—Master. You mentally broke him."

And it only took ten hours, using what I call the Needs a Cigarette approach.

My junior interrogator says, "He also thought Master might like to know where the brigade commander is."

We roll up the brigade commander. They let me handle the interrogation.

The technique I decide to use isn't intended to work; it's just for shock value. The brigade commander has been in prison for all of five minutes and I am already in his face. I slam the notebook and pen down on the table and say, "I'm gonna leave, and on that piece of paper you're gonna write down who the fuck you are, who the fuck you work for, and everything you fucking do. And may God himself have mercy on your soul if, when I come back, you haven't written anything down, or you're lying."

I leave, go back to the office, and I watch from the camera recording his interrogation. I'm watching him sitting there, staring at the pad. Half of them write, half of them don't.

He starts writing.

When he's finished, I go back into the booth and grab the notebook.

"I'm done," he says.

"Done what?"

"Running. I'm tired of running. You sons of bitches keep looking for me. I'm done."

Outside, I hand the notebook to my interpreter.

It's clear the brigade commander has spilled his guts. He's written down his real name, what he does for the Army of the Messiah, everything.

I go back into the booth. "Seems like you told the truth."

"I'll tell you whatever you want to know, but I have two conditions. First, you make sure my family is safe, get them out of town. Then you help us get to America."

Naturally, I tell him I'll help him and his family.

He talks heavy and hard. While I listen, I start thinking about a buddy of mine, a really good intel guy, this young superstar who recently returned home after a fifteen-month deployment. We saw a ton of potential in this kid, so we took him under our wing, trained him, tried passing on our knowledge to him, tried to make him the next generation because everyone knows he's "the guy."

Thirty days after he returned home, he put a bullet in his head.

This guy never had any mental issues, and he was always upbeat. But when you're in Iraq, you don't have any days off. If you're here for a year, it's 365 days, every day. You never get a break, and it takes years off your life. Big years. There's the physical demand—always being on patrol or being stuck doing time-sensitive target (TST) missions and not sleeping for forty-eight hours—and then there's the mental aspect of seeing all the shit you see, doing the shit you do. Sometimes you do things that don't feel right. You question your own morality. It's mentally and emotionally and spiritually draining.

Every. Single. Day.

As I listen to the brigade commander, a man who will turn out to be one of my most valuable sources, a man who will help us break a couple of other people inside the prison and help us in some other, more classified matters—as I listen to him spill his secrets to protect himself and his family, I realize I'm burned out. I've got nothing left. Here, in this moment, I know I'm done.

Years later, when people ask me about my time in the Army, ask me what I miss, I'll tell them I don't miss anything at all. I'll feel like an asshole when I say that—people miss things, I know, I get it. I can tell stories, laugh, and joke when I look back on my crazy, fun, weird, and scary times. I don't regret what I did, but I don't miss it. I don't miss a damn thing.

NATE HARLAN

Nate Harlan comes from a military family. His older brother served in the Marines, his father served in the Army National Guard reserves, and his grandfather served in France during World War I. He joined the Army National Guard at twenty-seven. Nate left the service as a captain.

On the morning of September 11, 2001, I get up early and drive south on the highway, trying to listen to the radio and keep my mind off the current state of my life, the fact that I'm a military spouse. I know I should let it all go, but I can't. It keeps lingering. Festering.

I got screwed.

I went to work right out of high school, took a job at a plastics factory. Wasn't a bad place to work, but I wanted to do bigger things with my life. One day in the break room my foreman said, "Nate, you and I, we're lifers here," and I literally said, "Fuck this," took off my shirt, and handed it to him. I enrolled at Kent State University, and then transferred to Holy Cross and eventually Notre Dame, to study communications. The only way to pay for it was Army ROTC. I had to compete for a scholarship. Luckily, I received one that covered about 80 percent of my tuition.

ROTC was a means to an end. But the more involved I got, the more I liked it. I really got into the military mindset. By my junior year, I was so serious about the Army and my communications major that I wanted to join the Signal Corps.

The summer before my senior year, I was on my way to attend the Advanced Leader Corps (ALC) and developed a nasty cold. The Army physician checked me over, said I had high blood pressure. I told him I didn't and to check my physical reports. He saw that I was right, and the Army let me go through advanced camp. I did well, graduated, and then went back to Notre Dame in the fall.

Then the colonel at the ROTC battalion called and told me I had to start getting my blood pressure checked twice a day, for five days in a row. I explained what had happened over the summer, but he insisted—and that stressed me out. I knew high blood pressure would disqualify me from ROTC. I went to my mother's doctor over Thanksgiving, and the woman told me my blood pressure was in kind of a gray area—140 over whatever. I told her it was a little higher than normal because I was stressed, but she didn't care. She sent over her report, and I got kicked out of ROTC.

Two good things did come out of it. First, they paid for my college. Second, I ended up marrying a girl from St. Mary's College, which is right across the street from Notre Dame. She was ROTC, Army, studying to be a nurse.

Now we're living in the DC metro area. She's working as an Army nurse at Walter Reed, and I'm twenty-seven and driving to my shitty sales job in Fairfax, Virginia, when I should be in the Army. My ROTC buddies are out, doing great things and kicking ass, and I'm a military spouse.

But maybe not for long.

I've been talking to a National Guard recruiter. A lot of time has passed since college, and he thinks I can enroll in Officer Candidate School because he believes my ROTC medical records didn't make their way into the Army's system. If I get into OCS, I don't have to travel. I can live with my wife, at our house in Fort Meade, and—

A breaking story comes over the radio about a plane flying into the World Trade Center. By the time I reach work, a second plane has hit, and another one has crashed into the Pentagon.

I go inside the company building and see everyone watching and then I realize what I need to do. I turn around and leave.

Highway north is a ghost town, not a single car on it. I drive 120 miles an hour. I'm not military but I need to get home ASAP and kick my wife in her butt and tell her to get to Walter Reed.

The entrance to Fort Meade is right next to NSA headquarters. It's mayhem, like something out of a disaster movie—people running with their arms in the air. I stop at the gate, and the guards draw their guns on me.

I roll down the window as bomb-sniffing dogs approach my car. *"I live here!"*

The guards get me out of the car. When they eventually

clear me, I pull onto the base and park. I'm about to enter my house when my wife comes out, bawling.

"Honey," I say gently, "you've got to get your shit together. You need to get to the hospital."

I'm helping her pack, wishing I were on active duty, when she gets the call. She's going down to the Pentagon to help with recovery. As I watch her drive off, F-16s doing six hundred miles an hour fly over the house. There is nothing more chilling than seeing fighter planes flying over your house when there is no other air traffic.

I enlist the next day. I'm twenty-seven years old.

The National Guard has a three-phase accelerated program. For the next eleven weeks, during basic training, where I'm the second oldest guy (first prize is taken by a guy who's thirty-three), I keep in close contact with my wife, who has been working nonstop treating the first responders in charge of recovering the bodies from the Pentagon. It's heartbreaking, listening to what she and the others are enduring, what they've seen.

For the next year, I drill with an infantry battalion and learn what's called PMCS—preventive maintenance checks and services. I go to Officer Candidate School, graduate a full-fledged lieutenant in the Maryland National Guard, and then I'm assigned to Bravo Company, 1st Battalion, 115th Infantry.

For the next four years, I do annual training in Japan for Operation Northwind, training Japanese ground self-defense force units that are getting ready to go to Iraq. My wife, now living in Maryland with our two kids, is planning on what our next duty station will be, so I know I'll be leaving the Maryland National Guard.

At the last minute, she decides she wants out of the military. She misses her family and wants to move back to Indiana. I go there and buy a house while my wife stays in Maryland with the kids.

The beauty of the National Guard is that I can go anywhere. I start the interstate transfer to join the Indiana Guard. I'm with the kids, setting up the house, when I get a call from Brian, my former commander at Bravo Company. He tells me he just got promoted to captain.

After I congratulate him, he says, "If we ever get deployed to Iraq, would you want to go with us?"

"Hell, yeah, Brian, of course I would."

He calls me back two days later, chuckling.

"Remember when I said, 'Do you want to go to Iraq with us?'"

"Are you shitting me?"

"We got a deployment order," Brian says. "Do you still want to go?"

"Absolutely. When do we leave?"

"Three weeks. But I want you down in Fort Jackson and then Fort Stewart, to get started on the pre-mobilization process."

In a normal deployment, when you're on active duty and receive your deployment order, you get six, maybe eight months to prep your families before you say good-bye. Brian is asking me to drop what I'm doing not months or weeks or days from now but *right now*. He's hoping he can rely on me to get in my car, drive from Indiana to Camp Fretterd, in

Maryland, and get the unit mobilized. He's counting on me to be his second in command.

I watch the kids playing in their new backyard, the phone pressed against my ear.

"I'll do it," I tell him. "I absolutely want to do it."

"Can you have the unit ready in three weeks?"

It's a tall order, what he's asking, and not to be taken lightly.

"You can count on me," I tell him. I hang up and watch my kids.

Having to leave them right now—it's a surprise, no question. But when you're a leader, sometimes you have to make sacrifices.

My wife drives from Maryland. I meet her at a rest stop in Pennsylvania to give her the keys to the new house and hand over the kids. We make the best of my shitty opportunity before I leave to drive to Maryland to link up with my unit.

We fly to Kuwait at the beginning of June of 2005. It's the middle of the night when we land at Ali Al Salem Air Base. When I get off the plane, I walk into a wall of heat so intense it instantly dries out the back of my throat.

This weird sort of quiet settles over the airfield. No one seems to talk as we shuffle from the processing center to a bunch of horrible briefings. We're given these strange shelf-stable meals called Jimmy Deans, and then we're loaded onto buses that will take us to Camp Buehring for two weeks of weapons training.

Coming here, I wasn't scared. Nervous, yes, but not scared. That changes once I get inside a bus. A designated shooter sits up front, and all the windows are covered with shades or curtains with tassels. Someone says, "Keep the curtains closed since we don't want people looking in, seeing you're Americans."

We drive for what seems like forever across the desert.

Dear God, where are we going? A lot of guys are dead asleep. I'm wide-awake, waiting for the barbarian horde to attack us. I'm still wired by the time I reach Camp Buehring. It's hot and windy as I go to my tent to try and grab some sleep. The air conditioners, we're told, aren't working. The first sergeant tells us we can sleep in.

When I wake up the next morning, I lie there on my bunk with my arms outstretched, sweating. It's pouring off me and there are pools of it underneath my hands because it's probably 160 degrees in the tent. Everyone inside lies there, unconscious, probably dying from heat exhaustion.

"Holy shit," someone moans. "This is misery."

When I head out of the tent, it already feels like it's 130 degrees cooler. I need water, and all the water is out in the sun. The water I drink is hot and covered in dust, and it has this plastic taste to it. It's terrible, not refreshing at all, and I keep drinking and drinking because you have to drink a lot of water, all day, every day, or you'll dehydrate.

When training is over, we're sent up to Camp Victory, a huge military city built by the good guys. My company is do-ing a handoff with a field artillery company that's been doing twenty-four-hour clearance on Route Tampa, a main supply route around what was formerly the Baghdad International Airport. The unit we're replacing—it's clear right away that they're beaten down, mentally and physically done. They lost several guys, and a lot more were wounded. Their vehicles are junk, practically trashed, and their weapons systems are in horrible shape.

My commanding officer wants me to go for a ride-along with the unit's executive officer, get the lay of the land.

"I don't have any ammo," I say.

"I'll get you some," my CO replies.

The executive officer's Hummer is covered in bullet holes and blast damage. I get into the back seat. The XO—executive officer—slides behind the wheel, looking spent. I wait for him to brief me, something along the lines of, *This is a hot IED area. We've been hit here before.*

"Hold on," he says. "And buckle up."

We roll out of the gate.

It's like a movie set for *Black Hawk Down*. A dozen or more vehicles destroyed by IEDs sit like blackened shells in the desert or by the sides of the road.

And then it hits me: this is for real. Until this point, everything has been another drill weekend—a really well-thought-out drill weekend with good special effects. I'm in country and this is the real deal and I'm starting to shake. It's really hot and I'm sweating, and I've got real bullets in my weapon. I have a round chambered. This is real.

What the fuck am I doing here?

We make a right turn, and suddenly the scene changes. The road, full of traffic, is carved through a small village, people walking everywhere. The XO drives like he's on a speedway; he hauls ass down the road, turning violently, throwing me around the back.

"We're going to do a snap checkpoint," the XO says as he follows the road into a stretch of desert. "You know: set up a roadblock and check all the cars coming through for bad guys."

He pulls up alongside a speeding Iraqi car and performs a PIT maneuver. He hits the car in the rear—

"I'm going to get there as fast as I can," he says.

—and the car spins clockwise, directly in front of us. The XO takes a hard right and floors the gas—

"I'm going to throw that checkpoint up."

—and I turn and watch the car, still spinning, careen off the road, into the sand.

"I'm going to be there for fifteen minutes," he says. "Then I'm going to collapse it and go back."

He hits and pushes more Iraqi vehicles off the road. I understand he's doing what he has to do because he's experienced the dangers of buried land mines and IEDs loaded along Route Tampa. He wants to get safely from point A to point B and back, but I still can't believe what I'm seeing.

We come to a stop inside another village. I see thatched huts and some small buildings and a guy pushing an actual donkey cart. The XO gets on the Hummer's loudspeaker: *"Get out of my way, motherfuckers."*

The locals, though, don't *habla* English. They ignore him and keep doing what they're doing as we get out and set up a checkpoint. We throw out some concertina wire and block off the area, and the entire time I'm watching, in growing terror, these guys walking around—guys with M16s and M4s. They're holding them John Wayne–style, by the pistol grip.

This is insane.

And it's only my first day.

*   *   *

My unit is quickly assigned to a bigger unit—the 2nd of the 70th. Logistically, they own us. We get our beans and bullets from them. My commander, Captain Borcove, calls a meeting and informs us we're going to secure a place called Sab al-Bour, a town of probably twenty-five thousand people. It's considered a black town, which means you don't drive through it, or you'll get shot at or hit with an IED.

"We're going to live in this government building that's half government, half Iraqi Police," Captain Borcove says. "It's divided by a wall. We'll take the government half, empty it out, and live there. We'll rotate platoons in and out."

A staff sergeant says, loud enough for everyone to hear, "He's going to get us fucking killed."

I grab him, pull him out of the meeting, and tear into him.

"You don't *ever* fucking say anything about what our commander plans in front of other soldiers. You do it again, I will beat your ass."

But deep down I'm thinking, *Oh, shit, he is going to get our asses killed.*

We head into town wearing brand-new uniforms, looking spiffy. We National Guard are literally the first unit in the country to wear them, these ACUs, with green tabs and green zippers. The Iraqis have never seen these uniforms before and think we are some crazy new unit. Our interpreters tell them we're Special Forces and the people are terrified.

This information operation works to our advantage. From

June to early September, we do battalion and company-level quadrant searches, get our hands on a lot of weapons, contraband, and, strangely enough, drugs. We end up really securing the town.

"I need you to go out on a recon," my CO tells me. It's almost seven in the morning, and I'm reviewing all the confiscated weapons. "Take my truck, grab a crew—and grab someone from the MP company to go with you. I don't care who. You need to leave in fifteen minutes."

Sergeants Zimmerman and El Daco roll out with me, along with a sergeant from the MP company, and we meet up at the battalion. We leave with four trucks: battalion S3, JTAC team from the Air Force, scout platoon leader in his truck, and mine. We're going to do a reconnaissance mission on a house near this traffic circle called the circle of death. We're supposed to capture some guy named Abu Bakker.

The joint terminal attack controller (JTAC) is with us as a show of force on the mission. They're going to drop bombs on this house, once we find it.

We do reconnaissance and drive around for hours and hours, taking pictures, looking for this specific house. Everyone is tired. We're heading down Route Islanders when I see a canal on the left-hand side with all these palm trees and reeds growing up really high. On the right-hand side there's a field and three large homes, and then a smaller house. A bunch of kids are playing outside it.

"Sir," Sergeant El Daco says, "I think I saw the house we're—"

An IED goes off and rocks our truck.

Everything seems really slow for a second. I'm aware of

spit coming out of my mouth and dirt flying around us. Then I'm snapped back to the present and everything hurts.

Drive, I tell myself. *Keep driving.* El Daco is dropping f-bombs over and over again, but he tells me he's okay. The sergeant in the back is groaning. I glance over my shoulder, see that his armored door is collapsed on him.

I drive another three hundred meters and then stop. The S3 traveling behind me stopped before the explosion; there's now a big gap between us. The JTAC team calls out that they've IDed the trigger person and are in pursuit. I see their Humvee tearing across the field, heading toward the house.

I'm on the nine line, calling for medevac, when two M1 tanks come over the horizon. They were right down the road and heard the explosion. I get out to help the sergeant in the back seat. The door is folded inward, squeezing him between the door and the bulkhead between the two back seats.

Medevac comes and gets the sergeant out. We get orders to fire at the most likely point of origin. If we do that, we'll end up killing a bunch of kids. I'm not going to allow that to happen, so we police the area.

We find a second IED.

"Call EOD," I say.

An explosive ordnance disposal unit arrives three hours later. I pull out some concertina wire. This little Iraqi guy in a white pickup truck pulls up to us.

I look to the interpreter and say, "Tell him to go away."

Terp tells him to go away.

The guy doesn't go away.

"Tell him again," I say.

Terp gets on the mic and says it again. The guy's still there—and now he's getting out of the car.

I tell my machine gunner to give the guy a warning shot with his 240 Bravo. He fires a twelve-round burst.

The Iraqi is still standing there. Now I have to confront the guy.

I stand about twenty feet away, can see how old he is, and yell, "Sir! Get back in your vehicle." Terp is telling him the same thing.

The Iraqi starts approaching me. And he's not saying anything.

This is not happening. I'm in the National Guard. This is not happening. My day is not supposed to end with a guy wearing a bomb vest. I draw my rifle and point it at him.

He doesn't get the message.

Now we're about fifteen feet apart, and he's coming closer. The warrior in me says to pull the trigger, not to take any chances. But the human in me is going through a whole bunch of what-if scenarios. We've made enough terrorists over here through our misguided actions, and I don't need to add to that.

Then I remember somebody saying how these guys aren't afraid of rifles, they're afraid of pistols. So I put the rifle down, pull out my pistol, and point it at him.

He stops.

Puts his hands around his neck.

Turns and leaves.

We call our compound the Alamo because we all think we're going to die here.

There are days when the Alamo is manned by different platoons, so there are different officers in charge of it. The day I'm in charge I get a call from a corporal who is a medic. "Sir, I need you to come out front and take a look at this guy."

He doesn't tell me anything else—doesn't have to.

Some of our battalion medics are positioned near the front gate, ready to help our wounded soldiers. Battalion has given us strict orders: under no circumstances are we allowed to see and treat Iraqi patients. Word of medical personnel has gotten out among the Iraqis, and the locals line up in front of the gate, begging for help. When I arrive, the corporal points to an Iraqi man and a boy standing on the other side of the gate. The boy is tall, around five six.

"Kid has a gunshot wound to the abdomen," the corporal tells me. "Small caliber, 5.56, somewhere in that ballpark."

"When was he shot?"

"Several days ago. Honestly, it's a miracle he's still alive. He's got edema—his ankles are swollen. I can't believe he's upright."

I go up to the father and, through the gate, ask him what happened to his son. The desperate man tells me the insurgents paid him five hundred dollars to have his son go out and dig a hole for an IED. Just a hole. An American unit saw his son digging the hole, shot him, and left him there. Just left him.

But I know the other side of it. The Iraqis are doing a lot of damage to us. American soldiers are out patrolling, see someone walking with a shovel, and mistake it for someone holding a weapon. I can see how someone could get shot.

"Why did you put your son up to that?" I ask the father.

266

"It's easy money—a lot of money. We need to feed our family."

This kid, his face and eyes—I can tell he's dying. But my orders are clear: no medical care. Iraqis have their own clinic for that, only we know there's no trauma care there.

Maybe making an exception is not such a bad idea. That would win the hearts and minds of the Iraqi people.

"I'm sorry," I tell the father. "I can't help you."

I turn around, feeling sick to my stomach—feeling like I'm about to lose my shit.

Don't you dare, I tell myself. *Don't you dare lose your shit in front of your men. Walk away. You need to walk away from this. You have your orders. That's it—walk. Now keep walking.*

Everyone returns home with something. I'm diagnosed with PTSD, traumatic brain injury, and tinnitus. The tinnitus gets worse and worse over the years, and I've got all these unwanted memories that keep coming back to me, again and again. I made a lot of decisions as a soldier and a leader in a combat zone; how could I not revisit them?

But the decision I made that day about the Iraqi kid—that one really sticks with me. I had a fourteen-year-old kid standing in front of me, dying from a gunshot wound, his father begging me to save his son's life, and I said no and turned my back on them. I get emotional every time I think about it, and I think about it every single day.

I don't know what's harder: making a decision or being forced into one. I had to make a decision for someone to live or die. I've got my own fourteen-year-old boy, and I think about that dying kid, his father begging me to save his son's life, and I chose death.

SHERRY HEMBY

Sherry Hemby's father served in the Army National Guard. After working in the civilian sector as a trauma nurse, an emergency room nurse, and, later, as a traveling nurse, Sherry decided, in 1992, to join the Air Force Reserve Command. She is the acting command nurse for the Air Force Reserve Command and is stationed at Robins Air Force Base, in Georgia.

I'm in a lecture room at the hospital, attending a scheduled in-service professional training day, discussing medical care geared to specific cultures in the diverse DC community, when I'm told that my Air Force Reserves supervisor is on the phone.

"A plane flew into the Pentagon," he tells me. "You need to report to the emergency room stat."

I'm trying to mentally absorb his words as he explains to me what little he knows about what happened at the Pentagon and what's going on in New York. It's the morning of September 11, 2001.

The Alexandria Hospital emergency room, where I work as a civilian, is three miles from the Pentagon. I arrive, get the equipment prepared, and help set up the hospital for mass casualties. We're not a level one trauma center or a burn center, so nearby hospitals that specialize in those areas will have to handle the critical patients.

None of us are sure if we're going to be dealing with casualties from a single aircraft. We're hearing reports that there could be more planes up in the sky. We also don't know what, exactly, we'll be dealing with in terms of the incoming patients.

There's also talk of anthrax.

My roommate, who is also in the reserves, pulls out her deployment bag and consults a medical reference book for the signs and symptoms of anthrax. I write a checklist for the doctors.

By the end of the day, we've treated twenty-five casualties from the Pentagon.

My Air Force supervisor calls me again, asks me if I'm okay. I explain to him what I've seen and done over the course of the day.

"When you get home," he tells me, "please call me immediately."

Okay, here we go. I take a deep breath. There's no doubt in my mind we're going to war. It's not a question of if; it's when.

The Air Force activates my unit a few months later, in February of 2002. We're going to Afghanistan, into a war zone, to bring out our wounded.

The guards salute me as I come through the gate. I tear

up a little, feeling so proud to be here, to actually do this. It makes me think of my father, who served in the Army National Guard for twenty-three years. He taught me about patriotism—to think of others. Service before self.

My dad stood six foot three. When he put on his uniform, he stood taller. I was a little girl, and I'll always remember my mother standing at the ironing board, making sure his uniform was perfect. Dad was so proud of his service. We all were.

As a flight nurse, your primary duty is to give each soldier the best care possible. To do that, you have to focus on the tactics—what medicines the patients need, how you're going to deal with the effects of altitude during treatment. You need to make sure they're stabilized, and you need to be constantly vigilant, watching for any signs or symptoms of possible adverse reactions.

To do all this effectively—to *really* focus—you need to put your feelings in a box. When I see how mangled the soldiers are, I remind myself not to let it get to me. If I do, I can't be effective. I can't do my job properly.

The C-141 aircraft is configured with stanchions in the middle and seats down along the sides of the fuselage. We place litters on each side. Each litter goes four high, and I have to climb over the ambulatory patients in the seats to check the patients on the fourth litter.

One fella looks like Radar from the TV show *M*A*S*H*. One arm is pretty mangled, so I put the IV with his antibiotics and pain medication into his other hand. I show him how he has to hold his hand a certain way.

"It's to make sure the IV fluid's going in properly," I explain.

"Yes, ma'am." Like the other soldiers on board, he's young—nineteen, maybe early twenties. I'm thirty-two, and what these young soldiers deal with in the war zone totally amazes me.

I make my rounds, see nine other patients, and also check in with the other medics to make sure they're eating and drinking plenty of fluids. If they don't, they'll physically crash, and they won't be able to take care of the patients.

When I come back to the patient who looks like Radar, to make sure the pain medicine is working effectively, I see he isn't holding up his hand the way I showed him. The IV fluid isn't really running.

"You've got to hold your hand like this." I demonstrate, and then I flash him a really big smile and decide to tease him. "Oh, now I get it. You just wanted me to come back and hold your hand, didn't you?"

He gets this sheepish little grin on his face.

The teasing, the joking, holding a soldier's hand—these soft moments make for more human interactions. It's important, too, because every single one of these young men and women want to know how long it's going to take for them to get better so they can get back to their troops. They still want to fight. Some of them feel guilty they got hurt. They feel like they've left their troops behind.

"Ma'am?"

The voice belongs to one of my critical care nurses. She's got what I call the caregiver-fatigue look written all over her face. I know what's coming.

"I don't know if I can keep doing this," she says. "I don't

know if I can handle three more months of seeing the same people hurt over and over again."

I tell her I'll do my best to find a replacement once we get home.

Shortly after we arrive at the base, I get a call from my husband's friend, who was the best man at our wedding.

"My neighbor's son was injured and put on an Air Evac that's coming to your base," he explains. "Can you please look in on him, make sure he's okay? His parents are worried sick. And his fiancée."

He gives me the soldier's name. I promise to check in on him and I hang up.

Getting this call has broken the barrier I've put in place. Knowing the patient's name, who he is, makes him very real to me.

I can't go to the hospital.

I go to my room and cry. I need to cry and then catch my breath before I go over and see the patient.

JOHN WALL

John Wall was born in Charleston, South Carolina, but grew up outside Birmingham, Alabama. A lot of men on his father's side of the family attended West Point. He is named after his great-grandfather, a West Point graduate (class of 1911). John graduated from West Point in May of 2006 and served with the 82nd Airborne as an infantry platoon leader. He got out in January of 2012, with the rank of captain.

O ur job is to deliver food and medicine and perform pop-up medical examinations for the locals—all without getting blown up.

Killed.

And that's a really hard thing to reconcile: risking our lives to help people who also want to kill us.

It's 2006, and the IED threat here in Afghanistan is massive. The thing that scares me the most—scares my men—is the actual driving when we go out of the wire. The uncertainty of what might be waiting for us on the road, the randomness of the attacks—you know it's going to happen to you at some point; you just don't know *when*.

Helmand, the largest province in Afghanistan, is a well-known Taliban stronghold. For the past twenty days, instead of doing humanitarian missions, we've been traveling in a huge armored convoy running resupply missions and providing combat support to our other line companies who are fighting to take control of the province. We've taken over the city, and the Taliban has fled to the nearby villages.

Now we're traveling from village to village, performing dismounted operations where we get out of our vehicles and go look for the bad guys. The people who live in these villages are supposed to be gone, but we find out that a lot of them stayed behind, making it really difficult for us to differentiate the Taliban from the civilians.

We've taken a lot of fire, a lot of casualties. My men are tired and keyed up as we head into another village. Coming in as their platoon leader two months ago was overwhelming. I didn't have any credibility as a young lieutenant, and that can create some adversity—even more if you're a West Pointer like me. All these guys had combat experience in Afghanistan and Iraq, and I didn't. Fortunately, I had a great platoon sergeant, a multiple Silver Star winner, who took me under his wing and smoothed the transition.

We've now been involved in multiple firefights. I've earned their respect, and they've come to trust me as their platoon leader.

When we started out that morning, it was dark. Now it's

light. Up ahead, I can see a bridge going over a small creek. We can't drive over it because there might be an IED. The only way forward is to drive down into a wadi, which is basically a dry riverbed.

The vehicle I'm in, an armored Humvee, goes first. As we drive down, I'm scanning the area for the enemy, any threat. I'm waiting for the sound of gunfire. In those moments, ten seconds seems like ten minutes. It's almost like watching a movie in slow motion, frame by frame. It's the most surreal thing when—

BOOM.

The explosion comes directly behind me. I turn and see the armored Humvee carrying our interpreter and our FS-NCO (fire support NCO), Sergeant David J. Drakulich, being pushed up into the air.

The convoy comes to a full stop.

Our interpreter and a few soldiers riding inside the Humvee are wounded.

David Drakulich, my good friend, is dead.

An IED explosion affects everyone differently—even more so when guys get hurt and killed and you can't find who's responsible for the bomb. And then there's the fact that you still have a mission to do. The mission must continue.

When we get back to the base, I address my men in a group and then try to talk to them individually. I try to figure out their needs, whether they're angry or extremely sad, if they were scared when it happened and if they're still scared now. I've got thirty-five different people, with different backgrounds and different feelings, and the hardest part is figuring out how to motivate and take care of each soldier. Everyone looks for leadership in a crisis.

Drakulich, I'm told, wasn't killed by an IED but from an anti-tank mine. I could have just as easily driven over it.

I've been struggling with undirected feelings of aggression, and now I feel an enormous sense of survivor's guilt.

I'm also told that Drakulich's parents have already been notified through the proper channels. As his platoon leader, it's my job to call and explain, to the best of my ability, what happened to their son. I've never met his parents, which is going to make this phone call even more difficult.

The hardest part is answering their questions. Because a lot of information is classified, I'm only allowed to say certain things. I have to work hard to find a middle ground that will give them the closure they need without overstepping my bounds.

It's the first of many such phone calls I'll make over the course of my military career.

Talking to families who lose loved ones, trying to comfort them—it's the hardest thing I've ever had to do. I did a great job with some. With others, questions will always weigh on me. Did I handle the situation appropriately? Am I doing the best I can to take care of them? Do they want to be called on Memorial Day, Veterans Day, anniversaries, and so forth? I want to be respectful, but I never want to reopen the wound.

No matter what they teach you at West Point, in basic training, at Ranger school—none of it ever prepares you for how to handle these situations in the moment. Or how to go on living with them.

PART FOUR:

ON THE HOME FRONT

TOM

Tom served in the Army for twenty years. He started out in communications and worked his way into special operations. He retired with the rank of master sergeant.

D ad, what's this?"
I turn around and see my sixteen-year-old daughter standing next to a group of dusty boxes in our tiny attic. We came up here to look for some old Christmas decorations.

She's holding my old field jacket, which she has taken out of a box.

"That," I say, "is my chocolate chip uniform."

"Chocolate chip?"

"They called it that because that camouflage pattern, those pale-brown shades there and the black spots, it looks like chocolate chip cookie dough."

"Yeah, it kinda does. Where's it from?"

"Desert Storm."

"When was that?"

"A long time ago. Before you were born."

Memories, most of them good, wash over me. I was a young soldier, all of twenty, when I showed up in Iraq in August of 1990. I was tasked with carrying the radio for the operations guy, Major Rod, who controlled all the battalion assets. The radio, all the other stuff I had to carry—I wore probably the heaviest rucksack on planet Earth on my back. People would sometimes have to help me get up and they'd walk behind me to make sure I didn't tip over.

"What was it like over there?" my daughter asks.

"Hot. Really, really hot."

"Were you, you know, nervous?"

"Maybe. Probably."

My daughter places the uniform on the attic floor and then turns her attention back to the box. "Was it scary?"

It occurs to me how we've never really talked about this. Desert Storm. My time as a Ranger, my Bronze Stars, with combat V device, which is awarded for valor in combat. Truth be told, I've never been good at talking with anyone, really, about any aspect of my twenty years of service in the Army. It's hard, talking about the stuff I saw, what I did. It seems braggadocious or something. I've boxed away my stories like my old uniforms and moved on with my life.

But there is something about the way my daughter is looking at me that makes me decide to tell her. She's certainly old enough. And after everything I've put her through, she deserves some answers. Maybe it will help her. Help us.

"When I was on the plane, flying over there," I say, "the only thing they told us was that Iraq's army, the Republican

Guard, was going to try to shoot down our plane. They didn't tell us anything else, like, you know, what to expect when we landed. So yeah, I was nervous. Then, when we landed, they told us to lock and load, and that's when…Yeah, I'd say then I was scared because in my mind I was thinking we were all going to have to start fighting our way off the airplane."

My daughter looks at me, wide-eyed. "Did you?"

"No," I chuckle. "We got off and set up a chow hall."

"What did you do there?"

"I was a signal guy. Communications. I followed this major around, carrying this big radio for him, so I got to sit down with all the commanders and listen to them plan the assault. That's when it got real—when we did the actual assault."

"And that's when it got scary."

I think about it for a moment. "I would say I was more nervous than scared. I had a lot of confidence in our leaders. I also had a lot of confidence in our guys. Our soldiers. I knew we could take on anybody and anything. After it was over, when I came back home…having followed these leaders around, I saw how they spoke and how they acted, what they did, and I knew I wanted to become a leader. So I reenlisted and went to Ranger school."

She reaches into the box, pulls out a black beret. "This is your Ranger hat, right?"

I nod, thinking about the day I went back to Fort Bragg wearing that old black beret. There I was a newly promoted staff sergeant with Airborne wings, a Ranger tab, and an 82nd combat patch. I'm on my way to the 1st Ranger Battalion. I remember feeling really cool.

I also remember meeting a lot of guys there who had leadership in their blood. I remember telling myself, *Dude, just be quiet. Just soak it up and watch these leaders lead.* Man, what a talented bunch of individuals.

"Did you go to war again?" she asks. "As a Ranger?"

"I came close. I got placed on what's called an RRF—a Ranger ready force—that was going to fly to Somalia, jump into an airfield, and take it over." I leave out the part where I was standing on the ramp wearing my parachute and signing my will. "The mission was given to another battalion, so I didn't have to go."

"Mom told me you went to war again."

"I did. In 2002. Afghanistan."

"Right after I was born."

I nod. She was born shortly before 9/11. I deployed a few months later.

"What was Afghanistan like?"

"Hot. Dusty," I reply. "We stayed at this place where I had to clean my clothes in a bucket for four months."

"Gross."

I laugh softly. "Showers came when the sun came out. You'd put water in a bucket and put it up on the roof, and after it heated up you could pour it on you." I remember feeling like we were out there living like some old Vietnam guys back in the day.

My daughter takes out my Ranger uniform. "Were you afraid that time?"

"Honestly, no, I wasn't. The people, the guys in my unit—they were the best of the best. Unstoppable. I didn't fear for a lack of ability. The only thing I cared about was making sure my ability matched everyone else's, because I didn't want to be a liability."

"What did you do there?"

"The first time? Reconnaissance. They'd drop us off somewhere, usually on a hill, and we'd have to walk miles to get to this field site. When we got there, we'd have to build what's called a hide site, which is a place where you can hide and watch the enemy. And that's what I did—sometimes for days. Watched the enemy and built these intel packets based on what we saw and heard and then handed everything over to the people in charge so they could make strategic decisions."

"How many days did you spend in one of these hide sites?"

"The longest was three. And man, it was so hot. So incredibly hot—at least 125 degrees, because there weren't a lot of trees in the place where we were. We'd hunker down there during the day, roasting, and later, when the sun went down, we could get out and move a bit."

I don't share with her the rougher aspects of the missions that followed—like seeing the guy right next to me get hit and go down. He ended up being fine—we patched him up and he returned to combat—but when I saw him go down it took me aback. I realized, right then, that none of us were invincible.

We lost guys. And it rocked me pretty hard. Our organization, even if you lost a guy that night, the next morning, you're right back at it. The tempo was unbelievable. Screaming fast. There were so many times when I wondered if we could physically keep up the pace.

I pull out another old uniform and smile softly, thinking

about how odd it is that a piece of clothing started this conversation with my daughter.

"Mom said you went to Iraq."

I nod. "I went there next. After Afghanistan."

"And kept going back."

I feel a wave of sadness and regret.

Those five deployments, as rough as they were on me, were even rougher on my wife. When you deploy as a Ranger, you don't really know when you're coming back. You don't know where you're going most times, either. There's also a really strong chance that you may not be able to call home for weeks, sometimes months, depending on the mission. It's really hard on a marriage. Many don't survive. Mine didn't.

My daughter took the hardest hit, no question. She's the reason I decided to hang up my spurs and retire, at thirty-eight. I didn't want to put her through that anymore. We're very close now, but it took a lot of work.

I put my arm around my daughter and hug her close.

"Those deployments," I say. "They helped me become a better man in the sense that...I was this ordinary dude surrounded by all these extraordinary human beings. They showed me how to get to the next level, whether it was fitness, being a good dad, a good Christian—a good whatever. These men, the experiences I had—they showed me what success looks like, the type of people I want to surround myself with. It taught me the true value of friendship."

"You should do something with these uniforms," my daughter says.

"Like what?"

"I dunno. Something. They deserve it."

Looking at my old uniforms, I wonder how many other veterans are out there like me, how many others just boxed up their stories, their unique experiences and sacrifices, and tucked them away in some dusty attic or cellar. It makes me think about those veterans who return home and take their own lives. I haven't been afflicted with that, but from what I've heard, the more they talk, the less they feel isolated.

What if I could help veterans share their stories by using their old uniforms? Could their uniforms help start conversations between family members, friends, and other veterans? Between officers and civilians?

"We should start a business," I say.

"Doing what?"

"Doing something good with these uniforms."

The business we created together, Eagles and Angels Limited, salvages the old uniforms of our brave men and women and transforms them into a unique line of high-end clothing and accessories crafted here in the US. Each piece carries the story of the soldier who wore the uniform, and each purchase helps support the families of our fallen heroes.

There are too many stories of courage tucked away in attics and old boxes across the country—secret even to the families of the ones who served. They deserve to be heard. And to be preserved.

KEVIN DRODDY

Kevin Droddy and his twin brother, Jason, entered the Army on March 18, 2009. They served six years with 3rd Ranger Battalion, 75th Ranger Regiment; deployed six times; and executed more than 150 missions each. When Kevin moved back home to West Palm Beach, Florida, he went into real estate with his brother. Their company, the Droddy Group, helps veterans buy and sell their homes.

I f you act like a man," my team leader tells me, "I'll treat you like a man."

He's twenty-four. My age. Only he's got all this life experience behind him because he joined the Army right out of high school and became a Ranger. My life was all about hockey—a year in Michigan; six years in Toronto, Canada; and then three years outside Philadelphia, playing in the NCAA. Last year, when I returned home to Florida, I worked, along with my twin brother, Jason, at our dad's tool and die company.

The country was in the grip of a global financial crisis—the worst one since the Great Depression—and while it affected my dad's company big-time, he refused to lay us off.

I loved the machine shop and working with my father, but it wasn't something I wanted to do for the rest of my life. Same with Jason. We always loved the military and knew this was our chance to do our part to protect our country while also helping our dad downsize and keep his company afloat.

My team leader, covered head to toe in sweat and dirt, picks up a bottle of water. He's just come back from combat.

As he drinks, he eyes me over the bottle, trying to size me up. He knows this is my first deployment.

"I'm your guy," I tell him. "Whatever you need." And I mean it. I'm going to put my age and everything else aside because he's seen combat and I haven't. Jason and I became Rangers because they see the most action. I'm going to be a sponge, soak everything up from this guy and the others.

"How long did you sign up for?" he asks.

"The max."

He looks at me a bit wide-eyed. You're given options when you sign up: three, four, or six years. Hardly anyone does six, the recruiter told us.

My team leader wipes his mouth on the back of his hand. I can tell we've reached an understanding. I think he can see that I will, in fact, do anything for him.

"Training gets you ready to mentally handle anything except combat," he says. "Live combat trains you for actual combat. First time it happens, it's gonna be real scary, but you can and will get through it. Remember that."

*   *   *

It's 2009, and we're in Afghanistan. Our small base is in Sharana, an extremely mountainous region in Afghanistan. As I unpack, I think about Jason, wondering how he's acclimating to his new company.

It's odd not having him here. We went through basic training together, then Airborne School and the Ranger Indoctrination Program, which is basic on steroids. Brutal. RIP is designed to break you. Over one hundred people signed up, and by the time graduation day rolled around, Jason and I were among the thirty or so left standing.

I realize this is the first time I've been apart from my brother for more than two days.

I find out I'm going out on the wire tonight.

My first mission.

The brief says we're supporting the third platoon. They'll be coming down a mountainside and pushing through a village. We're going to get dropped off on a particular mountaintop.

We find out the helicopter used for special operations isn't available. Another unit offers to take us out and fly us in. As they're briefed, I examine the helicopter. It's a Chinook, but it doesn't have the guns we typically fly with—or any armor.

There are three other people in my squad: the squad leader, the team leader, and a tabbed SPC 4, or tabbed specialist, which is what you are in battalion when you graduate from Ranger school. Our team leader speaks to us over the radio as we lift off.

"The mountaintop we're supposed to land on? These guys can't get us on top of it, so they're going to put us a mountain-top back. They can't land the whole aircraft, so they're going to hover the tail over the top of the mountain. You heard that right. The whole bird is not—I repeat, *not*—going to be on the ground, so watch your step."

It's around ten when we fly around to the mountaintop. As we prepare for our shaky landing, I see tracer rounds and then a rocket fly by the helicopter.

Is this really happening right now?

We're hovering over the mountaintop—and taking fire. I can hear gunshots. Getting out of my seat and coming down the ramp, I recall what I was told right before I deployed: *When you hear gunfire, you know you're getting shot at. When you hear a zip, it's close. When you hear a snap, it's even closer.*

The gunshots sound like little pops. Machine-gun fire—and it's a ways off. As I come off the bird, I see little sparks lighting up my night vision. They're coming from the rocks that I'm running to, and it dawns on me that the sparks are from rounds hitting the rocks.

I'm literally running into gunfire.

I run over and get beside my team leader and start returning fire at the mountaintop across from us. The enemy is camped out there, with machine-gun nests and RPGs. They're far away, so it's extremely hard to know if we're hitting people or if they're actually dead.

Our joint terminal attack controller (JTAC) gets ahold of the Apache to tell them about the enemy location, but it doesn't matter: the pilot and the others on board have already spotted the gunfire. With its thermal lenses, the Apache takes out the enemy. It's over in less than twenty minutes.

We've got to get moving—and we're at eight thousand feet. Oxygen is extremely low. My body hasn't adjusted to it yet, and we have to climb higher.

I'm not the only one who's sucking air. With us are a couple of guys who aren't with our unit as well as some onesies-twosies—guys working in pairs—from other units who are there for different purposes, and they're all falling behind. I'm sucking but I'm not falling out because my team leader is right in front of me, pushing me to keep moving.

"We're close," my team leader says, over and over again. "We're almost at the top."

Finally, we reach the top. We're the only two there. He gets on the radio to the tabbed specialist. "Where are you?"

The tabbed specialist is sucking big-time. He says he's still down a ways.

My team leader gets off the radio and looks at me. I'm on my knees, sucking wind.

"Run down there and get his aid bag and bring it up here," he says.

You've got to be kidding me. I just barely made it to the top and now I got to go back down and grab the first aid bag and carry it back up? He can't be serious.

The morning of graduation day at RIP, the cadre informed us he was going to get two of us to quit before we graduated. He smoked us all day. At that point, I was determined. He could do anything to me he wanted, but there was no way I was going to quit. I didn't then, and I'm sure as hell not about to now. I get to my feet and head back down the mountain.

But that's not the hardest part. That comes later, when I return home.

For six years, my life is a fast-paced routine: four to five months in Afghanistan, then it's back to Georgia, to Fort Benning, where I wait seven months to deploy again. Deploy, home, deploy, home, deploy, home. That's my life.

Only now there's talk of slowing down deployments. Some companies, I hear, may not even deploy at all.

My best days were deployments. I wasn't married and I didn't have any kids, so I couldn't wait to get back to Afghanistan. It's where I feel alive. It's the most freeing feeling in the world, being over there. You're not worrying about bills or shopping and cooking food or any other regular life stuff because there are things in place to manage all that for you. In Afghanistan, the mission at hand was your schedule for the day. It was a nonstop adrenaline rush for four to five months.

I'm addicted to it.

But with the slowdown of deployments, I don't know if I can mentally handle going back to the garrison life and just practice, hoping to be deployed again. I can't imagine being in a uniform and not deploying. That's like putting on my hockey uniform and just practicing, never playing. It's scary to imagine.

I decide not to reenlist.

My brother doesn't, either. Jason has a wife and a baby. I'm married, too, and my wife knows I'm thinking of doing some overseas contracting, to get back over there.

"Whatever you want to do," she tells me, "I'll support you."

I can't put her through that. As hard as it is for us overseas, I know it's even harder on the families back home.

I decide to stay home.

Jason starts selling solar panels. I go back to working for my dad, helping him with some machine work.

Going back to civilian life is tough. Deploying was one of the greatest times in my life, and now I don't know what I want to do. I've given away the thing I know and love the most. I don't carry a gun anymore, and I don't know what to do with my hands. Little stupid things I handled just fine before I went into the Army I don't handle so well now. Back here in the real world, people will walk all over you if you let them.

I have a lot of friends who do real estate. One of the guys I knew from my team got out a year before I did and went back to Pennsylvania, where he's selling real estate. I call him up and ask how he likes it.

"I love it," he tells me.

Jason thinks it's a good idea to try our hands at selling homes, so we do it together. We get our licenses and make the jump. I'm convinced we'll start making money right away, but we don't. Real estate takes a while. And I'm my own boss. I'm not in the Army anymore, so there's no formation, no line, no one there to tell me what to do and when, reprimand me when I screw up. This is all me.

My brother is struggling with the same feelings. He and his wife come across a Tony Robbins book. They read it and connect with Tony's message. They start looking into the seminars, see how it really changes people's lives. A seminar is happening soon in West Palm Beach. Jason thinks it can really help us.

I decide to go.

It changes my life.

Which is odd, since Tony Robbins doesn't say anything groundbreaking. He doesn't share some crazy equation or sprinkle me with magic fairy dust that turns me into a different person. What he does give me is a much deeper understanding of how the mind works. I become more aware of myself. It's not my circumstances. It's not that I came out of the Army and nobody cares about me, and now I can't get a job, or everyone should use me as their Realtor because I'm a veteran. It's not any of those things. It's *me. I'm* the one who has to change, and if I can change myself, my mindset, my life will change.

And over time it does. My friends and family tell me I'm night and day different than the person I was before, and I think it's because I have more of a sense of myself, and a sense of purpose. More than anything, I want to help other veterans, whether it's getting them a new home or just reaching out and talking to others who are struggling. Just help them with their mindset, because mindset is the biggest thing. Ninety percent of people want the direction of their life to change, but they forget they're the ones driving the car. You have to turn the wheel. Life isn't going to change for you, and no one around you is going to change. You have to change.

ROBERT LIVELY

Robert Lively grew up in suburban Washington, DC. When he graduated from Virginia Tech, he left for a six-month, 2,100-mile hike through the Appalachian Trail. When Robert returned, he went to work for a small trucking company, met his future wife, got married, and was then transferred to central Indiana. There, after much reflection, he decided that he wanted to live his true goals and visions and joined the Army. He was twenty-seven when he started basic training. After twenty-eight years and twenty-eight days of service and multiple deployments to Afghanistan and Iraq, Robert retired as a command sergeant major.

On June 17, 2001, I have my lower lumbar fused—L4, L5, and S1—the result of having slipped on a vehicle over in Europe and breaking part of my back. Now I'm looking at a long recovery at Walter Reed. I'm thirty-seven years old.

Here's my daily therapy back at Fort Bragg: walking in the

aquatic pool with eighty-year-old veterans and ladies, trying to get my back right. I've got only one shot.

Three months out, I'm walking down a hallway back at headquarters to hand off some paperwork. On one of the TVs I see a plane fly into a tower.

What the hell is that guy doing? It's a pretty day in New York City, not foggy or anything. By the time I reach the other end of the hallway, a second plane hits, and all the guys assemble around the screen in the squadron lounge.

We all know what has happened.

The command sergeant major of the squadron comes into the lounge. "Hey, fellas, it's on now. You know that, don't you?"

My first thought is, *I have six more months to recover*. Holy smokes, I'm going to miss going to war.

I get into my truck and drive to Walter Reed.

"I need to get an assessment on my recovery," I tell them. "I need a bone scan. I need to see how far this thing has advanced, what my recovery looks like."

They do a bone scan and tell me I'm looking really good. They agree to cut me loose for about thirty days of aggressive physical therapy. But I have to start *real* slow.

"That won't be a problem," I say. I have a solid athletic background—avid hiker and skier, and before I went to college I played football and trained hard to try to make the NFL—so, at some level, I know what I need to do.

Thirty days later, my squadron deploys. I miss them by about a week.

I call my doctor. "I'm feeling good. You need to let me go."

He pauses, thinking.

Then he says, "Put your gear on and go run a couple of sprints and tell me what it feels like."

I hang up, do a couple of sprints, and call him back.

"It feels pretty good," I tell him.

"I'm going to cut you loose. Go ahead and go."

The Army manages to get me a flight overseas. It leaves in six hours. I need to go home and pack.

My wife and I don't have cell phones. Right now, Cathy is at soccer practice in Pinehurst, North Carolina, with our girls. I call the Pinehurst police department and ask them to go get my wife and kids and tell them to come home.

We spend a couple of hours together. My kids are crying. They're old enough to understand where I'm going, what it means to go to war. I don't know when I'm coming back. I kiss them good-bye and then run off to catch up with my guys.

My first deployment to Afghanistan is short but intense, aggressive, and focused. I don't want to take a day off. I don't want to rest. I just want to be here. That's the Army's business strategy: deliver maximum sustained impact; come back, re-fit, recover, take on new responsibilities; and then be able to dial back in and go at it again.

Each deployment is different. Doesn't matter if it is six, nine, or twelve months: the environment changes, the enemy changes—everything changes. And for my personality, I love that.

When it comes to war, if you're going to pick up a gun, you cannot have an imbalance of commitment. You have to be ready to go, ready to fight, and ready to die. It's like my coaches used to tell me in football: you can't play like you're afraid to get hurt or you're going to get hurt. You have to be committed and you have to be all in.

I don't know of another woman, another mother or military spouse, who is any stronger or more committed than my wife.

I was never a big technology guy. During all my deployments between 2003 and 2005, even when I could Skype with my family, I didn't. What Cathy and I tried to do was let the kids be kids. Let them go to soccer, let them go to school. When I was home, we'd have a nice leave together, and then when it was time for me to go back, we'd go on a shopping spree and the kids knew it was time for them to up their team play at home: to pitch in better, to make sure they didn't give Mom too much trouble as teenagers. And when I got home in a few months, it would be like Christmas and we'd go on another vacation. I tried to bookend my leaving with two things that were fun and exciting.

And in the meantime, I expected them to be kids. I didn't want them doing stuff like military student programs. I just wanted them to be hanging out with their friends and not worrying about what's going on in another part of the world. They'll have the rest of their lives to worry about that.

During those three years, my mother died. Cathy's mother died and her father died. I lost several guys. Cathy's grandparents died and my grandmother died. I never missed a deployment, and I never got a single negative email from her. Cathy never said, "I need you home with me." She never complained. My kids were never late for school and never got bad grades. She never missed a soccer game or an athletic event or a school function. She carried that like no one I have ever heard of or seen.

I don't think anyone realizes what she did during that time frame and how well she did it.

We never really planned that she was going to be a military spouse someday. I never really planned to join the Army. This is just more affirmation that God has a mission or plan for people, and if you just watch it and try to listen to it, you'll end up there. Build a growth mindset and next thing you know you'll be handling things pretty well. You'll be able to have an impact on yourself and others in a way that you never dreamed you possibly could.

PATRICK KERN

Patrick Kern and his brother grew up north of San Francisco, in Marin County. Their father, who grew up in the projects, enlisted in the Army to become a dental technician. When Patrick graduated from high school in 1987, he attended West Point and chose the Army. His branch was Armor. His brother enlisted in the Marine Corps.

The FBI has me out on Staten Island, doing surveillance on these organized crime goombahs. I'm on my way home one day and see an M1 battle tank rolling down the freeway.

When you graduate from West Point, your obligation is five years of active service, four years reserves. My active service is done.

In October of 1992, a little over a year after graduating, the Army sent me, a brand-new second lieutenant, on my first combat tour along the Kuwait-Iraq border. The Kuwaitis and Iraqis were going at it. Department of Energy guys were there to issue us the ammo for our tanks—kinetic sabot rounds made with depleted uranium, designed to penetrate hardened steel and armor.

I did another tour there in 1993. When I came back, I did two years as a platoon leader and then another two as an executive officer. Then I punched out and went pretty much straight into the FBI, and now here I am working organized crime for the New York City field office.

As I watch the tank rolling down the highway, I'm thinking, *I don't know what unit that is, but that's the unit I'm going to join.* And that's how I get exposed to the 1st Battalion of the 101st Cavalry. It's an old unit from New York that became a tank battalion back in the day, and it's right here in Staten Island.

"You've got to turn on the TV," a friend of mine says.

I'm barely awake as I hold the phone to my ear. I was out late the night before and planned on sleeping in. I've got to go into work later in the day.

I sit up in bed, in my apartment in New Jersey. "What's going on?"

"Plane attacked the tower."

I turn on the TV, thinking back to an accident from the 1940s, when a B-25 accidentally flew into the Empire State Building. The plane my friend said flew into the tower—it has to be the same situation: an accident.

Then the second plane hits and I know what's going on.

I pack a bunch of extra clothes and then I grab my military uniform. I throw my dog tags around my neck, throw my shit in the car, hit the siren and drive my ass into the city. I'm about fifty miles out.

By the time I'm on the road driving into the city, the state troopers have already cleared the highways. I get a police escort for about thirty miles and then he breaks off and I go right through the Holland Tunnel and pop up into the disaster.

The FBI has a garage on the West Side Highway. When I arrive, I see a lot of FBI personnel already there. They're using the garage as a command post. It's mass confusion.

I meet with my supervisors and then we try to figure out where our people are. The big bosses are trying to figure out what they're going to do next while trying to get accurate information on what exactly happened.

The phones are limited. When I'm able to use one, I call my master gunner.

In 1998, when I took over company command, the Army had gone from eighteen active-duty divisions down to ten. A whole bunch of soldiers who got out of the Army were young, experienced, and still wanted to serve. During the mid-1990s, the Guard had an influx of these former soldiers. These guys are now cops and firemen and state troopers and corrections officers. Some are district attorneys. They're talented people with professional careers.

When I get ahold of my master gunner, I tell him to call up our guys, have everyone go to the Armory, post guards, and secure it. Two of my platoon leaders are there in a couple of hours. They roll the tanks out on the street, which somehow immediately gets back to the adjutant general in the governor's office. I get a phone call from some major who screams at me to get my tanks out of the street.

I hang up on him.

When I'm not talking to the agents and FBI personnel around me, I'm on the phone making more calls. Nobody seems to have a handle on what's going on—if another attack is coming, if there are more planes in the air.

Later in the day, the Bureau decides that agents will go on twelve-hour schedules. The National Security branch gets days. Criminal—my branch—gets nights. I'll be working from 10:00 p.m. to 10:00 a.m. every day, for the foreseeable future.

When the FBI releases me, I drive to Staten Island, report to my battalion commander, and help him get organized. By seven o'clock that night, all my guys have rolled in, dressed in their gear. They're ready to do what they've been trained to do. They operate well in this sort of environment.

Each day, when my twelve-hour shift for the Bureau ends, I head over to Battery Park, where my battalion commander has set up headquarters. There, for the next couple of weeks, I get tasked out to different military guard checkpoints surrounding the zone around the rubble.

The Bureau is my priority. Any free time I have I spend with the battalion commander or out with my guys.

We then get tasked to guard the Williamsburg Bridge. It's basically a security detail—nothing hard, just keeping an eye out and interacting with the civilians, who tell us how it gives them a sense of calm, seeing soldiers out there with M4s.

Our presence has another effect: it shuts down a known place where crack dealers meet up with all the junkies. The crack dealers and junkies are pissed off because the National Guard has taken over their site and shut down the drug trade.

I spend Christmas pulling a security detail on the Williamsburg Bridge. I think about the day the planes hit the towers. I think about my friends who died there and I think about agents like Lenny Hatton, who jumped on a fire truck and went down to the World Trade Center to help. That was the last anyone saw of him.

A lot of the FBI agents who were down near the WTC that morning and survived came right back to work all covered in dirt, filth, and dust. Some people can handle events like that. Others can't, like this kid in my unit. He'd been in one of the Towers, got out and survived, and now he's broken. Done.

We have to release him from the unit. He's not mission-focused, which makes him a liability.

Years later, I'll read this book, *On Killing: The Psychological Cost of Learning to Kill in War and Society,* written by a military guy named Dave Grossman. He'll talk about how courage is like having money in the bank. Everybody has money in the bank, but some have more than others. And every time you go out and get into a bad situation, you take a little bit of money out of this bank. If you keep taking money and don't put any in, you'll reach a breaking point.

There's no shame in it. Some people hit it earlier than others. When it happens, you need to step away and go someplace where you can recharge, put money back into that account. You have to step away and recharge so you can come back stronger.

When my command ends in 2002, my obligation to the Army is done, and I'm done with the military. The Bureau offers me what's called an OP, an office of preference, and I choose San Francisco. I'm a senior agent, and my FBI career is getting busier and busier. In 2004, I'm given an amazing opportunity: Oxford accepts me into its MBA program.

Mario, my old battalion commander back in New York, calls me and says, "Hey, the division has been alerted. I'm now the big dog who puts the whole shebang together for the commander. I want you to come over to Iraq and be my deputy."

"I'm going to Oxford."

"No, you're coming to be my deputy."

"I'm taking a year off and going to Oxford. I need a break."

"No, you're going over to be my deputy."

We go back and forth like this for days.

The Bureau isn't going to pay for my MBA. To go to Oxford, I have to take a leave of absence and go a year without pay, plus take out a loan to pay the eighty thousand dollars for this one-year MBA program. I start crunching the numbers and start thinking maybe I don't want to take on this kind of debt.

Mario keeps calling and pressuring me. I finally make a decision.

"I'll give you one year," I tell him. "I'll be your deputy G3 for one year."

I take a military leave from the FBI and ship back to up-state New York for training. When I get there, Mario tells me he gave my job away to someone else.

"You're now the CHOPS," he says.

"What the fuck? You said I can be your deputy G3, and now I'm chief of operations? That's a step below."

"There's another CHOPS—this other major. He's going to

be the senior CHOPS. You're going to be the junior. He'll get nights, you'll get days."

This is just getting better and better, I tell myself. I shouldn't be so surprised by Mario's actions. This is typical Army. No good deed goes unpunished.

In 2004, IEDs are becoming a huge problem in Iraq.

The 278th Cav is still equipped with the light Humvees. To give them some protection, they turn them into these *Mad Max*–type vehicles, bolting on steel and making turrets. When I go out on combat patrols, I sit on Kevlar blankets with these ad hoc steel doors, a little periscope for windows.

I travel to pretty much every major city in the four provinces. I file report after report back to the division commander and my G3 about the bloodbaths I see on the battlefield.

When the Iraqis are not attacking us, they're attacking the elections that are going on. A chief of police from one tribe gets elected, and the other tribe assassinates him. We have another election. Another guy wins, and then he gets assassinated. The Sunnis go after any Shiites who go out and vote. Suicide car bombs go off and kill anywhere from seventy to eighty people.

It's a daily occurrence.

When they're not killing each other, they're mortaring our forward operating base and using IEDs to try to take us out on the roads.

In the beginning, the IEDs are mostly old Soviet 155 shells planted in a road with wires. When they detonate one, shrapnel gets into the target vehicle. The explosions are not catastrophic.

Then they start using EFPs—explosively formed projectiles made in Iran. They're diabolical. A single EFP can penetrate an armored Humvee as well as Bradleys and tanks. We start losing drivers here and there. When the enemy buries a whole bunch of these EFP explosives in the road, it can shred a Humvee, kill four or five guys at one time.

When my deployment ends in 2005, we've sent seventy-two kids home in body bags.

What people have a hard time understanding is that Iraqi culture isn't wired for democracy. All these Iraqi tribes are basically interconnected. They're all brothers; sisters; third, fourth, fifth, sixth, seventh cousins—and yet they've hated each other for centuries. They're all at each other's throats, vying for power.

Their culture values death. They have no problem killing three hundred people with one car bomb—men, women, and children. Someone there had to explain to me that when an old man dies in the Arab culture, it's a tragedy because an old man is full of irreplaceable wisdom, knowledge, and experience. But if a child dies, their attitude is, "We'll make more."

Every day while I was over there, we would ask ourselves the same question: how do we deal with this situation?

To this day, I still don't have an answer.

LARRY GOMEZ

Larry Gomez was born in Long Beach, California, and raised in the small town of San Pedro, which is known as the Port of Los Angeles. During his freshman year at Cal State Long Beach, he pledged a fraternity, did a little too much partying, and, because his grades suffered, lost his 2-S deferment. Forty-five days later, on December 22, 1965, at nineteen years old, Larry was drafted into the Army to go to Vietnam. Larry started out as a private and shortly thereafter he became an officer through the Army's Officer Candidate School. He was commissioned as a quarter-master officer and specialized as a supply and services officer. He retired in 1993 after serving for twenty-seven years.

I'm in the commanding general's office at the 21st Theater Army Area Command, or TAACOM (the largest support command in the Army, located in Kaiserslautern, Germany), speaking to Lieutenant General Lewi, who is not only the commanding general of the 21st but also the quartermaster general of the Army.

"So," he says. "I hear you're getting ready to leave us."

"Yes, sir." After more than twenty years, I've decided it's time to retire, based on a series of events that happened the previous month.

On May 17, 1987, while I was assigned to the 21st, the Navy frigate USS *Stark* was struck in the Persian Gulf by two anti-ship missiles fired from an Iraqi jet aircraft. Thirty-seven sailors were killed. Their remains were going to be sent to the Army mortuary in Frankfurt. A whole team of identification experts from the States would be arriving to assist in processing the Navy remains. Fingerprint experts from the FBI, select armed forces identification lab technicians, and other contract specialists would all be dispatched to the Army mortuary.

Colonel Shellabarger, the 21st TAACOM assistant chief of staff logistics (ACSLOG) and my immediate boss, informed me that, as chief of the supply and services division, the mortuary fell under my job responsibility and staff purview. He directed me to go to Frankfurt to oversee this joint services operation. And because the operation was being run by the Army, he needed me there to oversee and coordinate everything as the Army proponent for the mission.

There was only one dilemma for me: I'd never had any mortuary experience, let alone handled a mass casualty disaster.

How do I go into this and quickly get prepared? That was the question I needed to answer before I arrived. I read up on everything I could from the Beirut bombing and other after-action reports from officers tasked to run some type of mass casualty operation. Fortunately, in their reports, these officers provided detailed information and lessons learned. I noted their lessons learned, experience, and recommendations so I wouldn't encounter the same problems. However, I found that many of those recommendations and lessons learned had not been acted upon, and as a result, I would face some of the same issues.

Arriving at Frankfurt and subsequently seeing, for the first time, some of the open body bags and the thirty-seven Navy dead lined up for processing was a temporary shock to my system that I had to quickly overcome. It would be a sight not easily or ever forgotten. Everything from receiving the remains to the process of removing the sailors' personal effects would become a difficult and lasting memory.

Sitting down next to the staff, I observed the care they took in inventorying the sailors' belongings. There were wallets filled with photographs of loved ones, of wives and kids; wedding rings; religious medals; and any number of things these sailors had on them at the time they were killed. Even more difficult was seeing the national news broadcasts with individual stories and pictures of these men and their families as their remains were being prepared to send back home.

In the aftermath of this operation, I wrote a very detailed action report that spelled out regulations and other procedures that needed to be changed when dealing with future military mass casualty operations.

As my years in the 21st assignment were coming to an end, I had hopes that I might be promoted from lieutenant colonel to full bird colonel. It didn't work out that way, and I decided it was my time to retire.

Now I'm in the CG's office with General Lewi, who says, "What would you like to do for your final assignment? Any thoughts on where you'd like to go?"

"Sir, my twins just graduated from high school. They'll be going on to college, so I'm hoping to be put in an ROTC assignment on some college campus. That would be ideal."

"I was thinking of something else," he says.

"You were, sir?"

"Yes. I need you to go to Department of Army and run casualty affairs and mortuary operations. Go in there and rewrite those procedures and regulations you outlined in your lessons learned and recommendations in the *Stark* after-action report you created."

"Sir, please don't make me the mortuary guy. I really don't want working mortuary operations to be the end of my career."

"I don't know anybody who knows the system better than you do," he says. "You know exactly what needs to be done, and I need you to do that for me."

I leave Germany and go to Washington, DC, as the new division chief of Army mortuary affairs and casualty support.

Early in that assignment, I get involved in a World War II recovery mission that takes me to the D-Day invasion beaches in Normandy, France.

A fisherman in Normandy files a report saying his net got hung up on a suspected sunken amphibious US tank. When he went down to unhook his net, he swore he saw skeletal remains.

By the time the international recovery assistance request

goes through all the appropriate channels and reaches me, it's late September.

The US lost twenty-seven amphibious tanks from the 741st Tank Battalion on D-Day. We were told this was one of the three sunken tank locations that had not been previously found.

In October, I take a team of six with me to Normandy. The team consists of three Navy deep divers and three Army scuba divers. We head out on a small boat. The weather is bone-chilling and the conditions are terrible. For the first couple of days, the sea is so rough we can't find the location. On the third day, we find the tank, but the conditions are still too rough to make a dive.

We mark the location with a buoy. It takes seven days to finally get sufficiently decent weather to attempt a dive.

The tank is, in fact, one of ours, and the deep divers go down to search for the remains. They find that the tank is filled all the way up to the turret with silt and sand. There's no way that fisherman could have seen skeletal remains in there.

We go home empty-handed, and I end up getting a slipped disc from the constant bouncing on the small boat in rough waters.

While continuing on as the chief of the Army's Mortuary Affairs and Casualty Support Division, I start hearing rumblings that we'll be going to war with Iraq. It becomes official during the early part of 1990.

Operation Desert Shield is the code name given to the operations leading up to the Gulf War. I begin briefing the Army deputy chief of staff personnel and attending briefings in the Joint Chiefs of Staff conference rooms deep in the bowels of the Pentagon. I'm usually the lowest-ranking officer, or one of the lowest-ranking, in the room. At one particular meeting, it seems that everyone around me is wearing stars. There are general officer representatives from each of the branches of service—Army, Navy, Marines, and Air Force—and a couple of other staff proponents.

Pentagon staffers have been analyzing multiple computer war scenario simulations: heavy attacks, heavy armament attacks, chemicals. I'm told I can potentially expect seven thousand dead in the first seventy-two hours of the war under the heavy-armament, chemical-attack scenarios.

Seven thousand? How the hell are we going to handle that in the middle of the desert? We don't have enough Army units to process those kinds of remains—and we sure as hell don't have enough equipment to put all those bodies through a chemical bath.

I'm the chief of mortuary affairs, and the Army has been named the executive agent for Operation Desert Shield. It's my responsibility to find a way to bring home whatever remains come out of this war.

But it's an impossible task. I've already talked to the Air Force about transporting our fallen soldiers. There's no way they're going to put remains that have suffered a chemical attack on their aircraft.

I reach out to the top scientists in the country: the chemical guys based out of Fort Detrick, in Maryland. I bring them into my next briefing so we can come up with a solution.

The Air Force's recommendation is to put all the bodies through a chemical bath even though we don't have the capacity to do it. One of the scientists speaks up.

"Even if you perform a chemical bath, you'll have the problem of what happens to these remains once they're in the air," he tells us. "The pores in the human body will off-gas once you get them up to twenty thousand feet. Nothing you do on the ground will get the chemicals out of their pores. If you have one hundred bodies in an aircraft and put them up at twenty thousand feet, they'll off-gas, and everybody on the aircraft will get killed."

The Navy's solution is to get these massive intermodal shipping containers made by Sealand, deep-freeze them, and bring them in frozen. Getting that done in the middle of the desert, however, is impossible.

The one-star public affairs general officer glares at me and yells, *"This is totally unacceptable."*

"Well, sir," I reply, "I understand that."

"So what's your *solution*?"

"Sir, I can tell you, but you're not going to like it." I take a deep breath and, with all eyes on me, say, "There's no way we are equipped to get seven thousand remains back here. It's impossible. We don't even have enough body bags right now—and we certainly don't have enough trained units and equipment to handle these kinds of numbers. We'll be in the middle of a desert war, and the remains, I'm sorry to say, are going to rot out there in those conditions unless we decide to incinerate them in place."

That sets off the public affairs officer. He starts yelling at me. "Can you imagine what CNN and the press will do with that coverage?"

"Sir, don't shoot the messenger. You just heard our top chemical warfare scientist explain why the Air Force can't transport these remains home. The Navy solution won't work, and the Army doesn't have a viable operational solution."

"This is totally unacceptable. It's your job—"

"Sir, you're a member of the Joint Chiefs of Staff. With all due respect, it's JCS's job to come up with the assets in order to complete this mission, and right now we don't have them."

A few days after the briefing, a decision is made to bomb any suspected target believed to house the potential capability to launch a chemical attack against US forces. Aerial and naval bombardments continue for nearly five weeks. As a result, our casualty rate is greatly reduced, and our forces are able to use conventional wartime collection methods to recover our casualties.

By the time the second phase of the Gulf War, Operation Desert Storm, begins, I've coordinated and assembled some two-hundred-plus people to augment the very capable and experienced mortuary staff at the port mortuary, Dover Air Force Base. The same team of people I had become acquainted with in Frankfurt for the USS *Stark* mission assist with the operation at Dover and the processing of the 383 fatalities that will come out of that war.

The whole process of bringing soldiers back home triggers distant memories of when I was drafted in 1965.

During eight weeks of advanced individual training (AIT), one constant theme was drilled into our heads: "There are two kinds of soldiers in Vietnam: the quick and the dead. You better learn how to fire those weapons and save yourself."

The life expectancy of a mortarman in Vietnam wasn't very good. I quickly realized I'd have a better chance of staying alive if I was an officer. Midway through AIT, I applied to OCS and was then selected. After AIT, I was sent to Fort Lee, in Virginia, where I graduated and became a quartermaster (logistics) officer. As a second lieutenant, I was shipped to Germany and assigned to a supply and services battalion.

I completed my required three years of service and got out of the Army as a captain, went back to school, and met my reserve requirement by joining a unit in Los Angeles. I missed the camaraderie of being a soldier. I'd listen to all my old buddies telling their war stories, and it bothered me, not having had their experience.

In 1972, I decided to accept an invitation to return to active duty—but, as I told the quartermaster assignments officer, the only way I'd go back in is if I went to Vietnam.

He made it happen, and I was assigned as the operations officer, Logistical Support Activity (LSA), in Pleiku.

Within weeks of arriving, a day came when we got word that one of our radio repairmen had been killed during a mission to a small remote firebase. His transport helicopter had been shot down by a surface-to-air missile, and the firebase had been overrun and captured by the enemy. We were on hold and waited for six long days until we got a call saying that a South Vietnamese Ranger unit had taken back the firebase and we'd have a brief window to recover the man's remains. I accompanied my two young grave registration soldiers on the mission. We hopped on a helicopter accompanied by two gunships and two attack helicopters assigned to watch over us.

Along the way—and a surprise to me—we picked up a full bird colonel, the senior Army advisor to the South

Vietnamese Ranger unit that had just taken back the firebase. He wanted to congratulate the Rangers and had just gotten an update. Our mission had changed. We were to recover not one but two sets of remains.

He looked at me and said, "That means, Captain, that you and I will have to help your men. We'll have to get in and out of there fast, as I'm not sure how long we'll be able to hold on to the firebase."

Then he turned his attention to my two young grave registration soldiers. "We're going to land on the outside of the perimeter of the fence line because everything's going to be booby-trapped. Don't touch anything. Don't try to pick up a war souvenir. The gunships will protect us as we retrieve the remains."

It seemed as though we were in the air for an hour or so before we were dropped off outside a war-torn barbed wire perimeter. Black smoke billowed from smoldering vehicles, and charred remains had been hung up in the concertina wire along the perimeter fence.

We took on mortar and rocket fire almost immediately. We headed for cover, leapfrogging to the main bunker, hitting the ground several times when we heard the whistle of incoming mortar and rock rounds coming at us. Once in the bunker, we came up with our plan to team up, locate and bag the two casualties, and get out.

As we made our way to the downed aircraft, the rocket and mortar fire intensified. Then came small arms fire. South Vietnamese rangers were running and retreating everywhere. Some had rockets. I thought, *Oh, shit, we're not going to get out of here alive.*

On the radio, the colonel screamed at the gunships and Cobras above that they had to take out that enemy fire. He motioned us to head back to the main bunker.

As I retreated, I heard that whistle sound overhead, and a rocket exploded at the base of a Conex container directly behind me. The explosion knocked me to the ground.

Dazed from the blast, images of my life flashed through my mind. I thought I was dead. I could see that the metal Conex container had been ripped open from the blast and I figured I'd been hit. I felt my legs to see if they were soaked with blood, but they weren't. I was okay.

I pulled myself together, got back up, and headed for the bunker. Out of the corner of my eye, I saw a retreating Ranger go down as small arms and machine-gun fire continued to come down on us.

While we were huddled in the bunker, our attack choppers eventually radioed the colonel and told him that they were running out of fuel and couldn't wait any longer. They had to leave. We were left sitting in the middle of nowhere, mortars and rockets coming after us and our South Vietnamese Rangers fighting to hold back an enemy just outside the perimeter.

Somehow we were able to make it through the night.

Two Air Force close air support jets arrived and were in radio communication with the colonel. They colored the sky with green tracer rounds to target the location where they unloaded their bombs.

Their first tracer pass was way off. The colonel redirected their fire and instructed them to come way back in and lay their payload right on top of our perimeter fence line.

Their second tracer pass pinpointed a location just outside our perimeter. They cautioned us to get as deep as we could in that bunker.

They lit up the night with their bombs.

Things got quiet after that. But it was decided that it was still too dangerous to send in a helicopter to pick us up. The enemy was still out there.

A new plan was created. We were advised that there were friendly tanks not too far away that would come pick us up. It would be the safest way to get us out of there.

We held fast until daylight and then got the radio call telling us the tanks couldn't make it; they'd been intercepted. The colonel, realizing we couldn't afford to stay much longer, made the decision to send in a chopper. It was our only way out.

"Okay, but once we're overhead, we have to go radio silent," the chopper guy advised. "Flash me with your survivor mirror so I can pinpoint exactly where you're located."

In the distance we could see a lone chopper. It flew way past us. The colonel radioed the chopper pilot. The pilot assured the colonel that he had us and began dropping below tree level a few miles up. We had been instructed to get on either side of the dirt road outside the firebase and watch for the chopper.

It was an unbelievable sight, how the pilot swayed that chopper from side to side just a few feet above the ground and weaved it up that winding road.

Once the chopper arrived, it rocked back momentarily. We swung the body bags into the bird. The crew grabbed us as we entered and the aircraft immediately took off. We flew out of there and looked at each other with tears in our eyes, grateful because we had somehow managed to get out of there alive, grateful because we had completed the recovery mission and were bringing our men home.

No man left behind isn't just a saying. It isn't just some BS motto people write on a wall. It's a deeply rooted core value that's part of the brotherhood of being a soldier.

And what better tribute could I have given at the end of my career but to have had the honor and privilege of being a quartermaster officer and playing a key role in making sure those valiant fallen warriors got back home?

JON EYTON

Jon Eyton grew up in a military family. His father served in the Air Force in Vietnam, and his uncle, a member of the 101st Airborne, completed four combat jumps in World War II. Jon served in the Army from 2003 to 2007. He got out as a staff sergeant and was assigned to Alpha Company, 4th Battalion, 31st Infantry.

When I return to Fort Drum in 2008, I decide to get out of the Army and move back to Boise, Idaho. I've got a plan: I'm going to open my own structural steel fab shop business. I don't really know shit about it, but I'm going to put my full force and energy into it while my wife stays at home raising the little ones.

Within three weeks of stepping off the plane, I've got everything I need to rock and roll.

Then 2010 shows up and the country is at the height of the financial crisis. My wife and I are fighting to keep our heads above water. Even with everything that's going on financially in my life and across the entire country, I manage to find a way to buy a house—I'm relentless, like a dog with a bone—and then the bottom drops out and I'm sitting in bankruptcy court owing forty thousand dollars to business vendors I can't pay.

Seemingly overnight, I've gone from being a former military guy who, while deployed in Afghanistan, was in a high-level leadership position—a guy with a high-functioning skill set and a ton of responsibilities; a guy who, on a daily basis, for years, dealt with IEDs, combat, and being constantly surrounded by people who wanted him dead—to being a guy standing in line at the Idaho department of welfare to apply for food stamps and Medicaid so my kids can eat and see their doctors. It's a very humbling experience.

On top of all that, nearly all work in the state has dried up because of the financial crash. Jobs are practically non-existent. Every night, my wife and I work our budget literally down to the penny to make sure the kids don't notice how bad the situation is.

I treat looking for a job as a job. I put in twelve-hour days. I calculate the miles I need to drive on specific days to see if I'll have enough gas because money is always tightest before the next unemployment check comes. This cycle goes on for months, until I land a job with a competitor of mine. I cash in my G.I. Bill and go to night school, to get my associate's degree in drafting and design, while working full-time.

Eleven months later, after Christmas break, I walk into work and see my boss.

"No need to go back to your office," he says. "You've been laid off."

Back to square one again. Back to government assistance.

Three months later, I land another job with a competitor, a guy who owns a big fabrication company. He's got a lot longer reach and a lot wider geographical range than my previous employer. He hires me as a project manager.

I end up getting my associate's degree and roll that right over to my bachelor's for construction management. I work during the day and go to school at night.

My wife decides to go back to school. We've got three kids in school and we're in school and the kids are all playing sports—and I'm coaching. I'm "enjoying the suck," as we say in the Army, and it feels good because my wife is just as relentless and stubborn and hardheaded as I am. We're both willing to do today what other people aren't willing to do tomorrow.

The Army gave me that attitude. Deployments gave me that attitude. Leadership and exposure to good mentors in the service gave me that attitude. There are no excuses, no bad days, no "Poor me." There's just no other way to be.

ANDY WEINS

Andy Weins grew up in a suburb of Milwaukee, Wisconsin, called Menomonee Falls. He served for fourteen years in the Army Reserve as an 88 Mike, motor transport operator; a 31 Bravo, military police; and a 31 Echo, corrections and detention specialist. Andy is currently a sergeant first class, his MOS 79 Victor, Army Reserve career counselor.

As a truck driver hauling fuel in Iraq, I'll always be a big, slow target. There's a damn good chance I'm going to die.

I grew up in the burbs, on a quiet street. I always wanted to join the military because, to me, the idea of becoming a man revolved around going to fight for your country—kill or die, if need be. I grew up loving that mindset. When 9/11 happened, it reignited my conviction to join.

Unfortunately, I needed two medical waivers. I'm fructose intolerant and I have really screwed-up elbows, and the military, I was told, allowed you only one waiver. I tried joining the Army in 2001, but they wouldn't let me in. In 2002, when I graduated from high school, I tried the Marines. No luck. I went back to the Army in 2003, tried again, and got rejected. My luck changed in 2004, when the recruiting standards dropped, and I'm able to get into the Army with two medical waivers.

I couldn't do infantry because of my fructose intolerance, so I asked the Army about the minimum amount of schooling I would need in order to get closest to the front lines.

"Go be a truck driver," the Army told me. "Those guys are getting blown up all the time."

Cool, I thought at the time. I already knew how to drive a truck.

But I never researched the job. I was so green I thought that you did whatever the Army told you to do. I went reserve because, at the time, I was told they were slotted to go to Iraq—and they are. It's February of 2006, and I'm flying on a C-130.

When I land at the Al-Taqaddum Air Base in the early afternoon, I'm hungry and kind of disoriented. It's hot and I've got motion sickness from the flight. They show us where we'll be sleeping, and after they give us all the basic supplies, we go to a convoy brief, where I find out I'll be going on a convoy the following night.

I go through rehearsal of concept (ROC) drills, learn that each vehicle in the convoy has its own job. I'll be one of forty vehicles hauling fuel to a Marine Corps base in Fallujah. The Marines protect the roads, and we deliver fuel to them since they don't have the necessary supply trucks and tankers.

We run at night, so we head out of the base at dusk. I'm all geared up—neck plate, all the different pieces and parts to my Interceptor Body Armor—and ready to get out there and kill the bad guys. The guy I'm with has been here for months. He's wearing a T-shirt and a soft cap. His uniform looks like shit. He's got this scowl on his face because he is so done and ready to leave this place and go home.

And now he's got to deal with me, the eager new guy. "Just drive the truck," he says wearily. "If the truck in front of you stops, don't hit it. And don't fall asleep. If you think you're gonna fall asleep, say something. I'll talk to you."

As we head out of the wire, I try to take in everything I can see while there's still enough light. Once it goes dark in Iraq, if you have a full moon unobstructed by clouds, there's tons of ambient light, and you can see forever. But if there's no moon, you can't see anything because there aren't any lights in the distance.

Because we're carrying fuel, we can run only on a hard-ball, which means we drive only on asphalt. It means that we can't use any bridges that aren't rated. It means that we can't take the shortest route: we take the safest route. The shortest route would be forty minutes. The safest route is four hours, and we may or may not get killed by insurgents along the way.

We arrive at the Marine Corps base at two in the morning. I'm exhausted.

"What do we do now?" I ask the guy driving with me.

"You eat or you sleep."

I fall asleep outside, between two tires. I learn to sleep that way for the rest of the year.

*　　*　　*

When I return in September of 2006, things are really heating up. During Ramadan, we get hit by IEDs in seventeen out of nineteen missions. When Ramadan ends, we get hit basically every time we go out on the wire.

I get hit.

Here's how it happens.

You're driving and all of a sudden you hear an explosion. It's loud and it's quick. You don't know what the hell happened, and you're disoriented and if you're the driver, you're trying to keep your truck on the hardball. You can't see through the thick plumes of smoke and dust and sand and debris but you keep rolling, hoping you're not going to run into a disabled vehicle and cause a massive pileup.

If you're the truck commander of the vehicle you're riding in, you reach for the hand mic clipped to your armor and more often than not you can't find it because it's fallen off. You grab the cord attached to the mic and fish it back into your hands as people in the convoy send reports over the radio. You tell the driver to keep rolling and you call the convoy commander and tell him you're alive and then you give him a LACE report: liquid, ammo, casualties, equipment. You're wondering about a secondary device or a secondary attack as people radio what they see, or saw, and because your vehicle is still moving, you slow down just enough that you don't lose the others.

Someone tries to blow you up and you keep driving. It's not that sexy.

When you roll in, you go to a special area so the vehicle

can be inspected. Usually it's a hot mess because all the fluids have pissed out of it. You have a raging headache and your ears hurt and more often than not you have whiplash. Someone comes and picks you up and you go get breakfast and then go to sleep.

Getting hit by an IED—to me, it's such a nothing burger. But yet I know it's such a significant time in my life. I know people who call these days their "rebirth date" or "the day they should have died," or something along those lines. To me, it's just another day in Iraq. That's it. That's my life every forty-eight hours.

And the only thing I care about is how many hot meals I can get. I want to be the first guy in line at breakfast, every morning. I always eat a massive breakfast: an omelet, four hard-boiled eggs, scrambled eggs, bacon, sausage, pancakes, waffles, and grits. Chow time is the one time throughout the day when I'm in charge. I can choose what I'm going to eat. For that twenty minutes or half an hour—that's my time. No one can fuck with me.

What I struggle with the most is the fact that someone wants to indiscriminately kill me and I can't fight back—I don't even have the opportunity *to* fight back. It takes away the edge of war. If you shoot at me and I shoot at you, the better man wins. But to lose just to lose? That's where I struggle. It makes it less personal, which also makes it *more* personal.

When I get back from Iraq, I become a tour manager for a band. I keep myself busy for the next eighteen months and then all of a sudden, in December of 2008, I lose my job. I find a bar and start thinking through my life.

I don't have a job or a girlfriend. I came back from Iraq, and instead of thinking through everything that had happened over there, I basically partied for a year and a half. And then everything hits me all at once.

I'm a hot mess for six months.

This time, I choose to deal with my demons instead of going to a bar. I go to counselors, psychiatrists, and psychologists for nine months. I don't get anywhere. It's all bullshit.

Every year, I schedule my PHA—periodic health assessment. Every year, the doctor tells me I have PTSD and need to go seek help and treatment.

I don't. What does work for me, though, is connecting with other struggling veterans on LinkedIn or talking to them on the phone. As much as I might be helping them, they also help me.

I'm very blunt and transparent. One year I tell my doctor I have homicidal and suicidal ideations every day because sometimes life sucks, and that's where my brain goes. He puts me on restrictive duty for thirty days.

Medicine, from what I've seen, treats symptoms, not the problem. When you walk into the VA with your problems, you leave with the same problems. My problem is, I miss being around people that have my back, that make me feel safe every day. That's what I miss. The symptom is, I don't trust people. The symptom is, I'm not very good at relationships. I don't open up to people. The symptom is, people in the civilian world will fuck you over every chance they get. How do I fix that?

I fix it by surrounding myself with veterans and people of the same mindset.

When you're in a military unit, you get everything. You've got your cooks, you've got your maintenance guys, your line platoon that go out and do their thing. You're self-sustaining. You're a tribe. You don't get that in the civilian world. You have to go out and create one for yourself—and I do. I create my own tribe. I also learn the importance of asking others for help because, as the Army's resiliency program taught me, asking for help is a fucking strength, not a weakness.

KAREN ZAKRZEWICZ

Karen Zakrzewicz grew up on a dairy farm in Thorp, Wisconsin, with three older siblings. Her father was in the National Guard and the reserve, as a combat engineer and an officer, and her grandfather was a drill sergeant during World War II. She is a sergeant in the Army Reserve, and her job is 68 X-ray, behavioral health technician.

In February of 2016, I'm working as a DOD contractor in Milwaukee, going to school for behavioral health, and putting in my time in the reserves when I get a call from my first sergeant.

"Do you think your soldier wants to go overseas?" he asks.

He's referring to Dan, the father of my daughter. I met him in 2013, and we had a kid. Our daughter was born in 2014. She's coming up on two, and Dan and I are looking to do the whole marriage thing and have more kids down the line.

"Absolutely not," I tell him. "I can almost 100 percent

guarantee you he'll say no. But I won't speak for him, so give him a call."

"Do you want to go overseas?"

"I sure do."

Twenty minutes later, I get a call from the company commander for the deployment. He's part of an MP unit heading to Camp Arifjan, in Kuwait, and he wants me to deploy as an augmentee to their prison staff. American soldiers, contractors—whoever it may be—that break the Uniform Code of Military Justice (UCMJ) while deployed are confined there for up to thirty days. If their sentencing goes beyond that, we escort them back to the United States to carry out the rest of their sentence at Fort Leavenworth.

"Are you interested?" he asks.

"I don't have any experience on the prison side. None whatsoever."

"But you do have a lot of clinical training. You've done intake interviews and know how to properly prepare files and how to put information into the Army's medical database."

I'm up-to-date on health documentation, and I've been keeping up with my interview skills and all the new data that's coming out on PTSD and traumatic brain injuries. I know the difference between chronic depression and major depressive disorder, as compared with transitionary issues when soldiers come home or are just getting to their duty stations.

"Don't worry about the prison stuff," the company commander says. "You can train with our unit at Fort Leavenworth, provided you're interested."

I tell him I am, and then in May, I'm off to Kansas.

Fort Leavenworth houses two prisons: the disciplinary barracks, or DB, where you stay if your sentence is ten years or longer, and the correctional facility, for those serving under ten years. For the next two and a half weeks during the month of June, I work with the prison's behavioral health sergeants and technicians, learning how to do intake interviews and understand the paperwork, how it works. I also learn the necessary combative skills and protocols in case an inmate puts his hands on me or attacks.

It's 2016. We get our orders to deploy in September. My daughter's birthday is at the beginning of the month. Fortunately, I'm able to attend her party.

Saying good-bye to her is extremely hard. She's two and really has no attention span—no concept that I'm going to be gone for nine months. She's just kind of like, *Oh, okay, whatever.*

The Arifjan base is two to three miles wide. The prison facility is moderately large. It can hold up to 175 people. There's literally no one there when we arrive—which means that our people are doing the right thing and following the laws of war and not violating the UCMJ.

Over the next few months, whenever an inmate trickles in—and it's usually a fourteen-day stay for insubordination, some kid who told his first sergeant and company commander to fuck off directly to their faces—I do the initial intake and then coordinate with the behavioral health clinic to sign off on his treatment or care plan.

I arrange my life so I can talk to my daughter. I call and video chat with her all the time. I go to the gym every morning at 3:00 a.m., which is about 7:00 p.m. back home, right about the time she's getting ready for bed. I'm starting my day and she's winding down, and after we chat for a little bit, I read her *Guess How Much I Love You in the Winter*. I bought her a copy, and I brought one with me so I can read her a bedtime story every single night as she goes to sleep.

Christmas is tough. I'm watching her open presents over video chat. It's late in the day for her, and she's tired and grumpy and just wants to go to bed. She's in a mood, and that's hard for me to deal with because, since I can't be there, all I want is to see her happy face as she opens the clothes and toys.

In the movies, when a soldier comes home, the family is waiting outside the plane and they come running up and everyone is in tears and you're in tears watching it. In July of 2017, I call Dan and tell him I'm coming home and what time I think I'll be arriving. He says he'll meet me at his mom's house.

Before I leave, I get dressed up and do my hair and makeup. Driving to his mom's house, I'm super nervous—actually shaking, as though I'm about to go out on a stage and give a huge speech to thousands of people instead of going to see my two-year-old daughter.

When I walk into the house, they're all inside—Dan and his mom and stepfather. All I can see is my daughter sitting on the floor, playing with her toys.

"Hey, baby."

She turns her head and sees me.

"Hey, Mom." She goes back to playing with her toys.

Which, in a way, makes sense. For her, I've gone from

being a face on a screen to now being a face in person. The only change is that I'm here.

But I've changed. I've learned a lot about myself. I've come to value my time with my friends and family a lot more. I'm willing to drive two and a half hours to see my family for their birthdays. If my sister texts me and says she had a bad day, I'll drive over just to sit and talk with her and share a bottle of wine. My time overseas makes me value my friendships and relationships with the people closest to me, and it makes me learn more about the people that I care about and the people I surround myself with.

BRENNAN AVANTS

Brennan Avants served in the Army.

We sing "Leaving on a Jet Plane" to our spouses from the bus as it begins to pull out of the parking lot on the base in Bamberg, Germany. It's February of 2004 and bitterly cold and there's snow on the ground and all the wives are huddled together.

The singing is about us banding together and steeling our nerves. We're going on our way to get loaded up on airplanes that'll take us to Kuwait.

My wife is a military brat. Her father is retired from the service, and her brother is serving in the Air Force; she knows the life. Still, I know how tough this is for her. Me going off to war—this isn't what she was expecting.

We got married right after I got out of the Army, moved back to Northern California. I had just signed up with a military reserve unit out of the Bay Area when 9/11 happened.

That day I dropped my job, put on my uniform, and reported for duty at the reserve depot. I wanted back in the action. My father-in-law convinced me that my best option was to get back in the service, so we packed up what we could into our two vehicles and drove to Texas to live with my wife's parents. I went to the Military Entrance Processing Station in Dallas and reenlisted. I got my former job back on a multiple launch rocket system crew. I kept my job, and I kept my rank, and I was assigned and shipped out to Germany.

I watch my wife until I can no longer see her.

I may never see her again.

They encouraged us to write a death letter before we deployed. Said it would help prepare us mentally for battle. I wrote mine, but I really didn't know what to say. What *can* you say? How do you condense all your love for your wife, your thoughts—your last thoughts of her—into one letter? How can a letter even remotely reassure her that I died doing something I believed in—something that I loved?

Last night in bed, I kept wondering if I would ever sleep in that bed again—if I would ever sleep next to *her* again. I kept wondering if she knew how much I—

Stop, I tell myself. *Just stop.* I can't think along these lines right now. I have to emotionally disconnect myself for the good of the unit, for my brothers and sisters. I have to detach myself from the real world. I have to create a wall around myself. I have to create an impenetrable shell.

I close my eyes, trying to get my head on straight, as the bus bounces along, taking us to the airport. To war.

Okay, this is real, I tell myself. *Once we get on the ground, it's all about the person to my left and the person to my right. I've got their six. I'm here to do whatever it takes to make sure they get home so we can all get home.*

We do a month or so of train-up at Camp Buehring. The Marines are getting slightly hardened doors for their Humvees while we're getting canvas. Everything is stuck in Conex boxes and inappropriately labeled at the port. We can't get them released, and we need armored doors if we're going to make it to FOB Summerall in one piece.

Corporal Malasko, one of my soldiers and a good buddy, and I travel around at night snagging any kind of fuel products—oils, lubrications, and greases. We use them to trade for slightly up-armored doors.

We make it to the FOB unscathed.

The 4th Infantry Division is cheering when we arrive. They look like something from a war movie about Vietnam—ghillie suits made out of their old uniforms, their living conditions very, very austere. We get them new uniforms so they'll look really good when they arrive back home.

We're ready. Motivated.

The enemy is, too.

We sometimes think the Iraqis are out of the Stone Age—a bunch of Neanderthals who don't know anything. But they do. They're not dumb. They clearly don't know our intel, but they've made a careful study of our units. They know when the new guys are in town, and when the old guys are leaving. They know when best to strike.

My battalion is actually FOB security, which means we're locked inside the base, manning all of the OPs and listening posts on the various locations. The enemy immediately starts "probing" the base with mortars, and sometimes rockets. The first time I take an incoming mortar, hear the sound of the ordnance hitting the cement—I'm terrified.

We quickly learn that the enemy is using the large, inoperable Iraqi water tower on our base as an aiming marker. Our engineers tear it down.

The more we're attacked, the more I realize the enemy's aim sucks—they miss us over and over again. We can figure out, in a relatively short amount of time, the mortar's point of origin and return fire from our own mortars. At night, it's hard to know the difference between incoming and outgoing mortars. I need to use a little bit of Tylenol PM just to help me try to get some sleep.

Reports of soldiers getting mild electric shocks in the showers start filtering through the base. The hot water tanks, installed by the local national contractors, are faulty, and command orders us to unplug them. We do, but some soldiers plug them back in, pranking someone with a little shock.

The 5th Artillery Battalion conducts presence patrols. They drive around in their crudely armored-up Humvees. They do security and try to initiate contact with the enemy while my battalion does base security. As the months pass, things start ramping up. There's a lot more IED activity, and Muqtada al-Sadr and his band are becoming very prevalent around the base.

I know they're preparing an attack. I can feel it.

The day it happens, I'm on the base, but I'm not working security at our main gate. I hear a large explosion. I turn, and as I see clouds of smoke coming from the front of the base, voices start screaming all around me, all over my radio. I run to the front gates. It's utter chaos.

A shocked NCO mumbles something about going to bed.

"What did you say?"

"VBIED," he replies.

Now I understand him—and what happened. The explosion was caused by a vehicle-borne improvised explosive device, or a car bomb.

"Contractors were all lined up outside the gate—lined up with their gravel trucks and dump trucks, you know, waiting to be processed through base security," the NCO says. "There was this white BMW riding really low to the ground and it wouldn't stop at the checkpoints. I was trying to get an interpreter to tell the driver to stop when the vehicle exploded." He looks at me, blinking, trying to process what just went down. "I saw an engine block fly past my head."

This event will go down as the first large VBIED attack on a US installation in Iraq.

Luckily, none of the soldiers are hurt. Two get Purple Hearts for their thankfully minor injuries—blown-out eardrums, that kind of stuff. The toll on the local nationals and on some of the Iraqi forces working with us, though, is crazy. Week after week working cleanup crew, we find hands and feet, charred flesh, and other human parts that similarly traumatize us.

I'm sitting on my bed, about to head to the shower only ten feet away, when my buddy Frank says, "Here's the new newspaper," and hands me a month-old *Stars and Stripes*. I flip through it as he heads off to the shower.

Someone screams. I don't react—it happens a lot, guys

dumping cold water on each other. Frank comes back, wide-eyed. Pale.

"I need your help," he says.

I follow him into the shower. My good buddy Corporal Marco Malasko is on the floor, unconscious. Unresponsive.

That scream I heard a moment ago—that was Marco.

I find out later the cause of death: electrocution. Someone plugged in one of the faulty hot water heaters, and Marco died.

A few months after the VBIED attack, we're assigned a mission: doing convoy and VIP security all over the northern part of Iraq. We form into personal security detachment units with our semi-up-armored Humvees. I'm assigned rear .50-cal gunner. I'm up in the turret of a Humvee driving in the back, my head literally on a swivel, looking for bad guys while we drive.

I develop code words with my wife, so she'll know when I'm on the road. I don't tell her where I'm going or that we're constantly encountering IEDs. I don't share how exciting it is to break the wire for missions nearly every day, being on these four-to-six-hour convoys, the roads strewn with potential threats—and *everything* looks like a threat. I don't share any of these details with my wife because I know how hard this is on her. Every night she goes to sleep with the computer, waiting for me to ding her over Skype or Yahoo Messenger so we can talk.

Today's mission runs later than usual. We're on base at Camp Speicher, outside Tikrit, escorting a VIP as part of his personal security detachment. The sun's going down as our convoy of six armored gun trucks leaves the base, heading back to FOB Summerall—an hour's drive, provided we don't encounter anything, or anyone, along the way.

We own the highway, head straight down the middle. It's like driving on I-95 during rush hour. If any drivers intermix with us, we find creative ways to push them off to the left or right. There's always the threat of somebody with a VBIED getting intermixed in our convoy and exploding. As rear security, I have a standoff distance of a couple hundred meters, and I have to use whatever signaling device I have to get vehicles to stay back, and that means shooting at Iraqis, whose attitude is *We own this road, too.*

The car I'm watching is doing this weird thing where it suddenly guns its engine and tries to approach the convoy...and then falls back. The driver does it again and again, which kicks my already tingling Spidey sense into high gear. I stomp on the ground—the code to let my vehicle commander know I'm going to fire a few warning shots—and prepare to shoot a tracer round from my M16 into the sand. Because I'm facing the rear, I can't see what's in front of me, so I look over my shoulder to make sure there aren't any kids with their little stands of soda, candy, and fruit.

I fire the tracer into the sand on the side of the highway.

The driver guns it, coming right at me.

He's fifty, maybe sixty meters away when I see his face.

I unload my weapon directly in front of his vehicle. It swerves and spins out.

Doesn't move.

Did I kill him?

Did I do the right thing?

Twenty minutes later, we roll back into our gate. I'm in complete and utter shock.

Staff Sergeant Rob comes up to me. "You all right?"

"I...I don't know what I just did."

"You did good," he says. "You did good."

It's still bothering me later. I have no idea what happened to the driver, what his fate was, whether he was a real threat or not. But to me he was a threat because he was harassing the tail end of our convoy.

When you're deployed to Iraq, you're constantly rotating through base security missions, through protective and service detail (PSD) missions, securing ammo dumps.

And the enemy...I'm surprised at how fast the bad guys evolve.

Someone hides a makeshift IED inside a pack of cigarettes left on the ground. Fortunately, it doesn't go off, but it's a reminder that the enemy can be anywhere, at any time. It's fatiguing, living with that heightened awareness all the time. It wears you down. So you stop looking at things closely.

Which is exactly what they want us to do. Threats become so commonplace that when you *do* encounter something out of the ordinary, your attitude is, *Whatever. If it's going to happen, it's gonna happen.* If you don't, you'll go insane.

I put on a false persona when I talk to my family back home. "Everything's good here," I tell everyone. "Everything's all right."

My wife is smart. She sees right through it.

"I told you not to sugarcoat things," she tells me. "If it's bad, tell me what you're allowed to tell me—and you *need* to tell me. So many servicemen and -women call home and say everything's rosy when it's not."

So I tell her what I'm allowed to say, and then I flip a mental switch and go back to work.

When I come home, it's not the easiest switch to flip back.

I'm a different person now. Mentally and emotionally. I'm distant, and when I get angry, I have these outbursts. I can't trust people, places, or things. All I want to do is spend time alone. And drink.

Prior to deployment, I was very outgoing and spontaneous. Now, if things aren't planned and structured, I don't want to go out. Not that I want to go out anyway. When I do, which isn't often, I don't enjoy myself. I don't have fun. The soldiers who died over there, the impact of their deaths on their families—those people aren't going out and having fun anymore. Why should I be able to go out and have a good time? How am I even still alive?

I think a lot about the loss of my close friend Corporal Malasko. It makes me so angry, thinking about how he went out. He didn't die on the battlefield. He got electrocuted. In a shower.

And that could have easily been me.

Eric, another military buddy of mine, became a mentor to me when I returned home. I told him I wanted to go to flight school, and Eric counseled me on the transition from being an enlisted multiple launch rocket system (MLRS) soldier to being a warrant officer flying Black Hawks. I had lunch with him at a Korean restaurant outside Fort Hood, and he gave me great advice about the application process.

Later that night, in bed, I texted him, thanking him and wishing him good luck with his advanced training while sirens wailed a few blocks outside my house. Hearing those sirens put me back on the rear attachment of the convoy, manning my weapon, looking for the enemy.

The next day, I find out Eric is dead. He got in a motorcycle accident the night before and was decapitated. Those sirens I heard belonged to the people responding to Eric's accident. As I was texting him, he was already dead on the side of the road.

I find out another soldier I deployed with died of an overdose in Baton Rouge, Louisiana. Another mentor of mine, this huge, massive sergeant first class with a heart of gold, was on Active Component to Reserve Component (AC-RC) duty and on his way to PT when his car somehow ended up in a culvert overflowing with rainwater. For some reason he couldn't get out and drowned.

Why are all these things happening around me?

I've never lost anybody to combat. I feel blessed, feel very thankful for that, and yet all these people I know, and love, and respect, are dying—and it makes me so *fucking* angry. I don't want to feel that—can't afford to feel that or anything else. I've got to lock away all my emotions. Joy can too easily spiral into absolute, utter grief. If I love people, I will lose them. I've got to protect myself. My career.

This new me, the way I look at life and interact with the world—I know the impact it's having on my wife and my family.

"You can't keep these emotions bottled up," my wife tells me.

We've had this conversation before. I know what she's going to ask me to do.

"You need..." she begins.

"No. I told you. I'm not going to do that."

"Brennan, you need to try to get back that piece of you that you lost over there."

I clear my throat and take in a deep breath.

"I can't."

"You need to *try,*" she says.

She persuades me to go to the VA.

I end up meeting some great counselors.

They tell me I'm allowed to feel my own emotions. I'm allowed to feel how I want to feel about anything because everybody is different. Own the emotions, feel them, they tell me, but don't keep them bottled up.

I tell them how I feel guilty doing normal things and how wrong I feel when I'm having a good time—and they tell me it's okay, it's perfectly acceptable and healthy to feel love, and happiness, and joy. It's okay to enjoy fun things on the spur of the moment. It's okay to enjoy life. Everyone has their own process, I'm told, but you have to go through *your* emotions. Not around them but *through* them. I have to go *through* the process.

And I do. I go through the process.

It leads me to humanitarian work.

Right now, I'm a disaster program manager for a chapter located in the Hill Country of Texas. We support eighty counties, over 6.8 million people. We respond to local disasters, like Hurricane Harvey, and national disasters, like the fires in Southern California. A lot of the people on my team are retired veterans as well. I've got back that camaraderie and brotherhood.

And I'm helping people through their darkest days and their darkest hours, when they have no idea what their next step is. "It's going to be okay," I tell them. "I know it doesn't seem like it now, but we'll all get through this together, one day at a time, one task at a time." It's so fulfilling. Humbling. I feel so, so grateful.

NICOLE KRUSE

Nicole Kruse grew up in Minneapolis, Minnesota. She was a junior in high school on September 11, 2001. Seeing what happened made her want to be a part of something that was bigger than herself. The following year, when she turned seventeen, Nicole joined the Minnesota National Guard. She is now a captain in the Army and a Black Hawk pilot.

My husband and I get married on my twentieth birthday. He's active-duty, with the 82nd. When he gets out, in 2006, he moves to Minnesota, and I get pregnant. I'm in my junior year of college.

One day after class, my professor of military science takes me aside and says, "Nicole, do you want to get out? Because you can."

"No, sir," I say, and mean it. I've always wanted to fly Army helicopters, and I'm committed to seeing it through. "This is what I want to do—this is my calling—and if you guys can work with me, my husband and I will figure out arrangements for our child so I can stick with this."

It's true. I really do want to stick with this. But I'm also trying to be realistic about my options. So I start thinking about corporate law. Tuition won't be a problem. The G.I. Bill will pay 80 percent, and because I'm half Native American, the money that comes in from the reservation I'm a part of will cover the rest.

I take the LSAT while I'm pregnant. I'm thinking about putting in an educational delay and going to law school when the professor of military science, a man who is an aviator and getting ready to retire, says to me, "You can be a lawyer at any point in your life, Nicole, but when will you ever again have a chance to fly Army helicopters?"

That hits a nerve. It makes me think of my mother. She always encouraged me to reach for the stars. Everything that I ever wanted to do in my life—none of it ever seemed impossible for me, no matter the circumstances. I truly believe anyone can make anything happen in their lives if they truly desire it—if they're willing to go the distance, do whatever it takes to get the job done. You have to be 100 percent committed.

"I think you're right, sir. Let me try for Aviation branch."

After I give birth to my son, Chastan, in the summer of 2007, I begin to pursue my dream.

It's not easy. Thank God for my family. We're super close, and they've always been my support system.

My mom works nights, so I bring Chastan to her house early in the morning before I have PT. I'm part of a Ranger Challenge group, and I have to get back into shape. I go back to school when Chastan is only a few weeks old.

It's ambitious wanting to accomplish all these goals as a new mother, but I know it will bring my son a better life than the one I had growing up. My mom raised me, and while she provided me with everything she could, I saw how much she struggled. Knowing that makes me even more determined to give my son the best life possible—even if that means also working up to thirty-six hours every week so I can get full health care.

But still, it's *a lot*. I'm getting very little sleep, so I'm exhausted pretty much all the time. But I know I'm also building up the sort of resiliency I'll need to get through some of the rougher times that I know are coming—like advanced camp. I missed it because of the pregnancy.

I end up doing advanced camp on the back end after college graduation, in May of 2008. That September, I find out I got Aviation.

I'm ecstatic.

In April of 2009, I go to flight school with my husband and son. It's rough. This is the first time I'm moving away from my family and not coming back. On top of that, my husband and I are having a lot of marital problems. We decide to use my time at SERE—the Army's survival, evasion, resistance, and escape school, which trains soldiers in how to survive in isolation or captivity—to give ourselves some space.

When I return from SERE, it's clear that my husband and I are not on the same path. We decide to get a divorce. He decides to move to Samoa to gather himself while he lives with his mother.

I stay at Fort Rucker, in Alabama, with my young son. I have to figure out how to watch and care for him while going to flight school.

Fortunately, there's day care, and the community of people and spouses at Fort Rucker help watch Chastan when I can't.

Then, when it's time for me to be a platoon leader and move to my first duty station in Hawaii, I'm fortunate to have one of my aunts move in with me. She's someone I can rely on and trust, and when I become a company commander at Fort Hood, she moves with me and helps out with Chastan. My son is very comfortable with her, which is a good thing because I've just been told I'm going to deploy, in January of 2012, as part of Operation Enduring Freedom.

I'll be gone for most of the year.

I'm twenty-five years old and I have no idea what it means to go to war.

I'm scared.

And on top of that, I'm leaving my son. The thought of being away from him for so long is crushing enough. Thinking about all these issues is overwhelming. Suffocating.

The soldiers I'm going with had all just deployed together to Iraq. They act confident, and their confidence gives me confidence of my own. Our mindset is: we're a family. We're going into this as a family. We're going to get through this together.

Our command aviation company is in Kandahar. Our assault battalion has three companies of Black Hawks: air assault, maintenance, and forward support. I'm with air assault, which means I'm responsible for bringing the ground force to the objective and then picking them up.

My first missions involve working with the Australian Special Forces. Our aircraft gets shot at. When we come back after an infiltration and inspect our aircraft, some of them have bullet holes. That's when the reality of what's going on here sinks in.

But I don't feel afraid when I'm in the air—on the ground, yes, but not in the air. One night I'm in the top bunk and I wake up to a siren going off. The base, I'm told, is receiving indirect fire. As I jump out of bed, I hit my head on the ceiling, and the fear sets in. When I'm in the air, it's like I'm in this other world where I feel like I'm in control. Not invulnerable or unstoppable, but in control of my area.

In April, we lose John, one of our crew chiefs—and it's due to pilot error involving weather, not enemy fire. That's when it sinks in that death is real. Someone I knew well and cared about is dead, and I'm not prepared for it.

How am I going to show my emotions? I'm a leader. I need to be brave for my soldiers, make sure they're all taken care of, and it's really hard to take care of them while also taking care of myself.

"We're going to do every mission for John," I tell them. "We're going to go forward, and we're going to make John's life count. His sacrifice."

John's death brings us closer, but I struggle with it for a long time because it's my fault he died. I recommended him for that particular mission. If I hadn't, he wouldn't have been there that day, and he'd still be alive.

When I Skype back home with my family and my son, I try to act like everything is okay because I don't want them to worry. Even to this day, they don't know what happened during my yearlong deployment. I don't tell them about my valor award or my combat action badge or my Air Medal. I think they realize the nature of my profession, but the things I've seen and experienced, I want to keep that separate from my family. I don't want to ever make them worry.

MIKE ERGO

The oldest of four, Mike Ergo grew up in the San Francisco Bay Area town of Walnut Creek hearing his grandfather's stories about the Marine Corps in World War II. An evangelical Christian from an early age, Mike always liked serving others. He went to Mexico to help build houses and one summer traveled to Slovakia to build a church. Mike served in the Marine Corps from 2001 to 2005. His MOS was 0311 Infantry, basic rifleman.

I stand up in front of the military board and say, "I don't want to do this anymore."

They're shocked. I understand why.

Going through boot camp, when I was asked by drill sergeants, instructors, and others what my MOS—my military occupational specialty, or career—was going to be, I told them I had chosen musician because I played saxophone and, after having auditioned for the Marine Corps band, had been accepted. I got laughed at the entire time. During boot camp, I had thought about switching from musician to infantryman. I loved weapons training and being in the field and training with a bunch of other soon-to-be grunts. I felt like I was in the real military.

I clear my throat, nervous. I'm eighteen, and everyone is staring at me.

"I'd rather be in the infantry," I tell the board.

Silence. I know what they're thinking: *People who join the school of music want to stay here. It's easy physically and the people here are nice to you and really fun to be around.* And they are. They truly are fun, nice people. But I want to go to war and be a part of something epic.

"Okay," says one of the board members. "Okay, yeah, we can do that for you, no problem."

Now I have to go back to the School of Infantry for a second time—only this time I'm going to do the actual infantry training. It's the summer of 2002.

I know they're going to push me far beyond my comfort zone and my perceived abilities. I know I'll have to earn respect. I know I can't rely on my dad's career as a partner in a law firm to give me a job. I can't rely on nepotism or favors from anyone. I'll have to earn everything myself, and I can't wait for it to begin.

The first time I deploy, in March of 2003, I'm part of the Army's 4th Infantry Division. The plan is to go through Turkey's airspace, land in Turkey, and then convoy down to Iraq.

I've let go of being scared. Whatever the heck is going to happen is going to happen. I'll just deal with it.

Turkey decides it doesn't want us coming through to go

into Iraq, so we end up floating around in the Mediterranean and watching the initial invasion on TV. We missed Afghanistan and now we feel like complete losers because we've missed Iraq.

Not that the war is going to last that long. We assume this one, like the Gulf War, is going to be over in four days.

We're wrong.

When I deploy again, in June of 2004, the insurgency has started to take off, and IEDs are the insurgency's signature weapon. We fly into Al Asad Airbase in western Iraq's Al Anbar Province and immediately get to work patrolling the deserts and some of the small towns. We get into a few small engagements, but nothing major.

The war gets real for me the following month.

My best friend, a fellow ginger, is moved over to a scout sniper platoon. On July 20, a day and a half later, after I had dinner with him in the chow hall, he's killed by an IED.

He can't be dead. I just saw him. A day and a half ago, we were joking around like we always did, and talking about what we were going to do when we got back home, and now he's *dead*? The shock turns to anger—what are we going to do to find the people responsible?—and then, eventually, gives way to guilt about my inability to stop my best friend from being killed.

The sobering reality of warfare hits me: this isn't a game. People get hurt and people get killed.

I don't have time to dwell on these feelings, let alone process them. I'm a twenty-one-year-old corporal. I have to go about my job, doing security patrols and meet and greets with local farmers out along the Euphrates River. Then I'm told we're heading down to Fallujah, to the base camp right outside the city, to start training for a big, massive invasion.

Al-Qaeda and all kinds of foreign fighters from all over the Muslim world have been flooding into Fallujah since April, when the insurgents, after ambushing a convoy containing four US private contractors from Blackwater, dragged the American bodies through the streets. The insurgents have been busy fortifying the city, getting ready for us to attack.

We invade the city on November 8. I have no idea I'm about to be a part of the largest urban combat battle the US has engaged in since Hue City in Vietnam.

RPGs fly over my head and explode against buildings. Smoke is pouring out of mosques, and insurgent fighters and squads are dashing across the street and making their way to the area my team has secured, the place in the middle of the city known as the mayor's complex.

In the midst of all the fighting, my team and I find ourselves totally exposed on the northwest corner of the mayor's complex. The rest of our company is situated on surrounding buildings, with some pretty good cover, but here we are on the ground. Did our company forget about us? Did they—

Women wearing hijabs and young girls appear right in front of us. Some are holding a white flag, the signal that they're civilians. The rules of engagement state that if they're waving a white flag, they're to come to us, and we'll get them out of harm's way.

My thirty-day crash course in Arabic taught me some basic phrases. I tell them to come to us. When they start walking, I see young men standing behind them. That's when I figure out that they're using these women and children as human shields.

Our rules of engagement are clear: if they don't come to us and surrender, we can open fire.

I turn to my men, my decision absolute. "Do not open fire. I repeat, *do not* shoot them."

Later that day, I find out one of our lieutenants got sniped through the side of his body armor, bled out, and died. I'll never know if one of the bad guys I let pass was responsible for it, but I regret my earlier decision of not engaging the enemy.

My idea of right and wrong is thrown into question. I'm also unsure of my grasp on being an effective infantry team leader.

Think about it like baseball, I tell myself. *Instead of being up at the plate and saying, "Okay, don't strike out, don't strike out," say instead, "Let's try to get a hit. Let's just focus on being here. Whatever comes, comes."*

We spend the next six days kicking down doors and clearing houses. We get shot at and we shoot back. Along the way, we get into engagements in the streets, and we shoot the enemy. Then the oddest, creepiest thing happens: they get hit by three or four rounds, jerk back, and then get up and run and scale a wall.

It's like we're shooting zombies.

The bad guys, we come to find out, are injecting themselves with some kind of stimulant that helps them keep going even when they get hit.

We do sector clearing all the way south. Then we're told to go back to the buildings we cleared and basically do mop-up duty, try to find the remaining insurgents who are playing cat and mouse with us.

Our platoon splits up to do the clearings. One of my junior Marines, who was off taking a leak, runs over to me and says, "Corporal, I saw these guys hiding behind a building. Then I saw them jump in it."

"Did you shoot 'em?"

"No, I came to get you." He gives me the location. The building is near where my platoon is currently located.

I take a makeshift team of four men, including myself: my point man, a guy from Grass Valley, California; the Goose, a combat engineer; and a guy carrying a light machine gun called the squad automatic weapon, or SAW. We hop over a wall, onto a street that's north of my platoon. I see the bad guys—there's four of them.

And they're moving to position themselves to ambush my platoon.

We start clearing the group of buildings. The first one is clear. Same with the second and third. They're empty of people.

There's one building left. They have to be in there.

We've just opened the back door to a courtyard when my point man says, "Shit."

"What?"

"I just realized there's a very small bathroom I haven't cleared." With his chin, he nods up the stairs.

"Check it," I say. "I don't want anyone sneaking up on us."

We go back inside. He heads up the cement steps. I trail him, my SAW gunner and the Goose behind me.

My point man kicks open the door.

Starts yelling and shooting.

And the bad guys inside return fire.

Then two guys shoot at us from a room across the hallway. We start shooting back. The place fills with gun smoke. The Goose, still behind me, gets shot in the helmet. Underneath all the shooting, I hear him yell and fall down.

It's complete chaos.

It brings to mind something my lieutenant told me: *When it comes to combat, you need to embrace the chaos because things are going to fall apart, and you need to be able to adapt.*

But we're pinned down—my point man and I are pushing up against each other. There's no place to go.

They throw a grenade.

This is the end.

I don't give up fighting, but I know I'm going to die. I don't have any urge to call out to God for help or to beg for my life. I don't pray. If this is how I go out, then I'm going out with my friends, these brothers I trust and love. This is the way *to* go out.

I surrender to it.

In that moment, I can feel my entire body. I can feel every single cell, even the hairs growing out of my skin. I can feel the air rushing into my lungs. And then I have this weird experience where I feel the world around me dissolve. I'm now in this timeless, peaceful place where I'm guessing my consciousness expands, taking me out of this building, away from the men shooting at us.

Right here, in this eternal moment, I don't have any worries. I know everything is going to be all right, and I'm at complete peace.

Somehow we manage to take these guys down. I survive, with a little cut on my neck from when the grenade exploded.

We stay in Fallujah for a little bit, living in the city and in other people's houses. Then we're sent to the Abu Ghraib prison and live there for a stretch while doing security patrols in the area. When I finally get back to the barracks, I go seek out two guys who went with me to the infantry school. We've become very good friends.

I find my friend Winters. "Where's Hawk?" I ask.

Winters shoots me a look. "You didn't hear?"

"No. Where is he?"

"Hawk is fucking dead, man. He got shot in the face."

Just when I think it's over and I can come back and meet with my best friends—nope, sorry, one of them is now dead. Death is the gift that keeps on giving.

I try my best to stay busy. Then, in 2005, near the end of January, I go back home to North Carolina.

The battle of Fallujah, what happened to my battalion, was all over the news, every single detail. I can tell that my wife and parents want to ask me about it. I'm grateful they don't.

How can I explain what it's like fighting to the death and seeing horrific shit like torture rooms where people were kept in cages? Or how can I explain how, when I got back to the barracks, I'd have hallucinations of people appearing in the bathrooms and then I'd go kick in the doors and leave feeling stupid because no one was in there?

And how do I explain what a huge shock it is for me to go from combat to living back in the United States, where people are living peaceful lives, where there's no gunfire or roads marked with huge craters from bombs?

Different sounds and smells, I discover, trigger my fight-or-flight response. My body gears up for something really bad to happen—something truly dreadful—even though the whole time my mind is saying, *No, no, no, everything is fine.*

In the summer, while I'm working for my dad's law firm and starting up at community college, I almost get extended for a third deployment. It doesn't happen, which is good. I know, deep in my heart, that if I go back, I'll die. And yet some guys I know have just deployed again as individual combat replacements to different units where they'll be the new guys, and it makes me feel guilty that I'm not there with them.

I worry about them all the time.

On top of that, I'm living in the civilian world without a purpose. I'm not around people who really know and understand what I've gone through.

I don't fit in here. What can I possibly do after fighting—and surviving—that huge battle in Fallujah? The only things that bring me joy are smoking cannabis and drinking excessive amounts of alcohol.

The cannabis does wonders for my anxiety. The booze helps stop some of the bad feelings and lets me tap into some of the good ones. It helps stop all these intrusive thoughts that are playing on an endless loop—getting a grenade thrown at me, shooting people and them shooting back.

I drink every single day, without fail, because I just want to stop feeling so bad. I go on some epic benders, too. Sometimes I wake up in the creek across the street from my house, dressed in my camis. Other times I feel so despondent that I hop on my motorcycle, drunk, and ride it around and black out.

Oh, my God, I think every time I wake up hungover, *I did it again. I'll never do this again.*

But I do it again. And again. My life is falling apart even though I'm going to UC Berkeley and getting good grades. I'm even getting some counseling, but I'm still not ready to face some of these intrusive thoughts, some of these difficult feelings. I'm not consciously aware that I'm purposely avoiding processing the traumas. I don't know I'm purposely avoiding getting close to people because I'm scared of going through the pain of losing someone again. I don't want to grieve. My friends are gone. I don't want to face that fact, or the feelings involved.

What complicates this even more is my friend Josh Munns. He went to Iraq to work as a contractor so he could buy a house for his fiancée. He got kidnapped, and the kidnappers mailed his fingers back to someone in the US forces to prove that they had Josh and he was still alive. He was held captive for over a year, and despite intense negotiations, he was killed.

Life, I know, is never going to get better; it's only going to get worse. All I can do is pump more booze into myself, and do more reckless things, and feel good once in a while, try to live for those fleeting moments the booze and drugs bring.

That changes in 2012, when I graduate with a master's degree in social work and start working with a vet group called Killing the Wounded Heart. The group talks about a principle called radical honesty. You have a choice, they say.

You can live with your shit and feel like shit, or you can decide to be brave and face your fears.

Listening to them, I feel this pang deep in my gut that this might be my only way out. One day I decide to go home and practice some radical honesty.

"I'm drinking a lot more than you think," I tell my wife. "I've been doing a lot of drugs, and I've been unfaithful."

My wife of four years stands there, glaring at me in shock. She just got home from work and I've verbally thrown up all over her.

That day she moves back home with her parents.

The next day, she calls me and says, "I want to stay together. But only if you give up every single drug, even cannabis. And no more booze. One more drop and our marriage is completely over."

The idea of living without alcohol or drugs—the only things that make me feel good—is terrifying.

"I choose you," I say.

We work on our relationship. I go to Alcoholics Anonymous and face all these feelings I've been avoiding, the grief and the intrusive thoughts, the post-traumatic stress—all of it.

It takes years before I start to feel better.

The real transformation begins on my thirtieth birthday, when a friend gives me a completely shitty present: a registration card for a half marathon. What kind of gift is that? The last thing I want to do is get in shape and run.

But for some reason, I decide to do it. About a week and a half into training, I feel good for the first time in a long, long time—all without using any mind-altering substances. I come to the realization that I can be here, in my own body, without having to disappear inside my head. I don't have to get blackout drunk or stoned out of my mind to feel like it's okay to exist.

I sign up for a half Ironman. I do a few of those and fall in love with the sport.

I sign up for a full Ironman. By that time, I've got a few triathlons under my belt, but for me it's still incomprehensible to go 140.4 miles without stopping.

Ironman sends out a short motivational clip of a woman named Lisa Hallett who lost her husband, John, in Afghanistan. In the video, she tells people that she was depressed and stuck in her grief and dealt with it by running. Running, she says, is all about physically moving forward, and that helped her move forward in her life, literally and figuratively. It helped her move forward emotionally and spiritually. She runs in honor of her husband and wears a shirt with his name on it.

In that moment, everything clicks for me. I'm able to shed tears of grief and joy. I'm so overcome by emotion, this freedom of not feeling ashamed or guilty that I survived. I don't have to feel this utter dread.

I can remember them. I can honor them by racing and carrying their names on my jersey. I can deal with my grief in a way that makes their families feel happy. I can do something I enjoy and do it with a purpose bigger than just completing a race, which in itself is a good enough purpose.

I begin to experience my own transformation and healing.

Ironman gets wind of how their events helped reshape my life. They ask me if I'd be willing to share my story in their upcoming footage for the World Championships. I jump on it. I want to let other people who are in my shoes know that they're not alone. Trapped. That you can find something that can change your life.

When Ironman announces its upcoming fortieth-anniversary celebration will take place in Santa Rosa, California, the company reaches out to me again, this time asking if I'd like to become their race ambassador. "Is there anything you'd like to do to make it unique or special?"

"Actually," I say, "I've been thinking of running a marathon for a gold star family. From experience, I know they get a lot of support during the funerals, but afterward they get ignored because the community doesn't know what to do to help support them.

"What I want to do is invite a local family to the event and run the entire marathon while carrying a flag with the name of their son or daughter on it. I think it might not only help other veterans who have survivor's guilt but also help the community make sure these gold star families feel welcomed."

And that's when the fear shows up. How the hell am I going to pull off running 26.2 miles while carrying a flag?

I tell myself I can do it—I *will* do it.

And I do.

CODA:

MEMORIAL DAY

SHIVAN SIVALINGAM

Shivan Sivalingam was born in Singapore. His family immigrated to the United States in 1984, and he grew up in Austin, Texas. While attending Texas A&M University in the mid-1990s, Shivan began serving as an intern in the federal government. After graduating, he received a commission in the US Navy Reserve. In 2005, Shivan left federal service to work as a defense contractor. He has been recalled to active duty on five occasions, most recently to serve as a liaison officer for the US Navy's 5th Fleet at Special Operations Command Central, in Tampa, Florida.

My friends,

Ten years have passed since I shared the story of my friend Roz with some of you. Others of you may have heard bits as we've met in the years in between. Roz and Shawn, two of my teammates in Afghanistan, set off on the Kabul-Bagram road ten years ago today. A short time after eight that morning, both were lost. There are many story lines that I think about from that day. The tremendous leadership from an unlikely hero. The friendship and community from Roz's family and so many others in the years since. Obviously, the guilt. But most of all, I think about the difficult fact that life will deceive us with relative predictability for long periods until, at the moments when we begin to feel the most comfortable, it unfolds, reminding us how powerless we all are.

As we approach Memorial Day, of course I remember Roz. However, on this day, we must be obliged to remember as many of our fallen friends as possible. While some of us by good fortune may not have a loved one or even acquaintance who has perished in the conflicts, isn't that all the more reason for those of us who have lost someone to share their stories? What follows are some stories of a few friends no longer with us.

MOHSIN

With much in common, Mohsin and I became fast friends at my camp in Kabul. We were both junior officers in a headquarters camp, both of South Asian descent, and both exceptionally charming young gentlemen for the times. Charm, we should be reminded, is one of those forgotten casualties of war. Mohsin, a Pakistani, had just completed a tour in Iraq and had gone home only long enough to get married before returning to harm's way. We ate dinner together most days, recounting the events of the past few hours and our plans for the day that was to follow.

Mohsin was especially excited during one of his first Fridays at the camp, as that was the day of the big bazaar. Vendors from all over the area would set up an open-air market just outside the camp, peddling everything from furniture and antique rifles to pirated DVDs and all manner of trinkets in between. After lunch, we walked to the bazaar, where he planned to shop for jewelry for his wife. For me, one of the grand wastes of time is watching someone bargain for anything at all, let alone alleged precious stones, so I excused myself. Mohsin seemed slightly displeased at this, expecting more hospitality from a friend.

When we met up for dinner, Mohsin, with unnecessary enthusiasm, displayed his prize catch of the day: a beautiful lapis lazuli necklace. He stayed on the topic some forty-five seconds longer than necessary to convey a message that I believe should never have exceeded ten. I took this as gloating, as implying that I should have kept his company at the bazaar. Never accused of refusing an opportunity to humble a good friend, I reminded him that the only difference between a jeweler and a thief is a handshake. Mohsin conceded, putting the lapis away.

During our chats, we often spoke about Mohsin's desire to go to the border region, where he felt he could put his language skills to better use. This would be a point of contention in our friendship. I tried appealing to reason, telling him that he could potentially get the attention of one of our seniors if he stayed in Kabul, thereby influencing the conflict at a strategic level. I appealed to emotion, reminding him of his obligation to his new bride and his family. None of my interventions worked.

The border region was unsafe for all Americans, but it would be especially unsafe for Mohsin. Locals he encountered there would quickly identify him as a native. For each local who displayed pride that one of their own had become an American soldier, there would be no fewer than three who would brand him a traitor. I thought that our enemies would not rest until they killed him. They would be relentless. Regardless, after a few weeks of trying, Mohsin got his desired assignment and left the camp in mid-August of 2008.

About a month later, I traveled home for my brother's wedding. On a random day, I looked at the faces of the fallen in the local paper. You don't ever look at that section expecting to see someone that you were just eating dinner with... not because the person was out of harm's path, but because you expect that you will get the bad news in a more direct way.

But Mohsin had arrived at our camp by himself, and he'd left by himself. In the few weeks he was at my camp, he got to know only a handful of people. When I got back to Kabul, I looked up the incident reports. Mohsin had been assigned to a camp where they frequently went out on missions. Our enemies had struck American convoys from that camp at a rate of just a couple of attacks per month in the months prior to Mohsin's arrival, but in the two weeks prior to his death, the enemy had targeted Mohsin's convoy four times in five attacks! Relentless indeed. Our enemies had been hunting for Mohsin.

MIKE

In November of 2001, some of the heaviest fighting of the then just six-week-old war occurred at Qala-i-Jangi (literally, "fort of war"), an imposing structure guarding the ancient Shia city of Mazar-i-Sharif from the west. It was here that General Rashid Dostum held some four hundred Taliban fighters, rounded up during a death march from Konduz to Mazar, across the Afghan northern plains. Dostum was one of several influential Afghans whom we enlisted for support after the 9/11 attacks.

One of my friends who had deployed there in October of 2001 shared a great account of General Tommy Franks speaking to Dostum on the phone about additional compensation for the assistance that the warlord was providing. *"What's got to happen first is the mission!!!"* Franks thundered before slamming down the phone on Dostum. Franks, having risen through the ranks during the lean Clinton years, was probably uniquely prepared to handle Dostum.

Dostum and his men picked up some four thousand Taliban on the way to Mazar, but only four hundred survived the journey. At Qala-i-Jangi, the prisoners were stuffed into the basement of a small building with pink walls. If a sardine had viewed the cramped, filthy conditions in that basement, he would have quickly reconsidered his plight and happily lumbered back into his can.

Mike and his partner arrived to question the Taliban prisoners. A few dozen of Dostum's men were all that stood between the two Americans and the prisoners. Initially, the prisoners, weary from the long trek, were likely just content to be off the container trucks, but perspectives and intentions would change quickly. Mike and his partner were focusing on the task at hand, not completely attuned to the changing attitude of the enemy, which was no doubt taking stock of scenes of friends being beaten and spirited off to unknown fates by Dostum's men. Recall that these were men who survived the death march—the march that had reportedly wiped out more than three thousand of their comrades.

Said another way: they were the strongest, toughest, and most resilient of the initial group. Even depleted in number, they still outnumbered Dostum's men by three or four to one and may have smuggled in weapons. Mike and his partner probably didn't know those crucial details. The prisoners began sizing up Mike, his partner, and Dostum's men. At a coordinated moment, when Mike's partner was away, they encircled Mike and began to pounce.

The ensuing battle featured these prisoners; Dostum's men, some of whom were on horses; British Special Forces elements parachuting in; and precision-guided aerial munitions dropped from ground attack aircraft, all within the confines of a high-walled desert fortress.

The picture in my mind is one from an eighties-era G.I. Joe cartoon, except Qala-i-Jangi really happened. Over the grand ramparts, inside the fortress grounds, the Afghan Army's 209th Corps would establish a garrison here a few years later. A huge wall bearing a disproportionately small door divides the fort in half, separating the working area from what amounts to a memorial ground for the fighting that took place here that November. The fortress was perfectly unpreserved, and stepping through the door, one quickly encounters rusted-out trucks, spent 12.7mm DShK shells, and the notorious pink house, the whole scene almost exactly as it was in the days following the battle.

When you walk Bull Run or Sharpsburg, much is left to interpretation and your imagination. In Qala-i-Jangi, the only things missing from 2001 are the bodies, the sounds, and the smell. A memorial for Mike stands in the veranda of the pink house, and the camp bears his name, a couple of miles to the south. Mike has the unfortunate distinction of being the first American killed in combat in Afghanistan after the conflict began.

FRANK

Some eight years after Mike was killed, Frank arrived at Camp Spann with a team of Navy personnel. They had trained together, done their pre-deployment workups together, and they had all traveled into theater together. In short, they were already a tight-knit group. Camp Spann was entirely enclosed within Camp Shaheen—the main garrison for the Afghan 209th Corps, with some command buildings a short distance away at Qala-i-Jangi. Shaheen was a perfect square, about three-quarters of a mile on each side, and Spann occupied a small corner of the larger camp, with its own perimeter fence.

We often place our camps within the walls of an Afghan camp to add a layer of protection... in concept. In 2007, I had deployed to Spann for six weeks. An unexpected treat of this duty was getting to run the roughly three-mile perimeter road of Shaheen. The weather in Mazar was pleasant, the air was clean, and the perimeter was perfectly flat, on soft gravel. In short, excellent running conditions, if one so desires. One loop was a typical warm-up or cool-down run; two loops was a regular running day; and on a three-loop day, with the greatest of intentions to complete the run, I would invariably begin evaluating the educational benefits of "walking it in" from just past the last turn, which featured a boneyard of old Russian ground combat vehicles on a road conveniently parallel to the perimeter.

Here lazy runners could break into a trot as they tried to distinguish old Soviet T-55s from T-62s while, more important, sparing their knees about a mile's worth of additional high-impact exercise. Running outside was not an easy option in Kabul, so being able to enjoy an outside jog while in Mazar was a welcome change. I did some form of running no fewer than three times a week, and I felt perfectly safe doing so.

Nearly two years later, Frankie and his teammates shared this mindset. A few months into their deployment, during a Friday run, Frank and his running partner in a foursome had dropped about fifty yards behind the lead pair. As the lead pair rounded that final bend, an Afghan soldier came down off a watchtower and shot at the lead group, mortally wounding one of Frank's teammates. Knowing that their friends were wounded, Frank's partner made a break for the clinic, which was perhaps a quarter mile away, while our beloved Frank stood with decision.

You see, he was at that last turn on the perimeter road, alongside the boneyard of tanks and APCs that would have offered ample protection from the bullets that would soon fly his way. At fifty yards and a moving target, he probably would have reached cover in the boneyard. But the proposition Frank faced that day, as life unraveled before him, was *Do I try to save my friends, or do I save myself?* He did not know that one friend was already succumbing to wounds.

It is a peculiar condition in humans, common even in the worst of pessimists, that when confronted with the prospect that one of our best friends has suffered a fatal accident, even one we have witnessed, we believe they are still alive. Some may explain this behavior as part of denial, but there is more to it. Our best friends are not mere mortals. They are our role models. They are our superheroes. Mere car accidents, or bullets, or IEDs cannot end them. Their superpowers will carry them a little longer.

In short, Frank charged the gunman that day believing he would save his slightly wounded friends. As he approached the gunman, Frank yelled out, running toward him but zigzagging as the gunman attempted to get Frank in his sights. Two of Frank's teammates survived injuries and live today because of his bravery.

Frank is buried at Arlington. I visited his grave site

a few Memorial Days ago with two good friends. One of them, a graduate of the academy, had just walked us over to the markers of a few of her classmates. It was a mini reunion of sorts for her school, but also a solemn reminder of the lives we have given in these conflicts. Folks were remembering Doug, Travis, and many others. And then we walked over to Frank's marker, a less-visited tomb, maybe a hundred yards away.

Along the way, I was sharing the account of Frank's bravery that I shared above. As we neared his marker, I noticed three young ladies whom I had never met, yet each was distinctively familiar. They looked back at the approaching group like sentinels standing a solemn watch, guarding especially hallowed ground. Indeed, they were.

Still a little shocked, I said "Hello, Brooke" to Frank's wife, who turned to his sister as if to say, *Who is this?*

Frank's mother then turned to me and, having no need to introduce herself, politely did so anyway. She admitted that she had overheard the story I had been sharing about her son. "Did you know him?" she asked, with a pause as if to indicate that, while she could not place me from all the years past, the pictures, the emails, and the visits, surely I must have known him from the detail of the story?

I replied with a resounding "No!," without offering explanation, knowing that there is always an incredible pride that falls over parents when they come into the company of complete strangers who speak so highly of their child's great deeds in life.

She smiled.

Roslyn "Roz" Schulte was from Saint Louis, Missouri. She was an officer in the Air Force and graduated from the Air Force Academy. She was residing in Hawaii at the time of her deployment. She was killed in action on May 20, 2009.

Shawn Pine was from San Antonio, Texas. He was a retired Army officer. He died of wounds on May 20, 2009.

Mohsin Naqvi was from Newburgh, New York. He was an Army officer. He was KIA on September 17, 2008.

Johnny Spann, a.k.a. Mike, was from Marion County, Alabama. He was a Marine Corps officer. He was residing in Northern Virginia at the time of his deployment. He was KIA on November 25, 2001.

Francis Toner was from Rhode Island. He was a Navy officer and graduated from the Merchant Marine Academy. He was residing in Hawaii at the time of his deployment. He was KIA on March 27, 2009.

From Manama with love,
Shivan

GINNY LUTHER

*Ginny Luther's son, Lieutenant Robert "Bart" Fletcher, served in
the Army. His MOS was Cavalry. He was a tank commander
based out of Fort Hood, in Texas.*

When Bart turns sixteen, he decides he wants to go to
Portugal as an American foreign exchange student. He
thinks being fluent in a foreign language will help him get into
West Point. Getting in will be a challenge. But Bart is a kid who
thrives on big challenges—especially personal challenges.

Challenging is the word I'd use to describe Bart. His father
and I separated after Bart was born, and I became a single
parent of two children—Bart and his older brother, Nick.
It was completely overwhelming. During the day, I worked
at a psychiatric facility with very young children who were
suffering from emotional disabilities, and I returned home
each evening to a child who acted like a tyrant. He was
defiant and disruptive and had major temper tantrums.

He was also very precocious—and very bright. At eighteen months, he was talking at the level of a four-year-old. People couldn't believe the stuff that came out of his mouth. He was enthralled with guns at a very early age. He would make one out of his toast and pretend to shoot me—and I was *mortified,* partly because I'm scared to death of guns. My dad took his life with a gun when I was fourteen.

I thought Bart would outgrow it, but his infatuation grew stronger. He kept asking me for a real gun, and I kept telling him no, and he kept having temper tantrums. His control issues were major—with me but also with babysitters and nursery school teachers. It was just difficult. He was a kid I couldn't take out in any public forum because of his insistence that the world go *his* way. One day when he was two, I was holding a wooden spoon and threatening to punish him when he turned around and pulled down his pants.

"Come on," he egged me on. *"Spank me, Mommy."*

Right then I had an epiphany: *I have got to do something different.* At that moment, I realized the negative impact I was having on him—that my responses were dictating his responses, having a *huge* impact on him. He was two. I was thirty-one! What if I chose to respond differently?

I was the one who had to change. Not him.

That moment started me on my own journey of shifting myself first. That meant to quit taking it personally and begin to see Bart's behavior as a call for help. I created a peaceful parenting business to help not only Bart but myself—and Bart became my first client. His defiant characteristics were actually the characteristics of leadership, and my job was to encourage him. At a very early age it became clear that he wanted to join the military. "I want to serve my country," he told me several times. "I want to support people's freedom."

And now here we are.

And I don't want him to go.

"Bart," I say, "you can't go to Portugal and do the whole West Point thing. If you go to Portugal, do you realize what you'll be faced with when you come back? You'll have to make up your junior year *and* do your senior year *and* apply to West Point."

He stares at me, incredulous.

"You know what, Mom? My agenda for my life is not your agenda. You either are going to support me in this or you're going to fight me in this. Which way do you want to go?"

My jaw drops. He's sixteen. He's sixteen and such a wise soul. He was always that kind of kid.

"I want to support you," I say.

"Okay. Good."

"If you really want this," I tell him, "then you have to create it."

When Bart was six, I married a man who had two children of his own. We have a loving, caring family, and Bart and I have a very, very deep relationship. When he returns home to Florida, fluent in Portuguese, we have a deep discussion about everything he learned overseas. He also tells me a lot of stuff I don't want to know—like how, when he arrived, the family that was supposed to sponsor him suddenly dropped him. They found him another family, but it wasn't an ideal situation. The neighborhood was rough, and the parents were working ridiculous hours and weren't around to supervise their children and Bart, which forced him to negotiate this unknown, dog-eat-dog environment on his own.

Bart has to make up for all the academia he wasn't able to enjoy over in Portugal. He does that while also jumping through all the hoops and doing all the things he needs to do in order to even *apply* to West Point.

"You know," he tells me, "I'm a man now."

"Tell me why you think you are."

"The thing I realized when I was over there was that I'm the one who's responsible for me. Nobody is responsible for me, and I'm totally responsible for every choice I make."

"Yes," I say, "you are."

"Now that I'm a man, I've fallen in love with Katie."

I'm not surprised. They met when they were fifteen and have been going out, or whatever the kids call it now, for a while.

"I would like to have sex with Katie," he says. "I want to have it here, at the house, so I want your permission."

"Excuse me?"

"Well, you know, I'm a man now, so . . ."

"That's great that you're a man now," I say. "I'm so glad you are. I appreciate you asking and the answer is no. I'm sure you'll figure something out, but it ain't going to be in my house."

Bart gets accepted at West Point with a caveat. His math score was a bit low, which isn't a surprise since math isn't his greatest suit, so in order to attend he has to take a summer course and do some other work for the math program.

"I'm not going," he says.

"What? Why?"

"I don't want to waste that time catching up. I'll be a whole semester behind."

Which isn't true. The truth is, he wants to stay with Katie. The truth is, I don't want him to go to West Point, either.

I'm holding the acceptance letter. I'm reading the part that says *"Do not accept this based on what your parents say to you. This has to come from you totally"* when I say, "You're giving up the opportunity of a lifetime. If you don't take it, I think you're making a big mistake."

"Mom—"

"I know they told you not to listen to your parents. But I'm telling you this because I don't want you to come back when you're twenty-seven and say, 'Mom, why didn't you...?' I'm going to say I did. I did tell you."

He chooses not to go.

He stays home, goes to a community college, becomes class president, and gets the perfect grades he needs to transfer to the University of Florida. He attends U of F and joins the ROTC. He becomes the top cadet, graduates from college with a 4.0 grade point average. He's eager to go to war.

Bart was in middle school when 9/11 happened, and even though it scared him, seeing what happened only fueled his desire to join the military. It's October of 2008 and we're still at war, and my son cannot wait to get to Iraq.

The hardest part about Bart going off is knowing he's going to be on the front lines. That has been his drive all along, to be on the front lines, and he's done everything he can do to become the best he can—paratrooper training, this training and that training, all these extra things to up his skills. Knowing he's going to be sent to war—it's indescribable, the inner angst sitting in the back of my brain and core of my gut.

Bart calls me from Fort Hood, in Texas. "It's time, Mom. I'm going to be deployed."

Underneath the warrior is a kid who played video games and loved watching the History Channel. A boy who, when he was three, asked for a G.I. Joe outfit and a tea set for Christmas. He loved playing house with all the little girls and loved to interact with them in such a positive way; he had such a positive little energy about him. After he put on his G.I. Joe outfit, the little belt and hat, over his pajamas, he opened the tea set and then sat down and asked to have tea. He didn't want to open any more of his gifts. In that moment he was so, so happy.

"Mom? You there?"

"Okay," I say. "When?"

"Next week."

"Okay. I'm flying you home for a few days."

Over the next few days, before Bart flies to Florida, I find myself thinking about an incident when he was sixteen.

Teenagers have a funny way of telling you they need to talk. When I returned home from work one night after ten, I saw Bart sitting on the couch, and I could tell he wanted to talk. It was either going to be a quick conversation or a very long one.

When I sat down next to him, he started to cry.

"I don't know if I'm making the right decision," he said. "I so badly want to serve and make freedom. But I'm not sure if this is the way to go."

I knew he was experiencing all kinds of fear about his decision to pursue a life in the military. He knew we were at war—knew there would be a good chance, if he joined, that he would be sent to either Afghanistan or Iraq.

"I want to be a hero," he said. "But there's a problem."

"What?"

"I know I'm not going to live a long life."

My heart was racing, my throat tight. "What do you mean?"

"I just know I'm not going to be on this planet for a long time."

I was completely stunned . . . and yet, from the time he was born, I'd been fighting that same feeling.

As I walk into the house, I realize this is going to be our last time together. It's very, very surreal.

Bart is in the home office, on the computer. This is it. I have to say something to him.

I run a business teaching parenting classes. Lots of discipline classes. On a shelf I keep a stash of little blue stars, glass trinkets I give to parents dealing with difficult children. The star is a reminder: *S* is for *smile* or *stop*. *T* is for *take a deep breath*. *A* is for *and*. *R* is for *relax*. I take one star and put a hand on Bart's shoulder.

He turns around. I put the star in his hand and say, "Bart, you are a warrior. You are a hero. There are going to be times when you're really scared, so I want you to have this star to remind you to breathe. Breathe deeply. For your soldiers and for yourself. If you don't remember to do that, remember I've got your back."

"Thanks, Mom."

A few days later, he calls me as he's about to get onto

the plane. He's going to lead a platoon that just lost their lieutenant.

"I'm scared," he tells me. "I don't know if I can do this."

"You can do this. You've got this, Bart. You've got it."

His tour ends in January of 2008. I want to go to Texas, where Bart is based, to be there when he returns to Fort Hood—to receive him and the other soldiers—but I can't because my mother is on the verge of dying. She has an aggressive cancer, and I'm her major caretaker.

A month later, Bart and his fiancée, Katie, come to Florida to attend a wedding near me and reunite with his family and his grandma. Bart is with me when my mother dies—a good thing, since she was close to him, too. We're able to help her pass and transition that weekend. Then it turns chaotic, with the funeral services and people coming from all over to pay their respects. There's no time to talk.

Bart feels he hasn't done his service to the country because his deployment was cut short. Since he didn't serve a full tour, he wants to make it up to his officers and the soldiers in his platoon. He does this by giving up his vacation time and picking up their slack, working day and night, weekends—anything and everything so people can get their deployment breaks, vacations, visitations, whatever they need. On top of all that, he's working to get everyone ready for the next deployment.

Two months later, Bart and Katie return home one weekend for a surprise engagement party. My family is gathered outside, on our patio. I sit next to Bart. It's the first time we've been together like this, without all the chaos.

"Was Iraq everything you wanted it to be?" I ask.

He looks at me for a long moment.

"You don't want to know," he says.

I can see there's a piece of him that's broken.

"I don't even know how some of these soldiers survived," he says. "But the thing is...It's not hard in Iraq, Mom. It's hard here. The soldiers here at home are hard to discipline. They don't respond to it. I'm dealing with domestic violence, stuff like that. I feel like I'm a social worker." He sighs, his gaze lingering on me when he says, "It's more dangerous here than it is in Iraq."

Two months later, I fly to Dallas to do a speaking gig. I want to drive to Killeen, where Fort Hood is based, to see Bart.

"I'm working long hours," he tells me. "We're trying to get ready for deployment. I'm going to be really busy. You're not going to see much of me."

"I'm okay with that."

When I meet Bart at Fort Hood, he seems so peaceful. I've never seen him so okay with himself, so at peace. He radiates so much joy as he takes me through his company and shows me the tanks. He's just so happy with who he is, what he has, and what he's done.

He climbs up on top of a tank. He's squatting, wearing his Stetson, and the sun is setting behind him. I wish I had a camera to capture this perfect moment, but my phone doesn't have one. He's looking at me and I'm looking at him, and I say, "Stay right there. I'm going to take a shot," and I put my fingers up as if I'm taking a picture and I make a clicking sound. He smiles, my beautiful son who is in all his glory. It's the most amazing picture, in my mind. It's the last one I'll ever have of him.

Two weeks later, two uniformed officers knock on my door.

"On behalf of the president of the United States, we regret to inform you, Mrs. Luther, that your son, Lieutenant Robert Fletcher, was killed by one of the soldiers in his company."

When I get to Texas to recover his body, I want to see my son, but the Army won't let me. They say he was shot in the chest and I want to drive to Dallas and see him, but they won't let me go there and see him.

"You're not going to cremate him now," I tell them. "We'll eventually cremate him, but we want to have an open casket just for the family."

My husband and I make arrangements to bring his body back to Florida—and I have to do it quickly. A major hurricane is threatening to hit Texas.

I go to the funeral home with my husband and Bart's siblings. As we drive, all I keep thinking about is all these plans Bart had for his life after the service—like how he wanted to become an ambassador. He was going to study international relations at Georgetown. He had all kinds of plans—and he had all kinds of skills. And his captain knew that. His captain told me how, the night before Bart died, he had been talking to Bart about one of the soldiers in the company, this man named Jodie, who had been suspected of stealing some highly sensitive night equipment and selling it on eBay. The original plan was for Bart to go to the captain's office and together they would travel to the soldier's apartment, which was off base, in Killeen. They needed to collect the goods, before the man was to be discharged the following day.

Bart, though, had another idea. "No, I'll do it," he told the captain. "You go to the office. I'll get up early, and I'll go."

And he did. Bart took a master sergeant with him. They weren't armed, because the apartment was off base. Jodie's apartment was in a motel-like complex, on the corner of the second floor. It had a balcony with an iron-rod fence. All the blinds were shut.

They knocked on the door. Nobody answered.

The master sergeant went to the apartment manager. "We would like to talk to him, but he's not answering. His car is parked in the driveway, and we're kind of concerned that maybe something's going on, because we know he's in his apartment. We can hear him."

The apartment manager tried to open the door, but it was locked from the inside.

Bart and the master sergeant became even more concerned. They knew Jodie was in there, and he wasn't answering. They were all thinking the same thing: *Had Jodie killed himself?*

The balcony had a sliding glass door. The blinds were drawn there, too. The apartment manager got his tools and they removed the kitchen window.

Bart felt all sorts of alarms going off in his brain as they looked through the blinds, into the kitchen area and beyond. The place was a mess—alcohol, guns, and all sorts of crap scattered over the counters, tables, and floor.

Jodie came out of the bedroom with a Glock in his hand.

Bart grabbed his phone. He dialed 911 and turned to the master sergeant and apartment manager. "Get off the balcony," he said.

They got off the balcony.

Bart did not. He spoke to the dispatcher, who urged Bart to get to safety.

Too late. Jodie stepped outside, onto the balcony, the Glock tucked in his pocket.

Bart tried to talk Jodie down. "Listen, we're just here to visit with you," he said, and then he tried to negotiate with Jodie a little bit, talk him down.

Jodie walked back inside the apartment. Now was the time for Bart to leave.

But he didn't. He thought he could talk Jodie down.

When Jodie came back out, he was more agitated. Then he heard the police sirens—and now he was even more alarmed. Jodie lost it and pulled his gun.

And went right for Bart.

Bart had nowhere to go, nowhere to run. He turned away and shots belted out from Jodie's gun. *Bam-bam-bam-bam-bam.*

The police arrived. Shots were exchanged. Then Jodie shot himself and fell on my son, who was carrying in his pocket the little star I had given him the night before he deployed. I'd always thought he'd thrown it in the garbage. I'm told he carried it with him all the time.

I arrive at the funeral home to see Bart.

As they open the casket, I recall what the captain told me on the phone: "You need to be prepared. Bart might not look...There might be a little shift in how he looks."

I thought he was shot in the chest. He can't look that different.

The person lying inside the casket doesn't even remotely look like my son.

That's when my husband sees a bullet hole behind the ear. "Oh, my God," he says. "I think he was shot in the head."

My husband and I and Bart's brother stand there, stunned. They said Bart was shot in the chest, not the head. But Bart was shot in the head not once but five times. Jodie literally blew his face off.

They knew. The Army knew what had happened, but they didn't tell me the truth.

They won't tell me why.

I never had to forgive my son's killer because, in my mind, Jodie was the person I feared Bart would become if I had not put in the hard work to help Bart go in the direction he needed to go.

Was I angry that this happened? *Yes.* But all I had for Jodie was empathy. Jodie had a background that was very stressful. He experienced lots of trauma. The reason he went to war was because of 9/11. He went to Washington and saw the devastation there and then he went to New York and saw the destruction and said, "I'm going to enlist, I'm getting into the Army, that's what I'm doing." And he did. Jodie had the same mission as Bart, but he wasn't there for the right reasons.

My work has always been focused on helping very young children be able to regulate social and emotional behavior so parents don't have to engage in warfare. Conflict always starts with an upset emotional state. If we can see it as a call for help, we can teach kids to regulate their emotions so they don't feel as though they need to be aggressive. Jodie never got his needs met. He was a homeless kid, living on the streets with his mother. No father in his life. He was very depressed and struggled all through school. He never got the support he so desperately needed. He never got a chance to learn resiliency, which is the ability to take disappointment and conflict and turn it into something better. Get through it.

Which got me thinking: what if we built a foundation of early-childhood centers that could help the Jodies of the world? These early-childhood centers are mom-and-pop places, and most parents can't afford the high-tech schools, the family privilege schools and nurseries that are out there. What if we could provide not only parents but also teachers with the critical skills needed to help children build resiliency?

That is the mission of my nonprofit, Bart's Blue Star Foundation: to transform aggressive, scared boys and girls into powerful leaders like my son.

Bart got to live his dream. That's the good news. My son lived his dream and always followed his heart.

And the military was so about his heart.

RORY PATRICK HAMILL

Rory Patrick Hamill grew up in Brick, New Jersey, the son of two Navy parents. Wanting to serve something bigger than himself, Rory joined the Marine Corps and, near the end of 2006, went to boot camp. He served from 2006 until 2012. He got out as a corporal.

'm doing desert warfare training out in Twentynine Palms, California, when the battalion commander gathers our company and tells us that fresh bodies are needed on the ground in Afghanistan to hit the Taliban, as part of President Obama's Operation Strike of the Sword.

"We're up next at bat," the battalion commander tells us. "We're going to Afghanistan."

Everyone around me is acting all *Yeah, fuck yeah!*

I'm like, *Fuck.*

I got married at eighteen. When I turned nineteen, in 2006, I had my daughter. I missed her birth because I had been deployed to Iraq. And now that I'm officially deploying to Afghanistan, I'm going to miss the birth of my son.

Afghanistan is constant, high-level stress. Every day when we leave our base to go out and patrol, someone in our area of operations is guaranteed to get shot at or blown up.

The first time I got into a firefight I didn't realize what was happening.

We were walking through a cornfield, which was a nightmare in and of itself. It was 130 degrees, the sun blazing hot, the air humid from the floods farmers had to create to keep the corn alive. When I heard a snapping sound, someone had the wherewithal to yell at me to *get down*.

That was when I realized: *Oh, shit, someone's trying to attack me and take my life*. And the adrenaline surge? Holy shit. I immediately unloaded my SAW machine gun.

The firefights are now happening almost every single day. We're taking casualties left and right. And I don't take cover the way I should. I always stay out in the open and shoot with my SAW and make myself a target. My technique looks borderline suicidal, but I want to make sure everyone is safe, everyone is covered.

The day we get ground intelligence saying there's potential enemy activity, a squad doing an adjacent patrol about two hundred meters distant starts taking on fire—potshots. The enemy withdraws, and our squad moves to flank them.

We cut through a graveyard and set up along a tree line. We now have the best avenue of approach to engage the enemy.

Only they get behind us quicker than we anticipate.

My team leader, Charlie Lee, points to a tree about five feet to the right and says, "Rory, I want you to set up over there."

I'm standing behind the tree, aiming out into the open field, when I hear a gunshot.

Where's that coming from? What—?

Charlie starts screaming. *"I got shot."*

I can see the damage: the round hit his shin head-on and blew out the back of his calf.

We react immediately.

Marine Corps rifle squads are designed so that if someone above you in rank gets wounded, you follow the succession of command, which, in this case, is me. I have to step up and become a team leader.

The firefight is intense—the single most frenetic situation I've been in up to this point in my career. We fight with tenacity and ferocity as the enemy ambushes us from three sides. I keep looking at Charlie bleeding on the ground and think, *Oh, my God, I failed him. I couldn't protect my team.*

We soon get bogged down and decide to pull into the other side of the canal. The enemy appears and we start getting shot at, which means we have to pull into the trench water. That is a major concern for us because Charlie has an open gunshot wound and a muscle and skin laceration on the back of his calf. That unclean water gets into his wounds, he's at risk of fatal sepsis.

We call in a medevac and a gunship and then take cover while the enemy keeps firing at us.

We wait an hour and a half until air support arrives. It feels like forever.

The medevac lands—directly in our field of fire.

Four of my guys drop their weapons, pick up Charlie, and start running through knee-high mud. I run alongside them and shoot anyone who pops his head out. The shooting gets so intense the crew chief door gunner jumps out and engages the enemy with his 9mm—ineffective in the grand scheme of things, but his actions say *Fuck you, I'm going to try*. His pilots are in harm's way, and he's got to protect them at all costs. Having a bird—this great big piece of metal—stranded on the ground makes us sitting ducks.

We get Charlie on the medevac. Later, when we exfil, the Cobras and Hueys move in and start pounding the area with Hellfire missiles, miniguns, everything. It's not a good day for the bad guys.

Today I feel like I became a man.

I think about the way the door gunner acted—how we all acted and came together to help Charlie and get him to safety. It's the greatest symbolism of love I've ever seen in my life. That might sound bad, since I have children, but the way these men came together—it's absolutely true: there is no greater love.

At the base, I receive the news that my son was born. I'm told the time of his birth, do some quick calculations, and discover that my son came into the world while I was out with my squad, fighting for our lives.

It's 2010. I'm twenty-two years old, married, and have two kids. While I have an amazing set of leadership skills and can operate under pressure, in extremely frenetic life-or-death environments, I don't have any actual skill sets that can translate into a job back home.

I decide to reenlist.

I'm told we're going back to Afghanistan—this time to a place called Maja.

When my platoon arrives, we start working in the area of operations, doing foot patrols. I'm a corporal and a team leader.

We get ground intelligence that an improvised explosive device is inside a compound. Sergeant John Moler, one of my best friends, turns to me and says, "You want to go get in some trouble?"

"Yeah, let's do it."

We set up a cordon around the compound. John fumbles as he tries to get the metal detector off his back. I can tell he's nervous. Shaky. This is his first deployment. I've been blown up six times: two IED strikes and four RPGs. I go into dad mode.

"Let me do it," I say.

"Corporal, I can do it."

"I know you can. I have no doubt in your abilities. I want to take care of it."

I take the metal detector from him and go into the compound. The floor is all dirt. I've swept about three quarters of it when I step on a low metallic pressure plate attached to an IED.

The bomb explodes. I'm launched ten feet into the air and then I hit the ground.

I try to draw a breath and can't because the bomb sucked away the oxygen. There's smoke and dust everywhere, and I can't hear anything.

Finally, my lungs inflate. I go to stand up, can't.

What the fuck? I look down and see my right kneecap dangling by some sinew and my femur sticking out.

The lower part of my right leg is gone.

I draw on some crazy muscle memory. I go to grab my lifesaving tourniquet in my right cargo pocket but the pocket is no longer there. The only thing I can do is try to cut the flow of blood the best I can.

I pick up my stump, pin it to my chest.

And that's when my new reality hits me: my leg is gone.

The pain comes.

I start to scream.

My guys run up to me. Even in pain, I'm locked in my training—my leadership mindset. *"Did you guys sweep for secondary IEDs?"*

"Yeah," they say when it's obvious they didn't. They just ran up to me.

I would have done the same.

As they drag me out of the crater, I touch my ass and the back of my leg. It's wet. "Doc, check my backside. I think I'm bleeding back here."

The doc hits me with morphine. This is his first deployment, too. I know he's scared—terrified—because he's just a kid. We're all kids, yet here we're performing to the best of our abilities in the worst possible environments.

After he gets a tourniquet on my right side, he rolls me over, onto my stump. The amount of pain I experience in that moment turns me into an animal. I don't feel human. I start clawing at everyone's faces. They pin down my arms while the doc hits me again with morphine.

The pain starts to subside. I calm down. "All right, all

right," I tell them. "I'm good. I'm good. Someone give me a cigarette."

They lean me up against the wall. I puff on a Marlboro Red, waiting for the helicopter to come.

"This is making me nauseous," I say, and spit out the cigarette. I see it bounce off my flak jacket, and the pain in my head kind of stops.

Everything gets really peaceful.

Quiet.

I can hear the birds chirping. The sky is so blue, and the sun feels great. It's so weird and perverse, having these thoughts, because the exact opposite is happening around me.

On the helicopter, I wind up flatlining for two minutes because of the amount of trauma and blood loss. I'm not a religious person. I don't experience the typical "great white light," but I do feel absolute peace. Like I'm one with the universe, or something. It's beautiful and terrifying at the same time.

I wind up at Walter Reed, which, oddly, is where I was born. It's ironic, this "full circle of life" kind of deal.

My stump, I discover, had been cauterized by the blast, so I didn't bleed out.

But my leg is gone. They couldn't reattach it.

A week later, after I'm stabilized, a nurse comes in and says, "You're going to have a special visitor today, so make sure you shave your face."

Great. Some Marine officer is coming to visit me. Whatever.

I have a full beard. I shave my face using a bedpan filled with water and a shitty two-blade disposable razor. I'm all cut up, sitting in my bed with pieces of toilet paper stuck all over my face, when I see President Obama.

Is this real?

He walks into my room with a cameraman and a Secret Service agent.

Oh, shit, this is real.

"Corporal Hamill," he says, pinning the Purple Heart medal to my hospital shirt. "I want to thank you for your service on behalf of this nation." He starts asking me questions: *How's your recovery going? Are you in a lot of pain? Is everyone here treating you well?*

I know we give people in positions of power a lot of shit, and I know we don't agree on politics, but I can tell he is a genuine dude. A normal human being who is shaking my hand and talking to me. It's an amazing experience, and extremely humbling.

The amazing thing our brains do for us is compartmentalize any kind of trauma.

And therein lies the problem: people don't address PTSD or what psychologists call a moral injury—the feeling of overwhelming shame and guilt, even rage, anger, or betrayal over compromising your moral conscience. If you don't address these actions and reactions, they come back to haunt you down the road.

I learn all this stuff later. Much, much later.

I get my prosthetic leg one day shy of three months after having my leg blown off. I don't want to sit in bed. I want to get up and move. I want to recover.

I have great motivation: my wife left me at the hospital.

She confessed she did some extramarital shit while I was deployed.

It fills me with such rage and anger that I decide: *I'm going to prove her wrong. I'm going to prove everyone wrong. I'm not going to be a statistic. I'm going to succeed in my new post-injury life.*

I do daily physical therapy and then go out and party at night with guys who have come back from deployment—guys who have seen others get killed, maimed, and eviscerated. We don't talk about any of that. We don't talk about how we miss being with our unit, with our guys, our problems with wives and girlfriends. We don't address anything that we're dealing with, which is why things start to go south for me mentally.

I get medically discharged and find a civilian job in New Jersey working on helicopters.

I get remarried.

The demons from all my deployments start eating away at me day and night. I can't sleep, and I'm drinking too much. I'm smoking like a chimney. I'm not seeing my kids, and I'm shirking my responsibilities—and it's all because I've been ripped out from the familial structure of the military. And I miss the camaraderie.

From day one in the military, your entire day is regimented. It's scheduled and structured down to the minute. You have a mission. You go out and get it done. Now I don't have anyone telling me to do anything. I don't have anyone keeping me in check.

My second marriage ends.

I find myself sitting outside a marsh by my dad's house in Atlantic City. I'm sitting in the driver's seat, holding a pistol.

I raise it to my head, about to end my life, when for maybe a half second my kids flash through my mind.

What the fuck am I doing?

I start crying.

I disassemble my weapon, take all the bullets out of the magazine, and throw everything out of the car.

I need to address this. I need to get some help.

I get diagnosed with PTSD. I start seeing a therapist full-time and get my head out of my ass. I quit binge drinking and stop smoking, which I've been doing since I was thirteen. I learn the importance of exercise and nutrition and taking care of myself. I begin to claw and scrape my way out of my self-loathing. I stop hating myself for everything. I stop blaming myself for my friends dying and every other shitty thing that's ever happened to me.

I start speaking to other people about my experiences.

Over time, I start to learn to love my fate. Instead of letting it control me, send me into a deep, spiraling depression, I discover a way to turn it around for good—to help others. If I can help one person every day, regardless of how I do it, then that's a win for me. If I can use my experiences, my story, to help a person every single day, then everything I've gone through in my life is worth it.

ABOUT THE AUTHORS

JAMES PATTERSON is one of the best-known and biggest-selling writers of all time. His books have sold in excess of 385 million copies worldwide. He is the author of some of the most popular series of the past two decades – the Alex Cross, Women's Murder Club, Detective Michael Bennett and Private novels – and he has written many other number one bestsellers including non-fiction and stand-alone thrillers.

James is passionate about encouraging children to read. Inspired by his own son who was a reluctant reader, he also writes a range of books for young readers including the Middle School, Dog Diaries, Treasure Hunters and Max Einstein series. James has donated millions in grants to independent bookshops and has been the most borrowed author in UK libraries for the past thirteen years in a row. He lives in Florida with his family.

MATT EVERSMANN retired from the Army after twenty years of service. His last assignment was as an infantry company first sergeant in the 10th Mountain Division during the surge in Iraq. He spent almost half of his career in the 75th Ranger Regiment and was a member of Task Force Ranger, the unit immortalised in the film *Black Hawk Down*. Eversmann and his family live in West Palm Beach, where he runs his own consulting company, Eversmann Advisory.

CHRIS MOONEY is the international bestselling author of fourteen thrillers. The Mystery Writers of America nominated *Remembering Sarah* for an Edgar Award. He teaches creative writing at Harvard.

THE KENNEDY CURSE

James Patterson
& Cythia Fagen

Across decades and generations, the Kennedys have been a
family of charismatic adventurers, raised to take risks and
excel. Their name is synonymous with American royalty.
Their commitment to public service is legendary. But, for all
the successes, the family has been blighted by assassinations,
fatal accidents, drug and alcohol abuse and sex scandals.

To this day, the Kennedys occupy a unique, contradictory place
in the world's imagination: at once familiar and unknowable;
charmed and cursed. *The Kennedy Curse* is a revealing,
fascinating account of America's most famous family,
as told by the world's most trusted storyteller.

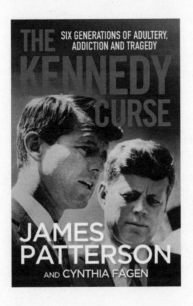

Also by James Patterson

ALEX CROSS NOVELS

Along Came a Spider • Kiss the Girls • Jack and Jill • Cat and Mouse • Pop Goes the Weasel • Roses are Red • Violets are Blue • Four Blind Mice • The Big Bad Wolf • London Bridges • Mary, Mary • Cross • Double Cross • Cross Country • Alex Cross's Trial (*with Richard DiLallo*) • I, Alex Cross • Cross Fire • Kill Alex Cross • Merry Christmas, Alex Cross • Alex Cross, Run • Cross My Heart • Hope to Die • Cross Justice • Cross the Line • The People vs. Alex Cross • Target: Alex Cross • Criss Cross • Deadly Cross

THE WOMEN'S MURDER CLUB SERIES

1st to Die • 2nd Chance (*with Andrew Gross*) • 3rd Degree (*with Andrew Gross*) • 4th of July (*with Maxine Paetro*) • The 5th Horseman (*with Maxine Paetro*) • The 6th Target (*with Maxine Paetro*) • 7th Heaven (*with Maxine Paetro*) • 8th Confession (*with Maxine Paetro*) • 9th Judgement (*with Maxine Paetro*) • 10th Anniversary (*with Maxine Paetro*) • 11th Hour (*with Maxine Paetro*) • 12th of Never (*with Maxine Paetro*) • Unlucky 13 (*with Maxine Paetro*) • 14th Deadly Sin (*with Maxine Paetro*) • 15th Affair (*with Maxine Paetro*) • 16th Seduction (*with Maxine Paetro*) • 17th Suspect (*with Maxine Paetro*) • 18th Abduction (*with Maxine Paetro*) • 19th Christmas (*with Maxine Paetro*) • 20th Victim (*with Maxine Paetro*)

DETECTIVE MICHAEL BENNETT SERIES

Step on a Crack (*with Michael Ledwidge*) • Run for Your Life (*with Michael Ledwidge*) • Worst Case (*with Michael Ledwidge*) • Tick Tock (*with Michael Ledwidge*) • I, Michael Bennett (*with Michael Ledwidge*) • Gone (*with Michael Ledwidge*) • Burn (*with Michael Ledwidge*) • Alert (*with Michael Ledwidge*) • Bullseye (*with Michael Ledwidge*) • Haunted (*with James O. Born*) • Ambush (*with James O. Born*) • Blindside (*with James O. Born*) • The Russian (*with James O. Born*)

PRIVATE NOVELS

Private (*with Maxine Paetro*) • Private London (*with Mark Pearson*) • Private Games (*with Mark Sullivan*) • Private: No. 1 Suspect (*with Maxine Paetro*) • Private Berlin (*with Mark Sullivan*) • Private Down Under (*with Michael White*) • Private L.A. (*with Mark Sullivan*) • Private India (*with Ashwin Sanghi*) • Private Vegas (*with Maxine Paetro*) • Private Sydney (*with Kathryn Fox*) • Private Paris (*with Mark Sullivan*) • The Games (*with Mark Sullivan*) • Private Delhi (*with Ashwin Sanghi*) • Private Princess (*with Rees Jones*) • Private Moscow (*with Adam Hamdy*)

NYPD RED SERIES

NYPD Red (*with Marshall Karp*) • NYPD Red 2 (*with Marshall Karp*) • NYPD Red 3 (*with Marshall Karp*) • NYPD Red 4 (*with Marshall Karp*) • NYPD Red 5 (*with Marshall Karp*) • NYPD Red 6 (*with Marshall Karp*)

DETECTIVE HARRIET BLUE SERIES

Never Never (*with Candice Fox*) • Fifty Fifty (*with Candice Fox*) • Liar Liar (*with Candice Fox*) • Hush Hush (*with Candice Fox*)

INSTINCT SERIES

Instinct (*with Howard Roughan, previously published as* Murder Games) • Killer Instinct (*with Howard Roughan*)

STAND-ALONE THRILLERS

The Thomas Berryman Number • Hide and Seek • Black Market • The Midnight Club • Sail (*with Howard Roughan*) • Swimsuit (*with Maxine Paetro*) • Don't Blink (*with Howard Roughan*) • Postcard Killers (*with Liza Marklund*) • Toys (*with Neil McMahon*) • Now You See Her (*with Michael Ledwidge*) • Kill Me If You Can (*with Marshall Karp*) • Guilty Wives (*with David Ellis*) • Zoo (*with Michael Ledwidge*) • Second Honeymoon (*with Howard Roughan*) • Mistress (*with David Ellis*) • Invisible (*with David Ellis*) • Truth or Die (*with Howard Roughan*) • Murder House (*with David Ellis*) • The Black Book (*with David Ellis*) •

The Store (*with Richard DiLallo*) • Texas Ranger (*with Andrew Bourelle*) • The President is Missing (*with Bill Clinton*) • Revenge (*with Andrew Holmes*) • Juror No. 3 (*with Nancy Allen*) • The First Lady (*with Brendan DuBois*) • The Chef (*with Max DiLallo*) • Out of Sight (*with Brendan DuBois*) • Unsolved (*with David Ellis*) • The Inn (*with Candice Fox*) • Lost (*with James O. Born*) • Texas Outlaw (*with Andrew Bourelle*) • The Summer House (*with Brendan DuBois*) • 1st Case (*with Chris Tebbetts*) • Cajun Justice (*with Tucker Axum*) • The Midwife Murders (*with Richard DiLallo*) • The Coast-to-Coast Murders (*with J. D. Barker*) • Three Women Disappear (*with Shan Serafin*)

NON-FICTION

Torn Apart (*with Hal and Cory Friedman*) • The Murder of King Tut (*with Martin Dugard*) • All-American Murder (*with Alex Abramovich and Mike Harvkey*) • The Kennedy Curse (*with Cynthia Fagen*) • The Last Days of John Lennon (*with Casey Sherman and Dave Wedge*)

MURDER IS FOREVER TRUE CRIME

Murder, Interrupted (*with Alex Abramovich and Christopher Charles*) • Home Sweet Murder (*with Andrew Bourelle and Scott Slaven*) • Murder Beyond the Grave (*with Andrew Bourelle and Christopher Charles*) • Murder Thy Neighbour (*with Andrew Bourelle and Max DiLallo*) • Murder of Innocence (*with Max DiLallo and Andrew Bourelle*) • Till Murder Do Us Part (*with Andrew Bourelle and Max DiLallo*)

COLLECTIONS

Triple Threat (*with Max DiLallo and Andrew Bourelle*) • Kill or Be Killed (*with Maxine Paetro, Rees Jones, Shan Serafin and Emily Raymond*) • The Moores are Missing (*with Loren D. Estleman, Sam Hawken and Ed Chatterton*) • The Family Lawyer (*with Robert Rotstein, Christopher Charles and Rachel Howzell Hall*) • Murder in Paradise (*with Doug Allyn, Connor Hyde and Duane Swierczynski*) • The House Next Door (*with Susan DiLallo, Max DiLallo and Brendan DuBois*) • 13-Minute Murder (*with Shan Serafin, Christopher Farnsworth and Scott Slaven*) • The River Murders (*with James O. Born*)

For more information about James Patterson's novels, visit www.penguin.co.uk